FRIENDS
OF ACPL
W9-DFT-281

Culture Wars and Enduring American Dilemmas

JUL 0 8 2010

CONTEMPORARY POLITICAL AND SOCIAL ISSUES

In 2008, John McCain, always known as something of a centrist or moderate Republican, picked the governor of Alaska, Sarah Palin, as his running mate. The moment he did so, the culture war returned to American politics. Although the economy was entering a tailspin and dangers were prominent around the world, once again we were discussing whether elites had lost touch with the common people by failing to appreciate religion and dismissing people's concerns with morality.

The Palin selection raised a larger question: Did we ever have a culture war in the first place? In this book, Irene Taviss Thomson offers an original and important new way of answering that question. Whether or not a culture war indeed existed out there in Middle America, just about everyone who wrote on the topic agreed that elites themselves were sharply divided between liberal and conservative views of the world. And, the argument went, the raging culture war was especially apparent in the media, whatever was happening in small-town America.

Rather than simply assuming the truth of this proposition, Thomson looks at the media—specifically, opinion magazines. Her research challenges the idea that our opinion leaders are engaged in an implacable war with each other. Culture has historically been defined as the common values that bind together a society. Thomson shows that this idea of culture remains very much alive. America remains a nation where agreement is more striking than disagreement. No matter how bitter and polarized our politics can seem, this truth should never be lost, and Thomson provides the evidence needed to back it up. Opinion leaders need to think about their own role in the culture war; Thomson has helped them do it.

—ALAN WOLFE

Putting Faith in Partnerships: Welfare-to-Work in Four Cities
Stephen V. Monsma

The New Imperial Presidency: Renewing Presidential Power after Watergate
Andrew Rudalevige

Self-Financed Candidates in Congressional Elections
Jennifer A. Steen

Trust beyond Borders: Immigration, the Welfare State, and Identity in Modern Societies
Markus M. L. Crepaz

America Beyond Black and White: How Immigrants and Fusions Are Helping Us Overcome the Racial Divide
Ronald Fernandez

America at Risk: Threats to Liberal Self-Government in an Age of Uncertainty
Robert Faulkner and Susan Shell, Editors

Barack Obama's America: How New Conceptions of Race, Family, and Religion Ended the Reagan Era
John Kenneth White

Culture Wars and Enduring American Dilemmas
Irene Taviss Thomson

Culture Wars
and Enduring American Dilemmas

IRENE TAVISS THOMSON

THE UNIVERSITY OF MICHIGAN PRESS
ANN ARBOR

Copyright © by the University of Michigan 2010
All rights reserved
Published in the United States of America by
The University of Michigan Press
Manufactured in the United States of America
♾ Printed on acid-free paper

2013 2012 2011 2010 4 3 2 1

No part of this publication may be reproduced, stored in a retrieval system, or transmitted in any form or by any means, electronic, mechanical, or otherwise, without the written permission of the publisher.

A CIP catalog record for this book is available from the British Library.

Library of Congress Cataloging-in-Publication Data

Thomson, Irene Taviss, 1941–
Culture wars and enduring American dilemmas /
Irene Taviss Thomson.
p. cm. — (Contemporary political and social issues)
Includes bibliographical references and index.
ISBN 978-0-472-07088-6 (cloth : alk. paper)
— ISBN 978-0-472-05088-8 (pbk. : alk. paper)
— ISBN 978-0-472-02206-9 (e-book)
1. Culture conflict—United States. 2. United States—Social conditions—21st century. 3. United States—Politics and government—21st century. 4. United States—Moral conditions.
I. Title.

HN59.2.T525 2010
303.60973—dc22 2009033205

TO MICHAEL

Contents

CHAPTER 1

Culture Wars and Warring about Culture

American culture appears to be deeply divided: those who believe there are absolute moral truths contend with those who place moral authority in individual judgment. Armed with these competing visions, "orthodox" versus "progressive" culture warriors clash on issues of abortion, homosexuality, feminism, school prayer, multiculturalism, popular culture, and university curricula. The population is increasingly polarized as a result.

The problem with this image is that it is not supported by survey data. American public opinion is considerably more ambivalent and internally inconsistent than the image of a culture war implies. Most Americans are moderate or centrist in both their political and religious beliefs. Very few are consistently for or against abortion and same-sex marriage, for example.

Proponents of the culture wars thesis acknowledge that most Americans occupy a position between the polar extremes. The issue, they contend, is not about what people think or believe, but about the public culture—the meanings and understandings enunciated by elites who seek to frame how we think. The competing moral visions of these elites inexorably pull all arguments into one or the other of the contending camps, effectively eclipsing the middle ground.

The question thus becomes whether American public culture is divided into the two opposing camps of the culture war, or whether both sides share the same American cultural ideas in propounding their differing visions. I find support for the latter view in my analysis of the 436 articles dealing with culture war issues that were published in four popular political magazines between 1980 and 2000. The culture war debaters in the pages of *National Review, Time, The New Republic,* and *The Nation*—magazines representing the mainstream American political spectrum, from *National Review* on the right to *The Nation* on the left—adhere to remarkably similar cultural principles.

Rather than dividing along the lines of "orthodox" versus "progressive" morality, the arguments of culture war partisans are nuanced and riddled with internal disagreements. There are abortion rights supporters who regret the immorality of abortion and antihomosexuality advocates who dispute whether or not homosexual behavior is a matter of morality. The symbols and rhetoric of the two sides often mirror each other. Consider the following statement: "A culture that is at once moralistic, self-righteous, alienated, and in a minority will constantly be tempted to break the rules of political discourse." Are these the words of a progressive describing the efforts of Christian Fundamentalists to influence American politics? No. This is a description of the Left written by a well-known conservative (Bork 1989, 27).

While there are doubtless persons for whom the binary logic of the culture wars is all-important, the elites represented in the pages of these mainstream media—the journalists and intellectuals, feminists and "family values" advocates alike—instead reflect shared cultural patterns. These discussions take place within the context of enduring American dilemmas—about the role of religion in politics and society, the tension between morality and pragmatism, how much individualism should be sacrificed for larger community goals, the meaning of pluralism in a "nation of immigrants," and how to reconcile the will of the people with standards enunciated by elites.

Though they disagree about specific issues and policies, the partisans on all sides subscribe to the following ideas: (1) respect for religion but uncertainty about its role; (2) use of moral frameworks but without "moralizing"; (3) belief in individualism but not to excess; (4) respect for pluralism but within one culture; (5) ambivalence toward elites; and (6) a high regard for moderation. The first five of these items represent dilemmas to which the high regard for moderation is something of an answer. Thus, religion is of great importance, but American society is both secular and diverse in its religions. Individualism is a supreme American value, but the needs of the community must be respected too. Ironically, the only unalloyed American virtue is that of moderation. Moderation, of course, does not constitute a dilemma. But the very vitality of moderation presents dilemmas for social movements. In a society that views as beyond the pale both ardent feminists and committed traditionalists, the strongly religious and atheists, fervent supporters and opponents of abortion, those who attempt to alter the culture are pressured toward a centrism that may be antagonistic to their basic beliefs.

While issues such as abortion or same-sex marriage may be new, the underlying dilemmas are of long duration. If every culture can be seen as "a kind of theater in which certain contrary tendencies are played out" (Erikson 1976, 82), these are classic American cultural conundrums. And though they may not be the only dilemmas in American culture, they are the ones that are central to the "culture wars."

Participants and observers alike contend that the culture wars originated in the late 1960s, when challenges to traditional values were dubbed the counterculture. The very idea of a "counterculture" suggests a new self-consciousness about cultural struggles regarding values and lifestyles. In the trajectory from the counterculture to the culture wars, what is new is not the political struggle over cultural issues but rather a heightened awareness of culture itself and those who seek to shape it. Both social scientists and the general public have come to think of culture as changeable and contested. And a self-conscious competition for cultural dominance has become more evident. While the "social construction of reality" has not become a household term akin to "charisma" or "lifestyle," an awareness of the provisional nature of social assumptions has "entered popular consciousness" (Wrong 1990, 28).

The Culture Wars

In one of the earliest and best-known portraits of the culture wars, James Davison Hunter (1991) described a fundamental split between orthodox and progressive views of morality and suggested that this divide cuts across class, religious, racial, ethnic, political, and sexual lines. In the eyes of one partisan, the culture war is apparent in the simultaneous emergence of "moral disarray" and "moral revival" symbolized by the success of both gangsta rap and gospel rock (Himmelfarb 1999, 117).

A year after Hunter put "culture wars" on the social science map, Patrick Buchanan popularized the idea in his speech to the 1992 Republican National Convention. He told the audience in Houston that "a cultural war" was taking place, a "struggle for the soul of America." The defining issues were abortion, homosexuality, school choice, and "radical feminism." In the aftermath of this address, the idea of a "culture war" became a journalistic staple.

But for all the credence given to the idea of culture wars in the press, public opinion analysts present a different portrait (see N. J. Davis and Robinson 1996a, 1996b, 1997; DiMaggio, Evans, and Bryson 1996; J. H. Evans 1997; Fiorina, Abrams, and Pope 2005; A. S. Miller and Hoffman 1999; C. Smith et al. 1997; Wolfe 1998; Wuthnow 1996). Only small percentages of Americans are consistently orthodox or progressive on such issues as abortion, stem cell research, the morning-after pill, gay marriage, and gay adoption (Pew Research Center 2006b). And while "the gap between the ideologically consistent liberals and conservatives may have widened a bit," there are now fewer Americans "in those fragments" than there were in the 1960s (Fischer and Hout 2006, 238).

Religious conservatives and liberals differ in their religious beliefs, however, and there is a loose correspondence between people's religious identities and their views on abortion, homosexuality, and school prayer (N. J. Davis and Robinson 1996; Wuthnow 1996). But their views do not clearly differ with regard to the values and moral orientations that are prominent in American culture. Both are guided by self-interest and by what feels good; both are dedicated to work and family and the desire to secure a comfortable life. Differences in political and social views are more related to people's religious activities than to their conservative or liberal religious philosophies. Those who participate actively in religion "are in substantial agreement on many aspects of their worldviews," whether they are liberals, moderates, or conservatives (Wuthnow 1996, 326). Furthermore, the religiously orthodox do not take a conservative stance on issues of racial and economic inequality (N. J. Davis and Robinson 1996a); three-quarters of the members of this group favor sex education in public schools, and almost half support making contraception available to teenagers (N. J. Davis and Robinson 1996b, 235; Kohut et al. 2000, 64). Even among people who identify themselves as part of the Religious Right, some 30 percent are Democrats, and 60 percent think abortion should be legal in some circumstances (C. Smith et al. 1997, 182). Among committed evangelical Protestants, one-third believe that abortions should be available to women in circumstances other than rape, incest, or to save the life of the mother, and 41 percent of committed Catholics believe likewise (Kohut et al. 2000, 64). The proportion of conservative Protestants who are so consistently pro-life that they reject abortion even when a mother's health is at stake is only 3 percent, a figure that has not changed in recent decades (Greeley and Hout 2006, 125).

Not only do the religiously orthodox show "little ideological consistency across a broad spectrum of attitudes," but their attitudes also differ by gender, race, social class, and age (N. J. Davis and Robinson 1996b, 237). This finding runs quite contrary to Hunter's thesis that the fundamental divide between orthodox and progressive views cuts across all other social categories. Nor is there evidence of enduring alliances across faiths, as conservative Catholics do not share sociopolitical attitudes with fundamentalist Protestants (Billings and Scott 1994, 180). Older alliances between religious groups and political parties continue; to this day, white Protestants are a majority of those who identify with the Republican Party, while Catholics, Jews, and black Protestants are much more likely to be Democrats (Layman 2001, 301). Even among the orthodox, younger people hold more liberal views regarding sexuality and reproduction, gender, and racial issues (N. J. Davis and Robinson 1996b, 242). And the role of moral beliefs in predicting voting patterns and party loyalties appears to differ by gender, again suggesting that something other than a culture war is at work (Kaufmann 2002; Layman 2001).

The division between the progressive and the orthodox camps is not monolithic even with regard to religious doctrines. Thus, some one-third of religious conservatives do not believe the Bible should be taken literally, while almost 20 percent of religious liberals think it should be (Wuthnow 1996, 326). An ethnographic study of one evangelical and one mainline Protestant seminary found that although they maintain competing moral visions, "the more intense battles are internal to each culture" (Carroll and Marler 1995, 18). Among religious elites, such as seminary faculty, neither side appears unified in opposition to the other (Olson and Carroll 1992, 778). Even if religious elites present positions as if they were internally consistent packages, group members show no such attitude consistency (Jelen 1990, 124). Furthermore, differences in religious beliefs are not necessarily reflected in actual behavior. Thus, the family behaviors of religious conservatives were not found to differ from those of religious progressives (Clydesdale 1997).

Within religious denominations, little evidence supports the idea of polarized views on culture war issues. Ironically, the one exception that has been found is among Evangelicals and Fundamentalists. These presumptively orthodox groups manifest intradenominational ideological polarization (Demerath and Yang 1997, 35).

Remarkably, the attitudes of religious conservatives and liberals on most social and political issues converged rather than further differentiated during the 1970s and 1980s (DiMaggio, Evans, and Bryson 1996, 729). Attitudes toward abortion may be the one exception. Evidence indicates greater polarization here, though this phenomenon peaked in the 1980s, and some analysts using different statistical techniques dispute the finding of polarization (Mouw and Sobel 2001). Evidence also shows increased internal division among both Catholics and mainline Protestants on the abortion question (J. H. Evans 2002). Yet in some ways, realistically, "there are not two political opinions on abortion—pro-choice and pro-life, but three. The third is 'It depends,' and is larger than the other two put together," with large majorities of the population favoring abortion if pregnancy was the result of rape or if the mother's health is in danger (Greeley and Hout 2006, 121, 123). Even with respect to this most polarizing issue, one recent poll found that 66 percent of Americans support finding "a middle ground," and only 29 percent believe "there's no room for compromise when it comes to abortion laws" (Pew Research Center 2006b).

Those who take extreme positions on the issue of abortion do not share a coherent worldview. Thus, pro-life supporters are deeply divided in their attitudes toward the death penalty, civil rights, feminism, and other social issues, while those most in favor of abortion are differentiated into liberal and libertarian camps. Despite their collaboration in antiabortion campaigns, the Catholic Church and the Southern Baptist Convention do not share cultural or religious outlooks, and even their antiabortion rationales differ substantially from each other (Dillon 1996).

The idea of multiculturalism also is less divisive an issue than some culture warriors suggest. Survey data show that while few Americans support the "hard multiculturalist" position that calls on the government to help racial and ethnic groups to maintain their original cultures, most Americans prefer an "inclusive nationalism" that "coexists with the widespread acceptance of pluralism in cultural practices." Faced with the option of having different ethnic groups "blend into the larger society" or "maintain their distinct cultures," 38 percent favored the melting pot position, 32 percent chose the cultural maintenance option, and 29 percent said neither. That a large segment of the public takes a middle position on this question suggests that many Americans do not view assimilating and maintaining elements of one's ethnic heritage as mutually exclusive (Citrin et al. 2001, 260). And while 63 percent favored designating English as the official language of the United States, only 37 percent agreed that ballots should be printed in English only (261).

Americans appear to manifest both a center-seeking tendency and strong ambivalence about culture war issues. Divisions between those who side with Ozzie and Harriet images of family life and those who align with Murphy Brown, for example, "do not take place between camps of people; instead, they take place within most individuals." In effect, "the culture war lies within" (Wolfe 1998, 111). While Wolfe's analysis is based on in-depth interviews with two hundred middle-class suburbanites, Fiorina, Abrams, and Pope report similar results based on national surveys of "tens of thousands" of Americans (2005, 8).

Perhaps such ambivalence is understandable in light of the contradictory pattern of American values. In the World Values Surveys, Americans' high level of adherence to traditional values (strong beliefs in God and religion, conservative family values, absolute moral standards, and national pride) resembles that shown by the populations of developing and low-income societies. At the same time, however, Americans are attached to self-expression values: "No other society is as traditional and as self-expression-oriented as America" (Baker 2005, 39). Since traditional values and the quest for self-realization may dictate contradictory behaviors, it is no wonder that Americans may experience conflicts over culture war issues and may simultaneously embrace both sides of the debate. Significant numbers of Americans, for example, believe both that homosexual behavior is immoral and that homosexuals deserve civil rights (Loftus 2001). Conservative Protestants are more willing to censure homosexuals but are no less supportive than are other Americans of hate crime laws designed to protect gay men and lesbians (C. Smith 2000, 226).

Data from the World Values Survey also suggest that between 1981 and 1990, Americans became almost evenly divided between "moral absolutists," who believe there are clear guidelines about good and evil, and "moral relativists," who believe that what is good or evil depends on the circumstances. This polarized distribution persisted through the 1995 and 2000 surveys (Baker 2005, 79). But such polarization does not indicate the presence of a culture war, since these moral visions are only loosely linked to attitudes and beliefs. Whether people are moral absolutists or relativists, they "tend to share similar religious beliefs, cultural values, and attitudes about social issues and policies" (104).

The orthodox and progressive camps thus are not polarized about social policies. Close elections may reflect not a deeply divided electorate but rather an ambivalent one that is closely divided about the choices offered by political elites who have become more polarized (Fiorina, Abrams, and Pope 2005, 8, 14–15). For example, a 2003 poll found that although weekly churchgoers are only half as likely to favor legalization of homosexual relations as those who never attend church, 40 percent nevertheless favored such legalization (89). And the single largest disparity found in 2000 between voters in "red" and "blue" states was the 16 percent difference between the 60 percent of Democrats who support gays in the military and the 44 percent of Republicans who do (26). There is little connection between party affiliation and views about abortion, despite the party alignments with "pro-choice" and "pro-life" slogans. The population may well be more divided over such labels than over the actual policy alternatives, just as women are more likely to approve of government policies to improve the status of women than they are favorably inclined toward the term *feminist* (Fiorina, Abrams, and Pope 2005, 63). Over time, as the labels have become more widely known, religiously orthodox people have become more likely to categorize themselves as "conservative," and religious progressives identify themselves as "liberal," even though their attitudes on issues have not changed. This phenomenon would account for "the paradox of a perceived increase in divisiveness despite a lack of empirical support at the individual level" (A. S. Miller and Hoffmann 1999, 728).

It is not clear that the majority of Americans attach great political significance to cultural issues. When asked to name the most important problems facing the nation or to discuss party differences, less than one-third of National Election Survey respondents in 1992 mentioned a cultural matter (Layman and Carmines 1997, 765), despite the emphasis on cultural issues at that time. Most churchgoing Protestants are not interested in fighting culture wars (C. Smith et al. 1997, 192), and attitudes among Evangelicals are as complex and ambivalent as they are among most Americans. The vast majority of Evangelicals, Fundamentalists, and conservative Protestants do not think that public schools should teach Christian values and morals or that teachers should lead classes in spoken Christian prayers. At the same time, however, members of these groups believe that public school instruction should include Christian views of science and history (C. Smith 2000, 206). Evangelicals disagree among themselves about whether to seek "Christian cultural hegemony" or to stress "liberty and pluralism" (36). Furthermore, no "single evangelical elite [speaks] in accord"; evangelical leaders are all over "the political and ideological map" (7).

For political attitudes and behavior to be consistent with the culture wars thesis, voters not only must see cultural issues as salient, they must also perceive the ideological or values standpoints underlying an array of different policy questions and must link a political party to a particular ideology. Such consistency of attitudes and viewpoints has not been commonly found in public opinion and political behavior. It is thus not surprising that an examination of the 1992–2000 National Election Studies finds that culture wars operate only rarely. And contrary to the culture wars thesis, such factors as race and religious denomination still make a difference. Thus, more religiously committed black Protestants are still more likely than their less devout counterparts to align themselves with the Democratic Party and with liberal political views (Layman and Green 2006). It would appear, then, that the culture war thesis does not apply to the majority of Americans.

James Davison Hunter has acknowledged that "most Americans occupy a vast middle ground between the polarizing impulses of American culture" and that "public discourse is more polarized than the American public" (1991, 43, 159). But he maintains that the culture war is not a matter of public opinion, about what is in people's heads or hearts. Rather, it is about the public culture. And in this culture, elites on both sides of the dispute force attitudes or opinions into their molds, thereby eliminating the middle ground. The two sides are in a struggle "over the meaning of America" (50). Individuals "become subservient to" or "must struggle against the dominating and virtually irresistible categories and logic of the culture war" (1998, 14). The culture war is "*not* reflected so deeply in public sentiment" (Hunter and Wolfe 2006, 93). But this does not mean that there is a centrist consensus. Rather, "the competing moral visions in public culture" are "a reality sui generis" (Hunter 1996, 246). Any coherent center that may exist is eclipsed by "the grid of rhetorical extremes" that either labels moderates as "wishy-washy" or judges them by the standards of the extremists—so that, for example, a moderate conservative on issues of homosexuality will still be dubbed a homophobe (247). Those who argue against the culture war hypothesis are engaged in "a denial of deep difference" (Hunter and Wolfe 2006, 36).

But to critics such as Alan Wolfe, a "culture war is not autonomous from the people who fight it. It has no reality of its own" (Hunter and Wolfe 2006, 100). There is also no reason to assume that people become "subservient to" the opposing logics of culture war rhetoric (Demerath and Straight 1997, 216). People can and do sustain inconsistency and ambivalence within their beliefs. This is not to deny that the opposing visions themselves have social effects. As A. S. Miller and Hoffmann (1999) have pointed out, people who come to identify with one side may feel increased antagonism toward the opposing side. Evidence suggests, for example, that anti-Fundamentalists harbor negative stereotypes about Christian Fundamentalists (Bolce and De Maio 1999a, 1999b). But people may also adhere selectively to the ideas of each side.

Hunter argues that the culture wars are about the power to define reality, to create and shape meaning. With competing worldviews in contest, the representatives on each side seek to project their "vision of the world as the dominant, if not *the only* vision of the world, such that it becomes commonsensical to people" (Hunter 2004, 5). If this is the case, a struggle over the soul of America is indeed taking place, despite the absence of polarization in the population.

How, then, can one determine the truth of the assertion of a culture war? How does one study the "public culture" or tap into the "deep differences" within contemporary American culture? Hunter's initial discussion of the culture wars focused on the advertising and persuasive literature emanating from culture war organizations and spokespersons. Yet scholars have long

3 1833 05534 8830

recognized that organizations and movements that seek public support tend to state their claims in exaggerated form. To overcome inertia and to motivate financial contributions, they emphasize the dire consequences of doing nothing or allowing the opposition to prevail. The public culture clearly encompasses more than the rhetoric of fund-seeking partisans.

Hunter recognizes that culture war issues filled "the nation's newspapers, magazines, and intellectual journals" (1991, 176), yet he focused on the sixty-second commercials, full-page advertisements, sound bites on the evening news, op-ed pieces, and direct mail letters that resulted in "much of public discourse" being "reduced to a reciprocal bellicosity" (170). Despite the "extremism and superficiality" of these sources, Hunter argued that they provided "the only objectification of the debate that really exists" (170).

But why should one make this assumption? Since the elites who shape the public culture express themselves in many venues, it seems rather arbitrary to define "public discourse" in such narrow terms. An analysis of the opinions and assumptions presented in large-circulation political magazines offers an excellent opportunity to test the culture war thesis. The journalists, academics, public intellectuals, and political figures whose writing appears in these magazines offer a representative array of the partisan views that constitute the public culture. I have also supplemented the magazine articles with selected works by writers whose names are associated with the culture wars—figures such as William Bennett, Allan Bloom, Dinesh D'Souza, Thomas Frank, Francis Fukuyama, Henry Louis Gates, Roger Kimball, and Michael Walzer.

Hunter has argued that "within the contemporary public discourse, one risks being branded a 'right-winger' by even invoking moral criteria. Indeed, the very word 'morality' has become a right-wing word" (1991, 323). And "the concept of religion or transcendence is also very often dismissed by secular progressivists as 'right-wing'" (324). My analysis of the writings of partisans on both the left and the right does not support such hyperbolic images. Rather, the spokespersons for both sides have "drawn on the same symbolic code to . . . advance their competing claims," as J. C. Alexander and Smith found in their analysis of discourse within earlier American civil debates (1993, 197).

An empirical test of the culture war hypothesis is of some significance to both social scientists and the general public. For the most part, empirical researchers have tended to reject the idea of a culture war based on survey data, while those who defend the hypothesis have done so without empirical research into the "deep culture" whose existence they claim. I hope that a systematic study of the public discourse about culture wars will shed light on the topic in a way that goes beyond the persuasive analyses of survey researchers.

There is, of course, an intuitive appeal—a surface plausibility—to the culture war idea, given the differences in the ideas espoused by Jerry Falwell, Pat Robertson, and Patrick Buchanan, on the one hand, and feminists, gay-marriage advocates, and abortion-rights supporters on the other. Even some social scientists are so wedded to the culture war concept that they behave like the proverbial pessimists who see only the doughnut hole. Thus, they see only divergences within the population where other analysts see convergences. John Kenneth White, for example, argues that a "values divide" exists in American politics, with one side emphasizing "duty and morality" while the other stresses "individual rights and self-fulfillment" (2003, 65). Citing a 2000 Zogby poll that asked whether there are "absolute moral truths that govern our lives," he reports that among those who classified themselves as "very liberal," 48 percent agreed and 46 percent disagreed, while among those who saw themselves as "very conservative," 74 percent agreed and 25 percent disagreed. He concludes that "the values divide between liberals and conservatives . . . has become a chasm" (66). But surely there is room for disagreement about whether this degree of difference constitutes a "chasm" or a culture war.

Why does it matter whether there is or is not a culture war? A society experiencing a culture war would face grave difficulties. It would lack common standards and assumptions, and as a result, the ability to make public policy decisions would be severely compromised. Indeed, a society without such common ground could barely function. It is instructive to recall that after *Culture Wars* appeared in 1991, Hunter's next book was titled *Before the Shooting Begins* (1994). My analysis of American public culture suggests that such images are unwarranted.

Warring over Culture

The culture war debates are embedded within a larger contention concerning the nature of culture itself. Unlike the culture wars, however, disputes about the concept of culture are not new. The term *culture,* used in the anthropological sense to describe how people think and behave, is generally traced to the 1870s. It was popularized in the 1930s and became an essential part of social science. Yet as early as 1952, some sociologists and anthropologists rejected the concept as "so broad as to be useless in scientific discourse" (Kroeber and Kluckhohn 1952, 5). Half a century later, the utility of the concept is questioned not because it is too broad but because it is too precise. Critics argue that *culture* implies a degree of structure, coherence, and stability that is not found in social reality (Brumann 1999).

The reigning image of culture in the 1950s was that of a set of basic values internalized early in life and shaping one's very being. By the end of the twentieth century, culture was more likely to be viewed as a "toolkit" (Swidler 1986), a repertoire of skills and styles, "a pastiche of mediated representations" (DiMaggio 1997, 267).

Even in the early 1950s, however, Kroeber and Kluckhohn were cautious about the sway of a unified culture. They noted that whole cultures are composed of varying and overlapping subcultures and that "each individual selects from and to greater or lesser degree systematizes what he experiences of the total culture" (1952, 157). In a complex society such as ours, there is overlap "only upon the broadest of issues" (114). Yet Kroeber and Kluckhohn assumed that values were the key to the unity of cultures. Without reference to values, any account of a culture becomes "a mere laundry list," they argued (173). By the late twentieth century, the idea that culture shapes behavior through values or ultimate ends was largely rejected, as was the idea of culture as something deeply internalized.

Beginning with Dennis Wrong's classic 1961 article, "The Oversocialized Conception of Man in Modern Sociology," the idea of culture as a deeply internalized "latent" pattern that accounted for most human behavior came under attack. Wrong argued that individuals had more independence from culture than sociologists recognized, if only because of biological characteristics or presocialized unconscious minds.

In the 1970s, Clifford Geertz reoriented the study of culture to public and symbolic meanings. He argued that culture should be seen neither as a "super-organic reality" that exerts pressure on people nor as the attitudes and beliefs lodged within people's hearts and minds. Rather, culture is the context within which things become intelligible. It contains "webs of significance," an interpretive search for meaning. "Culture is public because meaning is" (1973, 12).

A focus on public symbols allowed analysts to avoid questions of how widely shared or consensual the culture is (Swidler 2002, 313). The analysis of public culture also might fail to appreciate the extent to which some public cultures may represent "the authorized beliefs of a society about itself" (Swidler 2001, 213). Nevertheless, Geertz's work was very influential.

But Geertz's idea that culture should be understood "through the (recording and) interpretation of the publicly available forms in which it is encoded (the 'symbols')" did not come to grips with the problem that culture may no longer be "'contained' in a location and/or attached to a particular group" (Ortner 1999, 6–7). Television, for example, makes such containment problematic. Symbols are now "conveyed by media to individuals without the co-presence of other human beings" (Schudson 1989, 154). Television anywhere in the world contains an "articulation of the transnational, the national, the local, and the personal," making it difficult to continue to assume that any particular culture is the only or the most powerful way "to make sense of the world" (Abu-Lughod 1999, 129).

Given the multiplicity and complexity of cultural ideas in the contemporary world, the view of culture itself had to change. In the newer view of culture, as people draw on local, national, and global sources of cultural ideas, such "ideas never form a closed or coherent whole" (S. Wright 1998, 10). Cultural "worlds of meaning" are normally "contradictory, loosely integrated, contested, mutable, and highly permeable" (Sewell 1999, 53). Indeed, in complex contemporary societies, attempts to pin down the "mainstream" or "dominant" culture often lead to the "intellectually embarrassing" result that "homogeneity may vanish like a mirage" (Hannerz 1992, 80). It becomes "harder to say from what normative cultural world a particular sub-culture deviates" (Eagleton 2000, 75). However, at least one anthropologist suggests that distinctions between earlier and later conceptualizations of culture are exaggerated. Marshall Sahlins has argued that early American anthropologists were too individualistic to assume that cultures were monolithic or coherent. Rather, he suggests, contemporary anthropologists appear to be applying "the historiographic principle . . . of attributing to one's predecessors the opposite of whatever is now deemed true" (1999, 404).

Be that as it may, by the late twentieth century, earlier notions that a unified culture determined behavior were increasingly called into question. Research in cognitive psychology suggests that "our heads are full of images, opinions, and information, untagged as to truth values to which we are inclined to attribute accuracy and plausibility" (DiMaggio 1997, 267). Some ideas are more accessible than others, and cues in the environment may bring them to the surface. But the fact that the images are internally inconsistent does not appear to affect people's ability to retain and act on those images. Such cognitive research challenges earlier assumptions that culture is acquired only through socialization, and it suggests that people have the capacity to participate in multiple cultural traditions (267–68).

In 1986, Ann Swidler suggested that only a "loose coupling" existed between culture and action. Culture provides people not with a set of values or ultimate ends that shape their behavior but with "strategies of action"—skills, styles, and informal know-how. People draw selectively on these cultural "tool kits." Individual adherents to the culture absorb things selectively and inconsistently, remaining ambivalent toward some aspects of the culture or even adhering to some cultural codes in which they do not really believe (giving Christmas presents, for example) (Swidler 2001, 163).

Though the tool kit image suggests that culture does not determine human behavior, Swidler acknowledges that "when culture fully takes, it so merges with life as to be nearly invisible" (2001, 19). Conversely, an increased consciousness of culture may mean that there are fewer experiences of such "unmediated apprehension of how the world is put together and how we should conduct ourselves in it." Whenever "culture is recognized as culture," detachment and doubt result (Carey 1988, 11). Indeed, the very idea of culture wars suggests that such simple apprehension no longer exists.

A number of scholars have attempted to pursue a middle ground between a deterministic view of culture—in which culture shapes human action—and a more voluntaristic position that allows for greater individual agency in selecting from the available cultural repertoires. Schudson, for example, has argued that neither of these positions is entirely satisfactory. Instead, he suggests that "sometimes culture 'works' and sometimes it doesn't. Sometimes the media cultivate attitudes, sometimes not; . . . sometimes ideas appear to be switchmen, sometimes they seem to make no difference" (1989, 158). There is no "universal truth with respect to these problems" (Robertson 1992, 34). In a similar vein, Vaisey (2007) has argued that culture provides both motivations and justifications for action. The justifications are conscious and are chosen from the available tool kit, while the motivations may be deep-seated and largely unconscious. Swidler, in contrast, has argued that at least some of the time, culture may have powerful effects when it is *not* deeply internalized (2002, 315). Sheer knowledge of the public code exerts pressure on people to give Christmas presents or to acknowledge their secretaries during National Secretaries Week or their mothers on Mother's Day. In such situations, "one is constrained not by internal motives but by knowledge of how one's actions may be interpreted by others." If one does not follow the code, one "may need to negotiate a way around it" (2001, 163).

Struggles over the rethinking of culture are occurring in all the social sciences. Within sociology, the tradition stemming from Emile Durkheim's late-nineteenth-century images of culture as a thinglike external force competes with newer images of the "social construction of reality" (P. L. Berger and Luckmann 1966). And whereas religion has always been at the "core" of studies of culture, those who study the sociology of culture today tend "to ignore religion altogether" (Casanova 1992, 33). Presumably, if culture is no longer about deep-seated meanings, religious understandings are no longer central.

Within anthropology, earlier traditions of ethnographic accounts portraying culture as a whole contend with arguments about whether the concept of culture remains useful. An anthropologist notes that the discipline has largely avoided the study of popular culture even though those in "cultural studies" who do study popular culture use definitions that should be attractive to "an anthropology that attempts to think of cultures as fragmented, hybrid, deterritorialized, and mutually entangled" (Traube 1996, 128–29). But another anthropologist points out that while contemporary scholars generally view culture as "unbounded," "neither 'boundedness' nor its absence is *given* in the world." Therefore, "to say a priori that 'cultures' are not 'bounded' . . . is misleading since local discourses *do,* in fact, establish authoritative traditions" (David Scott 1992, 376).

A political scientist contends that "the concept of 'political culture' or 'common knowledge' with which most political scientists operate presupposes an internal coherence and stability that is indefensible empirically." Political scientists are instead urged to think of culture as the practices through which "social actors attempt to make their worlds coherent" (Wedeen 2002, 720). An American historian notes that following the demise of "consensus history" in the post–World War II period, the emphasis shifted from an examination of "static national values to contingent state structures and political processes" (Rodgers 2004, 32). In lieu of a stable culture, one now assumes change and contingency.

Nevertheless, older ideas of culture often remain "embedded in our teaching," as introductory textbooks portray cultures "with unproblematized boundaries" and describe them in terms of "uniform and internally integrated traits" (Goode 2001, 435). Such simplifications no doubt have their uses. But perhaps, too, they occur because people want to see culture "in precisely the bounded, reified, essentialized, and timeless fashion that most of us now reject" (Brumann 1999, S11). While we recognize that individuals share certain "commonalities in thought and behavior" because of their membership in the same family, gender, age group, social class, ethnic group, and so forth, there remain characteristics that many Japanese share and that differ from those of Americans (Brumann 1999, S7).

Just as anthropologists are denying the existence of cultural boundaries, people all over the world are consciously and conspicuously marking such boundaries (Sahlins 1999, 414). Within the United States, people increasingly differentiate themselves from others by using the term *culture*—whether it is the culture of a particular corporation, the culture of the deaf, or the cultures attached to various forms of popular entertainment. In contemporary Western discourse, "we now literally *experience* difference *as* culture" (David Scott 2003, 103). Perhaps the summation of one social scientist is apt: "we cannot do without a concept of culture" (Sewell 1999, 38).

In what appears to be the dominant view, then, culture is no longer seen as a total way of life that evolves among a distinct people and is transmitted to their children, who internalize and reenact it. Yet there is far from total consensus on the understanding of culture as something that is fluid, contested, and changing. Consider the following contrast. Swidler maintains that culture does not exert influence "via enduring psychological proclivities implanted in individuals by their socialization. Instead, publicly available meanings facilitate certain patterns of action, making them readily available, while discouraging others" (1986, 283). James Davison Hunter, conversely, contends that culture is a matter of "commanding truths so deeply embedded in our consciousness and in the habits of our lives that to question them is to question reality itself" (1994, 200). Here lies perhaps the ultimate culture war. Is culture a thinglike reality that exerts control over us, as Hunter sees it? Or is it "a contested area, . . . inflected with politics" (Suny 2002, 1485), a matter of struggle and inequality rather than consensus (P. Smith 1998, 3), "a political process of contestation over the power to define key concepts, including that of 'culture' itself" (S. Wright 1998, 14)? If the latter view is accepted, then culture wars and multiculturalism become normal features of society. Indeed, when "culture no longer refers to *shared meanings* that reflect a people's way of life," the political nature of culture becomes clear: "*cultural practices* refer to the many institutions, classes, and groups that compete in the articulation of the social meaning of things" (McCarthy 1996, 26). It is no wonder, then, that some analysts perceive not a culture war but a class war or a series of political conflicts.

Academic arguments about the nature of culture are thus not as far removed from disputes about culture war issues as they might appear to be. At the most fundamental level, whether a culture war is really taking place may hinge on how one understands culture. It is probably not accidental that the originator of the culture wars concept within sociology views culture as something unitary and internalized. Though he asserts that culture is always contested (J. D. Hunter 2004), Hunter nevertheless conceptualizes culture as a matter of internally consistent and deep normative structures. If the "deep culture" is a unified entity, disagreements appear as culture wars. By contrast, those who adhere to the newer views of culture do not see a single transcendent culture war. Instead, they perceive multiple spheres of contention, significant internal disputes, and a shifting array of players and policy disputes.

Furthermore, culture war contentions may appear and disappear over time. Some disputes are resolved by an emerging consensus, and new ones arise. Thus, some of the controversies originating in the 1960s (for example, whether wives should work and whether premarital sex is always wrong) have been largely resolved, while others (homosexuality and same-sex marriage) have become more salient (Fischer and Hout 2006, 229–30). At the end of the 1990s, even Evangelicals expressed more support for women's participation in both the labor market and politics than had been the case a decade earlier, though Evangelicals still prefer traditional family arrangements when children are involved. And though they are much less accepting of homosexuality than is the rest of the society, Evangelicals manifest greater tolerance than they did earlier (McConkey 2001, 169, 172).

Sometimes a culture war dispute disappears because the particular provocation is removed. Thus, the intense controversy over funding for the arts is "now over—not because we now have agreement on the meaning and value of the arts, but simply because there is neither a policy issue at stake, nor any sort of media attention on debates within the arts" (Kidd

2006, 6). Without specific provocations such as those surrounding Robert Mapplethorpe's photographs of gay men or Andres Serrano's photograph of a crucifix submerged in urine, the larger issue has been removed from public consciousness. The two-decade-long war over the university canon likewise appears to be of less concern now. The public is no longer engaged by the "canon wars"—disputes over what constitute essential or "classic" works to be included in university curricula.

Perceptions of the specific issues of contention in the culture wars are also significantly influenced by how one views culture. Multiculturalism, for example, is attacked or defended through the lens of one's understanding of culture. Curiously, multiculturalism has been attacked for both underestimating and overestimating the influence of culture. The idea of multiculturalism has been found wanting by those who subscribe to both older and newer understandings of culture.

James Davison Hunter alleges that multiculturalists fail to recognize that culture is a matter of norms and values that are deeply embedded within us. "Within multiculturalism literature, culture is essentially reduced to life-style (choices about how one lives) or, at best, customs (practices that have the sanction of tradition but are not insisted upon as inviolable)." Multiculturalists assume that the individual is "free and independent from culture, unencumbered by moral commitments defined by virtue of one's membership in a community. But culture is much more pervasive, powerful, and compelling than is allowed for in the liberal understanding of the self. . . . By reducing culture to a product about which individuals may choose, multiculturalism further renders culture as a trifling matter" (1994, 200–202). Bernstein argues similarly that multiculturalists do not really know or care much about culture: "The paradox is that the power of culture is utterly contrary to the most fervently held beliefs and values of the advocates of multiculturalism. Multiculturalism is a movement of the left. . . . But culture is powerfully conservative. Culture is what enforces obedience to authority, the authority of parents, of history, of custom, of superstition. Deep attachment to culture is one of the things that prevents different people from understanding one another" (1995, 6). And a historian has argued that in our zeal to imagine "a soft multiculturalist notion of a syncretic America," we may well minimize "the pain of cultural brokerage, . . . leaving Pocahontas Disneyized." Those cultural brokers "who were once reviled as 'half-breeds' of treacherously inscrutable loyalties, emerge now as transcultural virtuosos, able to shift performative identities at will" (Rodgers 2004, 39).

Multiculturalists are also criticized for failing to appreciate the unity and integrity of culture. "A culture is, after all, a complete way of thinking, feeling, and viewing the world. It is not a smorgasbord from which the diner can select his favorite bits and pieces at will." Multiculturalists operate with "a general ignorance of what a culture is" (O'Sullivan 1994a, 40). "A moral tradition is an organic whole," says another conservative; one cannot accept only some of it. Making homosexual activity acceptable, for example, will generate questioning of the whole tradition (Klinghoffer 1998, 26).

From the vantage point of those with the newer view of culture, however, Hunter, Bernstein, and others are "cultural fundamentalists" who are frightened by "the flimsiness of a culture where everything is in motion and authority has perpetually to prove itself . . . and the fragments of identity are on sale everywhere from the university to the mall" (Gitlin 1995, 223). Multiculturalism appears to make a mockery of deeply implanted normative structures.

Critics who accuse multiculturalists of overestimating the significance of culture, however, allege that multiculturalists make every group appear to have a culture of its own, so that we become incapable of understanding each other across cultural barriers. As one observer puts it, the multiculturalists "have created a cult of incommensurability. But if the differences between individuals and groups were as thick as the multiculturalists think, then not even multiculturalism would be possible. Everybody would be shut up in subjectivity" (Wieseltier 1994, 30). In "the exaggerated postmodernist perspective" to which some multiculturalists adhere, human beings are "pure products of cultural context," so that no understanding or communication between cultures is possible. This idea not only is false but "provides intellectual backup for a political outlook that sees no real basis for common ground among humans of different sexes, races, and cultures" (Ehrenreich and McIntosh 1997, 15, 16). Multiculturalists treat culture as if it were "a fixed entity, transmitted, as it were, in the genes, rather than through experience" (Chavez 1994, 26). Left and Right converge here in critiquing the exaggerated influence that some multiculturalists impute to culture.

As these critics of multiculturalism see it, no contemporary group can maintain a firm culture. "The onslaught of economic, organizational, and technological change inexorably erodes the very ground on which one's parents walked" (Gitlin 1995, 206). While multiculturalism harbors the "presumption that grandparents are destiny," contemporary individuals can choose their cultural affiliations. Though there is "a common prejudice to the effect that affiliations based on choice are somehow artificial and lacking in depth, . . . superficiality does not follow from volition any more than authenticity follows from submission to tradition and authority" (Hollinger 1995, 119). After all, "the depth of . . . involvement is often greater among converts than among birthright members of a particular religious community" (121). And the allegation that those who change religions are not "morally serious" is belied by such phenomena as the pro-life activists who convert to Catholicism or those who switch religious denominations because of agreement with the "moral culture" of their new groups (R. S. Warner 1993, 1076–77).

Given the hostility toward multiculturalism from those with very different understandings of culture, it is perhaps not surprising that no commentator in our twenty-one-year sample of political commentary defends the basic concept of multiculturalism. To be sure, some writers are more hostile to the idea than others, and some offer support for educating students about cultural diversity, but enthusiasm for the fundamental concept is strikingly absent.

Arguments about the workings of culture are also implicated in the culture war debates concerning popular culture. Reflecting the greater likelihood that progressives will adhere to the newer view of culture, most commentators on the left do not see any one-to-one relationship between popular culture and actual behavior. By contrast, those on the right are more likely to see popular culture, art, literature, and other symbolic fare as directly affecting behavior. An editorial in *National Review,* for example, argues that people who watch TV talk shows "will find it harder to reject other kinds of behavior that are wrong but less extravagantly perverted, like conventional adultery" (Editorial 1995b, 18). A liberal commentator, by contrast, suggests that although "the culture now has a surfeit of coarseness, from noxious rap lyrics to the Jerry Springer Show," there is no evidence of moral decline (Whitman 1999, 18).

Progressives similarly attack what they see as a "simple one-to-one correlation between books and behavior" in the debate over the university canon. If people are divided, as they have always been, about "what kind of country they want," then "books cannot mold a common national purpose" (Pollitt 1991, 331). It is also wrong to treat works of art as if their purpose is "therapeutic." "Imbibe the Republic or Phaedo at 19, and you will be one kind of person; study Jane Eyre or Mrs. Dalloway, and you will be another" (Hughes 1992a, 47).

Progressives thus appear to attribute greater autonomy or agency to individuals in the face of cultural symbols than do the conservatives. Yet at least one conservative, unwilling to tolerate government censorship of cultural materials, suggests that the sex and violence in contemporary popular culture do not have dire consequences. He agrees with those who argue that "as an influence on the development of my children, my words and my example outweigh . . . anything Britney Spears does. . . . It's the culture—but it doesn't matter; it does no great harm" (Derbyshire 2000, 34). Similarly, at least one progressive acknowledges that cultural imprinting can have significant effects. Although we are aware of the social construction of cultural categories, they often act "as needless calcifications," he says. We know that "cultural definitions of sexual and gender unorthodoxy have shifted over time. . . . Most of us, alas, however attracted to the theory of infinite malleability, have been trained in a culture that regards sexual appetite as consisting of two, and only two, contrasting variations—gay or straight. And most of us have internalized that perhaps false dichotomy to such a degree that it has become as deeply imprinted in us—as immutable—as any genetically mandated trait" (Duberman 1993, 22).

Commentators from all sides acknowledge the pervasiveness of popular culture and the difficulty of disentangling one's own thoughts from those disseminated by the media (Gibbs and McDowell 1992; Labi 1998; Morrow 1994a). Conservative writers are more likely to find these influences pernicious and to attribute power over the culture to the Left. "Culture shapes our lives and affects every action we take," says one such commentator, and "the current epidemics of drug use, AIDS, and crime are testimony enough to the power of culture to influence our lives. Just think how implicated the cultural agenda of the Left has been in these disasters," since the Left's literature, music, and films have "glorified every kind of libertinism and polymorphous perversity" (Lipman 1991b, 53).

Despite disagreements about where power lies, most commentators subscribe to the idea that culture is ultimately made by people in their ongoing social interactions. Though conservatives assume that "most people aren't pleased to have their most cherished values challenged" (Hyde 1990a, 26), while progressives assume that traditions are or should be "open to criticism and renegotiation" (G. Graff and Cain 1989, 312), the idea that culture is socially constructed and changeable appears to be shared by all. Writers on the left and in the center may use the language of "social construction" more frequently than those on the right, but all seem to share some version of the following idea: "Each of us in our daily lives helps shape the cultural images and assumptions that define the limits of the permissible" (Pollitt 1990, 24). Debates about the meaning of Columbus, for example, are seen as a way of reinventing ourselves, overturning earlier myths and replacing them with new ones (Gray 1991). More generally, "America is a construction of mind. . . . America is a collective act of the imagination whose making never ends" (Hughes 1992a, 44). What is discussed in the culture wars is a matter of the redefinition of morality—"a process in which all Americans, from born-again to New Age to agnostic, are already participating" (Judis 1999, 56). A *National Review* writer notes that if we capitulate to the demands of the multiculturalists, we might "create a self-fulfilling prophecy" and produce a multicultural society, though none currently exists in the United States (Chavez 1994, 26). And a well-known conservative describes the process through which a culture can erode over time. He argues that the essentially WASP American character, rooted in hard work, civic-mindedness, and individual consciences, has come under attack. "The danger is not that a new post-WASP personality will emerge. A nation's character is not so mutable; it takes major upheaval—revolution, conquest—to transform it. What is possible, however, is that the character America already possesses will slip into chronic malfunction. Most of us will keep behaving the way we always have, without knowing why, while the rest will act differently, simply for the sake of being different." (Brookhiser 1993b, 79). We are not powerless to change the culture, another conservative suggests, as the example of smoking illustrates. In the not-very-distant past, "the culture and its sustaining icons (Humphrey Bogart for example) loved smoking. Today smoking cigarettes is disreputable. . . . Change the myth and the values follow" (Morrow 1995, 90).

The Culture Warriors

Those who participate in the culture wars are, of course, intensely aware of the struggle for control. As each side attempts to define the culture while fearing its opponents' ability to do likewise, a kind of mirror imagery appears in descriptions of the struggle. The Left says that at issue is "a powerful movement to impose intellectual and cultural hegemony on the whole society. The New Right agenda not only includes compulsory prayer; it demands compulsory heterosexuality, compulsory sobriety, compulsory racism, sexism, and imperialism" (Editorial 1984, 308). The Right, in turn, explains "the Left's cultural agenda" as consisting of "primitivism, feminism, racialism, multiculturalism, and sexual radicalism. The Left wishes to . . . destroy every traditional social habit and institution, including churches and ending with the family" (Lipman 1991b, 38). If a critic on the left portrays the culture war as a contest between questioning authority and *Father Knows Best,* between self-expression and deference to norms (Ehrenreich 1993b, 74), an observer on the right suggests that what "drives the culture war" is "the power of rationalization" that convinces people that "heretofore forbidden desires are permissible," whether such desires are homosexuality or abortion (Reilly 1996, 60).

The two sides fear each other's influences in very similar ways. A commentator on the left cries out, "How long are we going to let conservatives define the national agenda on social issues?" (Tax 1995, 378). And from the right, the question is, "Why is culture formed so completely by the Left, rather than by the Right?" (Lipman 1991b, 38). Those on the right argue that support for the traditional family goes against "the reigning orthodoxy" (Marshner 1988, 39) and subjects one to "the charge of being a bigot, a religious nut, or just hopelessly out of touch" (Tucker 1993, 28). On the left, the contention is that "it's even harder to get a serious public hearing for a radical critique of the family than for a radical critique of capitalism" (Willis 1996, 22). The Right accuses American society of a form of religious intolerance, suggesting that "culture makers" bear a "disdain bordering on contempt . . . for the deeply religious" (Krauthammer 1998, 92). The Left argues that it is not possible in American society to "mock religious belief as childish" or to "describe God as our creation" because such sentiments violate "the norms of civility and religious correctness" (Kaminer 1996, 24).

Both sides fear that their opponents have gained the upper hand in framing the debates, in constructing the cultural realities. On the right, there is concern that the gay movement has succeeded in defining a reality that makes opposition to homosexuals appear to be bigotry (Editorial 1998c, 16). On the left, there is fear that the Christian Right's definition of acceptability has made all gays seek to demonstrate that they're just as worthy (Ireland 1999, 16).

Each side sees inadequacies in its own efforts to shape the culture. Conservatives worry that their relative absence in the culture-producing industries—the arts and entertainment—has left audiences more vulnerable to the opposition's influence. Without leadership from conservative culture makers, audiences have continued "their passive consumption of cultural artifacts and thus acquiescence in the dominant values" (Lipman 1991b, 53). Progressives, conversely, are worried that they have been so absorbed in calling for cultural diversity that "we on the left no longer know what we want from cultural life, nor what we should demand from culture" (Kriegel 1984–85, 714).

There is mirror imagery, too, in the motives that each side assigns to its opponents. The Left argues that the culture wars are a right-wing effort to distract attention from the increasing inequality of income and wealth. "It's the culture, stupid" (di Leonardo 1996, 25). The Right, in contrast, suggests that for the Left, "culture—or rather cultures—replaces economics as the engine of revolutionary social change"; "power to the cultures" replaces "power to the people" (Lipman 1991a, 40).

Each side accuses the other of "politicizing" culture. If the Left has argued that "the personal is political" because issues of feminism, abortion, and gay rights cannot be handled on a purely individual or personal level, the Right sees this as "politicizing." The Left politicizes everything, conservatives have argued, by taking private behaviors—such as homosexual acts—and bringing them into the public sphere. "The idea that one must be either in the closet or out of it is an invention of those who would politicize sex and abolish privacy" (Short 1990, 44). When conservatives see politicization within their own ranks, it is with dismay. Thus, "the politicizing of religion" is seen as disastrous for both public life and religion (Neuhaus 1988a, 46). For the Left, however, the Right "politicizes" culture when it disputes revisions of university curricula or the funding choices of the National Endowment for the Arts. As seen by the Left, the campaign against funding the National Endowment for the Arts is part of "the populist right's broader agenda" (Editorial 1995a, 152); it is based on "an amalgam of high culture reactionaries, antigovernment ideologues and faux populists" (Pollitt 1997, 10).

The Left accuses the Right of denying its own—inevitably political—stances. Thus, conservatives' "uneasiness and sometimes distaste for minority subcultures: blacks, women, gays" goes along with "a tendency to advance a supposedly depoliticized (which means strongly political) view of culture that sees it as a museum of fixed consensual values" (Howe 1984, 29). The Right, in turn, accuses the Left of being "determined to politicize" culture to undermine and destroy traditional habits and institutions (Lipman 1991b, 38).

The mirror images of the contending culture warriors—the idea that criticism of the family is not acceptable versus the idea that the traditional family is out of fashion; the idea that one cannot criticize religion versus the idea that serious religious conviction is out of bounds; the idea that culture wars are a cover for increasing economic inequality versus the idea that they compensate for the failure of egalitarian ideas—reflect an underlying social reality in which both sides are true. Americans are highly individualistic, yet they endorse the importance of the family far more than their European counterparts do (see van Elteren 1998, 70). Americans are highly religious but uncomfortable with extremists of any stripe. Americans are egalitarian in ideology but uncomfortable talking about class; thus, cultural issues cover for economic ones. The values of both sides in the culture war appear to be strongly present in the American population.

Perhaps only in America does a conservative who sees the traditional family as in tune with "the facts of human nature" nevertheless feel it necessary to argue that teaching children about family values does not inhibit self-expression. We need to train children in these traditional family values to help them understand their own nature, she argues. Children so trained are nonetheless free to reject these values when they mature, which is "why, contrary to what the relativists insist, instilling them is not oppressive" (Marshner 1988, 40).

American Culture

Can one subscribe to the newer view of culture and still speak of an entity called American culture? Can one refer to American culture without doing violence to empirical reality? To some extent, nations exist as "symbolic communities" and "define themselves in opposition to one another." Being anti-American, for example, may help to define some French people (Lamont and Molnar 2002, 185). But is there some essence that defines American culture?

If one contends that there is no "war" over "the meaning of America," how is this meaning to be defined? Over the years, various analysts—most notably, perhaps, Robin Williams (1957), Herbert Gans (1980), and Seymour Martin Lipset (1996)—have produced lists of core American values. However credible these lists may seem to be, they remain both static and simplified. They fail to indicate the ambiguities and contradictions attached to each particular trait.

While most adherents to newer understandings of culture reject the idea of values as central in understanding behavior, I argue that the values discussed are rarely held without ambivalence. It is not simply that people's actions do not reflect the ideals of the culture in a straightforward way. Each value is accompanied by competing concerns, ambivalences that do not allow for simple enactment. As Slater has noted, every culture frustrates some needs by emphasizing others. Thus, American individualism repeatedly frustrates needs for community and dependence (1976, 8–9), and such frustrated needs inevitably exert cultural pressures.

If Americans are notoriously individualistic, what exactly does that mean? Survey data over many decades substantiate an American devotion to laissez-faire policies and the belief that each individual is responsible for his or her fate. But individualism is not a unitary phenomenon (Fischer 2000; Halman 1996). If Americans are supremely devoted to economic individualism, they are simultaneously concerned about the excesses of individualism and the need for community. They also place more credence in traditional authorities than the citizens of other advanced technological societies do.

American devotions to religion and morality, to pluralism and populism, are likewise riddled with inconsistencies and paradoxes. If Americans are more given to religious and moral thinking than are citizens of most other technologically advanced nations, they have never resolved how much religion and morality should be matters of public consensus and how much should be left to the individual conscience. Americans have wrestled with issues of religion and morality in ways that manifestly differ from those of their European counterparts, who have not experienced the extremes of a constitutional amendment banning alcohol or the outright ban on prostitution, for example.

Lipset and others have argued that unlike other nations, whose citizens belong as a matter of birthright, the United States was born out of revolution, and its unity hinges on a shared creed. In Europe, for example, "one cannot become un-English or un-Swedish. Being an American, however, is an ideological commitment. It is not a matter of birth. Those who reject American values are un-American" (1996, 31). Lipset's critics reject the idea that a set of enduring values can explain American history and politics, maintaining instead that values result from at least as much as they cause institutional practices and historical events. Lipset acknowledges the role of institutional factors in producing values, noting that "a new settler society, a Bill of Rights, Protestant sectarianism, wars, and the like" have produced American values. Nevertheless, he asserts that these values "result in deep beliefs, such as deference or antagonism to authority, individualism or group-centeredness, and egalitarianism or elitism, which form the organizing principles of societies" (25). Such an approach minimizes the roles of both human agency and power differentials and exaggerates the degree to which one end of each polarity is dominant.

Some adherents to newer understandings of culture question the utility of the concept of values. Swidler argues, for example, that American individualism should not be seen as a "value." Rather, it represents the idea that action depends on individuals' choices. And the "individualistic way of organizing action can be directed to many values, among them the establishment of 'community'" (1986, 276).

If many contemporary scholars are willing to abandon the concept of values and to question the idea of well-defined cultures, others continue to assert that "deep culture is more than the epiphenomenal product of political and economic arrangements" (Wuthnow 2006, 28) and that cultural assumptions often make change difficult. Assumptions about "individualism and the American dream," for example, may "make it difficult to confront inequality and discrimination" (Wuthnow 2005, 363). Yet as Bennett Berger has observed, culture entails "a continuing historical process" in which "the meaning of none of the key terms is fixed over time" (1995, 39). Indeed, many aspects of the "American Creed" can be seen as persisting while being subjected to change, conflict, and the evolution of new meanings. American culture is embodied in enduring dilemmas rather than enduring values.

To some extent, the very religiosity and morality that appear to inhere in the American Creed may help to generate conflicts. Many scholars have argued that Americans are among the most religious people in Christendom because voluntaristic sects rather than hierarchical churches have dominated American religious institutions. "The sectarian is expected to follow a moral code, as determined by his/her own sense of rectitude, reflecting a personal relationship with God." The American sects have thus "produced a moralistic people" (Lipset 1996, 19–20). Conflicts about public policy are "intense" and "morally based" as "people quarrel sharply about how to apply the basic principles of Americanism they purport to agree about" (26).

From this perspective, the contemporary American culture wars can be seen as an outgrowth of characteristically American culture patterns. Cultural politics are certainly not new in American life, even if earlier manifestations were not labeled as "culture wars." Contentions regarding the abolition of slavery, the prohibition of alcohol, and the reading of the Bible in public schools, for example, were of major importance in earlier American politics.

Like earlier cultural politics, the contemporary culture wars take place within the parameters of some enduring cultural patterns. These patterns are a matter not of stable values but rather of a series of dilemmas that are revisited as new issues or situations evoke them. Dilemmas about the role of religion and morality, about individualism, pluralism, and populism, constitute American culture. In each case, as my analysis of public discourse in the culture wars shows, there is no simple solution. American culture is not a matter of either/or but rather of both/and. There is thus no simple or unitary "culture war," no "struggle for the soul of America."

If the contemporary culture wars differ from those of the past, it is only because we have become increasingly aware of such contention and increasingly conscious of the tenuousness with which all cultural ideas are held. One does not need to be a sociologist to recognize the speed with which ideas about sexual practices, for example, have changed. Premarital sex has become the norm. Homosexuality has lost its exoticism. Indeed, gay activists were well aware that the more their members came out of the closet, the less difficult the struggle for acceptance would become. Self-conscious efforts to shape cultural meanings are now part of the political agenda.

The chapters that follow explore each of the American cultural dilemmas in which the culture wars are embedded through the lens of two decades' worth of political commentary. Where data are available concerning public sentiments on these issues, these data are incorporated into the narratives. Also addressed are historical and theoretical arguments concerning the larger issues—for example, questions about American religiosity and civil religion, the nature of American individualism and pluralism, and how multiculturalism is related to individualism. Although there is more agreement among the cultural antagonists than is usually imagined, there is also more internal disagreement within each camp than is usually acknowledged. These internal divisions are explored in the penultimate chapter, which assesses the current forms of polarization in American society, whether they result from an "American exceptionalism," and whether the 2000, 2004, and 2008 presidential elections demonstrate the significance of the culture wars. A brief concluding chapter offers observations on ongoing cultural change.

CHAPTER 2

Respect for Religion but Uncertainty about Its Role

When Alexis de Tocqueville visited the United States in the 1830s, he observed that the American case belied the eighteenth-century philosophers' assumption that religious faith would decline in the face of broader freedom and knowledge: "In America, one of the freest and most enlightened nations in the world, the people fulfill with fervor all the outward duties of religion" (1848/1961, 1:319). He also noted that although a politician could attack a particular sect without being damaged, "if he attacks all the sects together, everyone abandons him" (317). In this regard, little appears to have changed.

The Public Sphere and Civil Religion

In keeping with the general American tendency to view religion as a positive force, all of the journals of political opinion show a respect for religion. Although *The New Republic* editorializes against the Religious Right's "conflation of religion with morality," it nevertheless chides liberals not to assume "that the godless have nothing to learn from the godful" (Editorial 1994a, 7). However, it is not only the Religious Right that conflates religion and morality. Five years after that editorial appeared, an article published in the same magazine argued that we are now "more moral" than we were earlier. The writer's progressive sympathies are clearly indicated by his measures of moral progress: declines in sexism, racism, ageism, and discrimination against homosexuals and the disabled. Nevertheless, he also lists as indicators of moral progress a slight increase in church attendance and prayer and no decline in religious belief (Whitman 1999, 18).

A broad consensus holds that religion contributes to civil society. As one commentator sees it, if all religious claims were to be deemed inadmissible in the public arena, we would be "depluralizing our polity," to its detriment. Religious ideas and communities encourage civic participation, mutual assistance, and humanistic values. And it is not possible for "persons of faith" to "bracket their beliefs when they enter the public square." Much of the animus against religious participation in public life comes from the style of that participation, which should be altered to be intelligible to those who do not share the faith (Elshtain 1996, 25).

Articles in magazines across the political spectrum suggest that debates in the public square must be based on secular reasons, not on faith. Because religious reasons are not persuasive to the nonreligious, the secular reasons must be debated, even in matters such as abortion (Editorial 1994a, 7). Whatever public policies arise from religious understandings "will have to be justified, in the public square, on other grounds" (Pollitt 1996, 9). To be sure, some conservative religious spokespersons contend that religious debaters can bring "a nuanced appreciation of complexity and a level of public reasoning that can elevate the otherwise debased moral discourse in American society" (Neuhaus 1986, 46).

Articles by William F. Buckley Jr. and Harvey Cox nicely illustrate the convergence between Left and Right in their support for religious discourse within the public sphere. While Buckley writes in *National Review* that public figures should be able to say that greed or adultery is wrong, as the New Testament tells us (1996, 63), Cox argues in *The Nation* that religious discourse can enrich political discourse and that either politics is "linked to morality or it withers" (1996, 20). A conservative writer in *The New Republic* also argues that "conservatives are not the only ones who are troubled" by the question of "what happens to a free society when a major source of its values—religion—declines" (Krauthammer 1981, 25).

Of the forty-six articles that deal with aspects of religion other than the creationism disputes, half maintain a favorable view of religion, while only six are clearly negative. The remaining seventeen articles are neutral. Even within the sample in *The Nation,* six of the articles addressing religion are neutral or positive (three of each), while five are negative. In the discussions of creationism, only three of the nine articles are clearly hostile to religious encroachments against science; two are neutral, and four support religion's claims to be heard in the classroom, albeit not as science.

Support for religion in the public sphere includes the idea of strengthening American civil religion. The American civil religion—including a belief in God and the hereafter, religious tolerance, and the notion that virtue should be rewarded and vice punished—has enriched the nation for two centuries, one writer argues. Though it is now jeopardized by the "Holy War" between the Fundamentalists and the secularists, its purpose is "to infuse American life with a sense of transcendence, not to impose a religious order on individuals." (Krauthammer 1984, 19). Keeping God out of the public schools, says another commentator, "prevents people from drawing on this country's rich and diverse religious heritage for guidance and it degrades the nation's moral discourse" (Gibbs 1991, 68).

Though calls for the rejuvenation of American civil religion are essentially calls for consensus and unity, the concept itself is fraught with controversy and conflict. Attacked as a form of national self-righteousness, defended as a transcendent standard of judgment for the American polity, the idea of American civil religion embodies the long-standing connection between religion and politics in the United States. Despite American devotion to the separation of church and state, civil religion has served to legitimate and sanctify both the government and various social movements. As numerous commentators have pointed out, the very language of the Declaration of Independence contains tenets of American civil religion, suggesting that God's laws rule over humans and that God has given us "unalienable rights." But the very "elasticity" of civil religion "as a symbolic resource means that its content is contested" (Rhys H. Williams and Alexander 1994, 4).

While the phrase *civil religion* originated with Rousseau, who saw it as a creed developed and implemented by rulers to assure citizens' loyalty, its use has also reflected the Durkheimean understanding that every social group has a religious dimension. The application of the idea to American society received its classic form in the work of Robert Bellah in the late

1960s. Bellah defended his concept against the accusation that it represented "national self-worship" by arguing that its central idea is "the subordination of the nation to ethical principles that transcend it and in terms of which it should be judged" (Bellah 1970, 168). In Bellah's understanding at the time, the references to God in our currency and in our pledge of allegiance to the flag, in the oath of office and in the inaugural addresses of most American Presidents signify that though sovereignty is in the hands of the citizenry, it ultimately rests in God. There is thus a "higher criterion" by which to judge the will of the people (171). The beliefs (including the idea of America as the promised land and the idea that "God has led his people to establish a new sort of social order that shall be a light unto all the nations") (175), the symbols (the flag), and the rituals (the presidential inauguration, the Fourth of July, and Memorial Day) together constitute a civil religion that is nonsectarian and is not tied to Christianity, though they may share some ideas.

Bellah recognized that the American civil religion could be used for good or for ill. Though it is "difficult to use the words of Jefferson and Lincoln to support special interests and undermine personal freedom," the theme of the American Israel was used to justify shameful treatment of the American Indians, and "an American-Legion type of ideology that fuses God, country, and flag has been used to attack nonconformist and liberal ideas and groups of all kinds" (1970, 182). Yet his tone remained guardedly optimistic. Even a decade later, he asserted, "I am not prepared to say that religious communities, among which I include humanist communities, are not capable even today of providing the religious superstructure and infrastructure that would renew our republic" (1978, 200). This is of great importance, Bellah argued, because civil religion is "indispensable" to the existence of a republic—a government in which there is an active political community that has purpose and values (197).

But by 2001, when analysts saw a resurgence of American civil religion in the aftermath of the September 11 attacks, Bellah was clearly skeptical of the uses to which civil religious themes were being put. He was highly critical of an address given by President George W. Bush at the Washington National Cathedral, calling it "stunningly inappropriate . . . because it was a war talk" (Broadway 2001, B09). The use of the concept had clearly now become so identified with conservative causes that Bellah and other liberals no longer felt tied to it. Bellah's initial discussion of civil religion had appeared during the liberal era of the 1960s. At that time, he cited as an example of American civil religion President Lyndon B. Johnson's 1965 address calling for a strong voting-rights act, which concluded, "God will not favor everything that we do. It is rather our duty to divine his will. I cannot help but believe that He truly understands and that He really favors the undertaking that we begin here tonight" (Bellah 1970, 181).

Twenty years after this use of civil religious language to promote the cause of civil rights, noted theologian Martin E. Marty asserted that civil religion "has been transposed in public perception, from moderate and liberal contexts to conservative and nationalist ones" (1985, 16). Robert Wuthnow proclaimed that there were now two versions of American civil religion: conservative and liberal, with the former emphasizing biblical origins and economic and other freedoms and the latter concerned with peace and security and America's role in the world (1988, 281). Both sides talk of "higher principles" that govern what America should be (Derek H. Davis 1997), but the Right emphasizes "one nation under God," while the Left stresses "liberty and justice for all" (Guinness 1993, 232). While it may seem like an oxymoron to talk of competing civil religions, Bellah et al. argue that the two do not represent "a polarization of American civil religion." Rather, American popular culture embraces the values proclaimed by both sides; it's not a matter of either/or (1991, 215).

In the wake of the September 11, 2001, terrorist attacks, "the ailing civil religion" seemed to come back to life. Large numbers of Americans went to church for comfort and displayed American flags everywhere—"an instinctive melding of the religious and the civil" (McClay 2004, 16). Those on the Christian Right, such as Jerry Falwell and Pat Robertson, who viewed the attacks as evidence of "God's displeasure at America's having turned away from its Judeo-Christian roots" were "quickly and soundly rebuffed" (Machacek 2003, 157), their credibility damaged (McClay 2004, 6). Perhaps, one analyst argued, "a great many Americans" understood that "their brand of narrow-minded religiosity is not, after all, the 'American way'" and that American civil religion can be inclusive of all Americans (Angrosino 2002, 265).

The search for a "common faith" remains (McClay 2004, 19), as does the desire for a more expansive civil religion that affirms "religious diversity as a positive value" (Machacek 2003, 157). Civil religion is seen as providing "a second language of piety" within a pluralistic society where "religious believers and nonbelievers alike need ways to live together" (McClay 2004, 19).

Struggles over how to define the civil religion are certainly not new. Indeed, "it is doubtful whether America ever existed as an ideological whole" (Demerath and Williams 1985, 163). The Durkheimean image of moral integration and cultural consensus was probably never accurate. Our newer understandings of culture make it clear that the unifying characteristics of a civil religion have been exaggerated.

Though Bellah disputed any necessary connection between Christianity and American civil religion, such connections clearly are often made. As one historian has noted, the idea that "Christians have a proprietary relation to the United States" dies a very slow death (Hollinger 2002, 863). Efforts at greater inclusion through the use of the term *Judeo-Christian* are not persuasive in a twenty-first-century America whose population includes many Hindus, Muslims, Buddhists, Sikhs, and members of other faiths. In such a religiously pluralistic society, no "religious common denominator" is possible, "no faith can be shared, public, all-American—and transcendent" (Guinness 1993, 233–34).

While members of both the contemporary Left (as represented by Bellah) and Right (as represented by Guinness) view civil religion as requiring a standard of judgment that transcends the social system, some earlier observers defined American civil religion as the equivalent of a "folk religion" (D. G. Jones and Richey 1974, 15). Thus, for Will Herberg, the American Way of Life "is a civil religion in the strictest sense of the term, for, in it, national life is apotheosized, national values are religionized, national heroes are divinized, national history is experienced as . . . a redemptive history" (1974, 78). To critics such as Bellah and Guinness, this is little short of idolatrous. Indeed, the very Durkheimean understanding of religion as a kind of societal self-worship makes civil religion "inescapably idolatrous" (Guinness 1993, 225). Another critic points to the contradictory elements in American civil religion. "Can American civil religion be anything other than the patriotic cult of the manifest imperial destiny of the American nation or the cult of a nation made up of individuals pursuing their own private utilitarian forms of religion? Both would undermine republican virtue" (Casanova 1994, 60).

The few efforts to test the idea of American civil religion with empirical data have not produced convincing evidence. A study of editorials in one hundred newspapers during the Honor America Day celebrations of July 4, 1970, found surprisingly few mentions of any of the themes of American civil religion as enunciated by Bellah. The references that existed did not contain religious connotations but were purely secular—for example, discussion of human rights without any suggestion that they come from God. Contrary to researchers' expectations, civil religious content was more prevalent in large urban newspapers than in newspapers in small towns and rural areas. Perhaps, the authors suggest, "a well-defined thesis of civil religion may be more the creation (and fantasy) of the liberal political intellectual elite than active faith among the masses" (Thomas and Flippen 1972, 224). American churchgoers may well see public values as being Christian or secular rather than a matter of civil religion (223).

Another study, using a small sample of conservative religious Protestants, does find support for a separate civil religious dimension (Wimberley et al. 1976). However, from the vantage point of more than three decades later, the indicators for this civil religious dimension would likely be seen as anathema by substantial portions of the American population. Far from being a matter of cultural consensus, they would likely provide little more than evidence of "culture wars." The agree/disagree items in question include "We should respect the president's authority since his authority is from God"; "It is a mistake to think that America is God's chosen nation today"; and "National leaders should not only affirm their belief in God but also their belief in Jesus Christ as Savior and Lord" (893).

More broad-based adherence to civil religious ideas is found in a 1975 North Carolina survey that called for agreement with the ideas that America is God's chosen nation; that the flag of the United States is sacred; that human rights come from God and not merely from laws; and that if government does not support religion, government cannot uphold morality. In this study, while both religious and political conservatives show more adherence to civil religion than do others, a majority of participants in liberal religions and more Democrats than Republicans and independents also support civil religion. But while support for civil religion is found across most social segments, those at or near the top of both social and religious hierarchies—"professionals, ministers, and officials"—are not supporters (Christenson and Wimberley 1978). Bellah suggests that questions asking respondents whether political leaders or institutions have a religious or sacred quality do not tap civil religion. Instead, he argues, we should be asking if respondents agree that all men are created equal, that they are endowed by their creator with certain inalienable rights, and that governments derive their just powers from the consent of the governed (1976, 155).

Perhaps the main conclusion to be drawn from this brief review of four decades' worth of discussion of American civil religion is that the idea of viewing political issues in religious and moral terms remains a significant element in American culture. Whatever the ongoing contests, however varying the interpretations of civil religion that reign at different times, there is the continuing tendency to seek divine legitimation for American political ideas and social movements. If today the conservative uses of civil religion seem dominant, it is well to remember the role of civil religion in the Populist movement of the late nineteenth and early twentieth centuries. William Jennings Bryan declared in 1896 that "every great economic question is in reality a great moral question," and the Populists condemned economic inequality "as a violation of God's 'natural order'" (Rhys H. Williams and Alexander 1994, 6). They repeatedly recalled the image of Jesus throwing the moneychangers out of the temple. "American Populism—so often considered an 'economic' ideology—was also a religio-moral enterprise" (12).

Despite—or because of—the perceived conservative domination of civil religious thought in the contemporary period, several articles in *The Nation* discuss the contributions that religion can make to progressive causes (Cox 1996; Ferber 1985; Kazin 1998). These articles note that the "religious revival" in contemporary American society includes movements for social justice and disarmament. All agree that the Left must not relinquish the terrain of values and transcendence to the Right. "We must recover some of our own lost traditions—such as the Romantic rebellion against early industrial capitalism—which were infused with moral and religious themes." Moreover, the secular Left needs the Religious Left. Religious institutions "provide a space that is relatively untouched by the commercialization of the larger society" and can thus serve as "centers of a counterculture, pockets of resistance [to] the dominant bureaucratic culture" (Ferber 1985, 12). "To rule out religious imagery is to ignore a discourse that at its best can speak out powerfully against greed, ennui and coldness of heart." Religion can help us "to imagine creatively different ways of organizing economies and politics" (Cox 1996, 23). "The bashing of religious faith serves neither our democratic principles nor the practical need to build a culturally inclusive mass movement" (Kazin 1998, 19). Railing against "popular religion violates the first principle of democratic politics: Empathize with the concerns of everyday people, even if they are not your own" (16). The writer identifies himself as a Jew and an atheist but sees his own beliefs as irrelevant in view of the need for democracy and democratic social movements to take religion seriously. Barack Obama's 2008 campaign clearly heeded this message.

Whether one believes that religion should speak to public issues is perhaps less a matter of what one's religion is than a question of what the issues at hand are. During the 1960s, mainline Protestants advocated taking public stands, whereas evangelical and fundamentalist Protestants more often do so now (Regnerus and Smith 1998). Nevertheless, some highly religious evangelicals would prefer "religious separationism" (Jelen and Wilcox 1997, 286). And recent evidence suggests that their numbers are growing. In 2008, 36 percent of white evangelical Republicans thought that churches should keep out of politics, an increase of 16 percent since 2004 (Pew Forum 2008b).

Dilemmas of Church-State Relations

Those who argue that religion has an important role in civil society must nevertheless deal with the question of how exactly church and state are to be separated. Many commentators insist that religion must not be ruled out of public life. Thus, an opinion piece in *Time* suggests that "a healthy country would teach its children evolution and the Ten Commandments" and that biblical creation should be taught not as science but for its "mythical grandeur and moral dimensions." Furthermore, although "creationism is back door to religion, brought in under the guise of . . . science," secularists have been doing the same thing. Teaching the proper way of using a condom "is more than instruction in reproductive mechanics. It is a seminar—unacknowledged and tacit but nonetheless powerful—on permissible sexual mores" (Krauthammer 1999, 120). An article in *Time* about the separation of church and state argues that "for God to be kept out of the classroom or out of America's public debate by nervous school administrators or overcautious politicians serves no one's interests" (Gibbs 1991, 68). Supreme Court rulings against prayer in the public schools, says one conservative, go against "the intended meaning of the First Amendment from its inception." It "was the work of people who believed in God and who expressed their faith as a matter of course in public prayer" (M. S. Evans 1995, 76).

In the enduring American view, religion provides the basis of morality, moral behavior, and social values. Thus we are told that the rigid wall of separation between church and state mandated by recent Supreme Court decisions has helped to bring "deterioration in American life" (Buckley 1994, 86–87) and that "how the nation defines itself spiritually will have much to do with its future political directions and with the strength of its moral foundations" (Ostling 1989, 94). "It is a mistake to assume that rejecting the lunacy of the far right means we must deny the value to society of a religious sensibility" (Krauthammer 1981, 25).

A commentator on the right suggests that "the bent condition of human existence in these closing decades of the twentieth century is an affliction resulting principally from the decay of belief in an ordered universe and in a purpose for human existence" (Kirk 1983, 626). And one on the left proposes that "the Christian left offers Americans something its secular counterpart no longer seems to favor: a sincere faith in moral progress" (Kazin 1998, 18).

Articles in both *Time* and *The New Republic* decry the fact that religion has been relegated to a minor role in school textbooks. The writer in *Time* suggests that schoolchildren deserve "a more profound image of, say, Thanksgiving than as a pumpkin-pie party with the Indians" (Bowen 1986, 94). The discussion in *The New Republic* suggests that for the most part, history textbooks "place religion at the lunatic fringe of American society" and that liberals should view this situation as a serious deficiency (Pasley 1987, 20). Some scholars, however, dispute the contention that contemporary textbooks give less attention to religious history, a point to which I will subsequently return.

It is also a sign of respect for religion that various commentators are dismayed by the use of religion for purposes of therapy, "lifestyle," or other reasons of social utility. One writer notes that from Norman Vincent Peale in the 1950s through Robert Schuller in the late 1980s, religion itself has been transformed "into primarily a social and therapeutic activity. . . . [R]eligion has become a lifestyle strategy," as when a Dallas Cowboys representative told a talk show host that "being a Christian has become Deion

[Sanders]'s lifestyle" (Judis 1999, 56). Another commentator suggests that one must be careful to avoid "using culture, as many have tried to use religion, as a kind of social therapy" (Howe 1991, 47). Creationists who say that adopting Darwinian ideas would deprive life of its meaning are taken to task for their admission "that the moral and social utility of religion is what recommends it" (Editorial 1999, 11).

Perhaps, too, the sheer amount of attention paid to religion in these magazines signals its importance in American life. The two ends of the political spectrum, represented here by *The Nation* and *National Review,* tend to devote more attention to attacking the views of their opponents than to affirming their own positions. Thus, for example, *National Review* published seventeen articles discussing the general idea of multiculturalism, while *The Nation* published only one. Similarly, *The Nation* printed two articles about multicultural education, compared with eight in *National Review.* By contrast, the number of articles dealing with "family values" was greater in *The Nation* (seven) than in *National Review* (four). On religious matters, however, the two magazines published almost identical numbers of articles: on church-state relations, *The Nation* has five and *National Review* has six; on internal religious issues, six pieces appear in *The Nation,* and seven appear in *National Review.*

Of the nine articles in our sample that discuss creationism, four appear in *Time.* Two of these works offer straight reporting on the struggles between the two sides, one is clearly hostile to religious intrusion into scientific education, and the remaining article advocates teaching the Bible for values and morals, not as fact or science: "if we were a bit more tolerant about allowing the teaching of biblical values as ethics, we'd find far less pressure for the teaching of biblical fables" (Krauthammer 1999, 120). An editorial in *The New Republic* sides with "science," suggesting that any effort to "delegitimate" it "is a counsel of despair and an American disgrace" (Editorial 1999, 12). The three articles in *National Review* argue that science and creationism (or intelligent design) can be reconciled (Buckley 1997; Glynn 1999; Kirk 1983). The one article in *The Nation,* perhaps surprisingly, advocates teaching both evolution and creationism as an object lesson in what science is about. If students receive the tools to evaluate a scientific theory—ideas of falsifiability and the ability to generate reliable predictions—there is no doubt which theory will emerge as superior. Liberals and pro-evolutionists seem to fear that religion will undermine scientific belief, just as the religious feared the teaching of evolution in 1925. But creationism needs to be taught because "it has a hold on the minds and emotions of large numbers of Americans" (Postman and Postman 1986, 5).

A 2005 national survey by the Pew Research Center found 64 percent of Americans amenable to the idea of teaching both creationism and evolution. This majority included secular respondents and liberal Democrats as well as conservative Christians, those who believe in natural selection and those who do not. A majority of those who accept natural selection theory (62 percent) support teaching creationism along with evolution. The public apparently favors having more viewpoints offered where there is controversy (Pew Research Center 2005). The well-publicized debates on this issue apparently have increased uncertainty in the population. Between 1985 and 2005, the proportion of Americans who were not sure about evolution increased from 7 percent to 21 percent, while those accepting the idea of evolution declined from 45 percent to 40 percent and those rejecting the idea declined from 48 percent to 39 percent (Jon D. Miller, Scott, and Okamoto 2006, 765).

Only a small number of commentators seek a reduction in religious influence. They express frustration that remarks that are deemed "offensive" to religion are not tolerated anywhere. Contrary to allegations about "liberal intellectual elites who disdain religious belief and have denied it a respected public role," it is not possible to attack religion in American society without being seen as violating the norms (Kaminer 1996, 25). This sentiment echoes Tocqueville's observation that in America, "those who do not believe conceal their incredulity," whereas "those who believe display their faith" (1848/1961, 1:324).

At the same time, supporters of religion claim that American society excludes "anyone who takes seriously religious belief or traditional moral norms" (Wagner 1986, 28). Though we tolerate all who treat their religion as if it were no different from any consumer preference, there is intolerance for those who take religion seriously; we tolerate only "people who don't believe in anything" (Krauthammer 1998, 92).

Given the American taste for moderation, it can be argued that both the supporters and the detractors of religion are correct. Thus, four-fifths of Wolfe's small middle-class suburban sample believed "there is such a thing as being too religious" (1998, 83). National surveys between 1988 and 1996 found that approximately one-fifth of the respondents expressed intense hostility toward Christian Fundamentalists, rating them no more highly than illegal aliens (Bolce and De Maio 1999a, 39). At the same time, however, a 2003 national survey found that "from a list of groups that also includes Muslims, recent immigrants, and homosexuals, Americans name atheists as those least likely to share their vision of American society. They are also more likely to disapprove of their children marrying atheists" (Edgell, Gerteis, and Hartmann 2006, 212). In interviews, respondents portrayed atheists either as "immoral people who threaten respectable community" from below or as "rampant materialists and cultural elitists that threaten common values from above" (227).

Americans reject not only extremes in religious beliefs but also what they perceive as extreme views concerning the role of religion politically. Thus, in a 2006 survey, 69 percent of respondents answered yes to the question, "Have liberals gone too far in trying to keep religion out of schools and government?" At the same time, 49 percent said yes to the question, "Have conservative Christians gone too far in trying to impose their religious values on the country?" (Pew Research Center 2006a). Similarly, 48 percent of the population in 2008 believed that religious conservatives have too much power over the Republican Party, and 43 percent believed that nonreligious liberals have too much power over the Democratic Party (Pew Forum 2008b).

Historically, of course, religious groups have spoken publicly about most of the major issues facing the nation. Sometimes, as in the case of the slavery debate, they have been arrayed on both sides. And those who decry the excessive liberal influence in keeping religion out of American schools and government cut across party lines: large majorities of Republicans, Democrats, and independents share this view; only those who identify as liberal Democrats do not (Pew Research Center 2006a). Americans' uncertainty about the role of religion is well illustrated by a January 2007 Gallup Poll that asked whether the influence of organized religion on the nation should increase, decrease, or stay the same. Thirty-nine percent of the population want the level of religious influence to remain the same, 27 percent want an increase in religion's role, and 32 percent favor a decrease (Feldman 2007, 13). The complexity of American attitudes toward religion in the public sphere is compounded by the fact that Evangelicals are themselves ambivalent on the subject, given their concerns for individual spiritual conversion and their sense that the political sphere does not deal in the eternal (McConkey 2001; C. Smith 2000; Wolfe 1998). Some analysts have argued that evangelical Protestants abandoned their reluctance to get involved in politics when the Republicans articulated concerns about moral decline in American society (Leege et al. 2002, 89).

The relatively small contingent of political commentators who are opposed to religious influences argue that there is no true separation of church and state in American society. Rather, they contend, we "live in a society that favors all religions equally" (Pollitt 1983, 24), a society in which religious institutions are exempt from equal opportunity statutes and do not lose their tax exemptions when they use their money for political causes (Pollitt 1983; Vidal 1997). "The official American civil religion" currently appears to be that "what religion you have" is "your own business, . . . but it's society's business that you have one" (Pollitt 2000, 10).

These critics argue that there is neither equal treatment of the nonreligious in American society nor recognition of the connections between church and state powers. In the United States, one critic asserts, even those on the left tend to be more respectful of religion than is the case in other societies. Elsewhere it is recognized that "the Church is part of the material reality of the ruling order" and that "temporal ruling elites" need religion in some form to "convince themselves that they rule in the interests of all." In the United States, by contrast, "the left is either actually religious or secular in a semi-apologetic way" (Hitchens 1984, 230). Another critic of religion argues that as religion and politics "are once again mingled, . . . it is time that humanists wipe the respectful smile off their faces when organized religion is discussed." There are, after all, "no events on record where the orthodox acted more humanely or nobly than the unorthodox" (Koning 1980, 501).

This critic of religion and others argue that the nation's laws and institutions are public, but beliefs "are purely private matters." They "may give comfort to those who hold them, but they have no brief to give discomfort to those who do not. They have been private matters since the last public burning of a heretic" (Koning 1980, 501). Put with more civility by another critic of the sacredness of religion in American life, "Secularists are often wrongly accused of trying to purge religious ideals from public discourse. We simply want to deny them public sponsorship" (Kaminer 1996, 32).

Supporters of religion, by contrast, do not see such mingling of religion and politics. They contend that religion is effectively ruled out of the public sphere. While "every manner of political argument is ruled legitimate in our democratic discourse, . . . invoke the Bible as grounding for your politics, and the First Amendment police will charge you with breaching the sacred wall separating church and state" (Krauthammer 1998, 92).

The idea that religion needs to be protected from too close an alliance with politics or the state can also be seen as an aspect of the American respect for religion. Thus, an editorial in *The New Republic* argues that we must be vigilant about the "crevices" in the wall of separation between church and state not because "American democracy is . . . crumbling before American religion" but because of "the damage that politics may do to religion." Religion is cheapened and trivialized by things like "Jesus Day" (proclaimed in Texas by Governor George W. Bush). "A faith that requires the support of a government is an infirm faith," and believers must recognize that "the freedom from religion is also the freedom for religion" (Editorial 2000b, 9).

To be sure, those hostile to religion also see this connection. They contend that school prayer may help undermine religion, since established religions generally have less public support than religion has had in American society (Editorial 1984, 308). If schools must scrupulously avoid religion, there is the possibility that religion will gain "the romantic aura of the forbidden—Christ is cool" (Pollitt 1994b, 788). Once again, one can hear echoes of Tocqueville in this discussion. The American clergy, he argued, perceived that to avoid the vicissitudes of politics, it was wise to renounce state support. As a result, religion in American society may be less powerful than it has been elsewhere and at other times, but "its influence is more lasting" (1848/1961, 1:323).

Conservatives, too, suggest that religion must not succumb to political involvements. Indeed, one conservative argues that "conservative activism has contributed powerfully to the politicizing of religion that most conservatives deplore. . . . Far from providing a common resource of belief, tradition, and moral judgment, politicized religion turns societal conflicts into crusades. This is bad for public life; it is worse for religion" (Neuhaus 1988a, 46). When religion and politics are too closely aligned, religion is compromised (Gibbs 2000, 38). The mainline Protestantism that has defined the spiritual and moral ethos of American society for more than three centuries is in decline, in part because of "a preoccupation with political and social issues at the expense of good old-fashioned faith"(Ostling 1989, 94).

While various writers on the left value the moral critique that religion can offer to society, some conservatives fear that a politicized church can no longer serve moral purposes. Today, "churches that once served as sources of clear moral guidance are . . . grappling uncertainly . . . as they try to decide whether their sexual standards will derive from biblical tradition or the fluid folkways of modernity" (Ostling 1991, 50). In contemporary theological discussions, everything seems up for debate—homosexuality, premarital sex, even adultery. "The obvious secular explanation for this hubbub is that America's churches are internalizing the mores of a developed society. . . . Like most obvious secular explanations, this one is shallow. American churches don't just passively receive ideas from the general culture. They also stimulate them." In fact, innovators and traditionalists within the church disagree about sex, as they do about everything else. "The disputants are primarily motivated not by policy considerations, but by what they believe to be right. That is what makes this fight so all-American, and so angry" (Brookhiser 1991, 70).

Those who see churches as yielding to the norms of secular society fear that this process is ultimately self-defeating. The "watering down of moral requirements" and the "substitution of politics for morality" produce a "kitsch religion" that is "free of troublesome moral obligations." This dilution provides a feeling of spirituality without requiring orthodox belief and action. The result is that the church loses members to such alternatives as the gym, politics, and New Age movements (Klinghoffer 1996, 52). If the religion that is currently flourishing is "religion on our own terms," then "secularization has triumphed after all," since religion of this sort "is devoted to need-meeting rather than truth-telling" (Neuhaus 1989a, 20).

Along with respect for religion and a tendency to cast issues in moral terms, Americans often manifest a great reverence for the Founding Fathers, and disagreements on issues of the separation of church are state are often formulated as different interpretations of the intent and religiosity of the Founding Fathers. People have commonly argued that the Founding Fathers were attempting to protect religion from political influences (Editorial 2000b, 9), to prevent the establishment of a national religion that would threaten the religious diversity of the states (M. S. Evans 1995, 58), to invoke God to give "America's rights a Source beyond the state's power to modify or amend" (Editorial 1994b, 18), to remind people that our rights derive from natural laws and "Nature's God" (Brookhiser 1994, 84). The dissenters—those who would reduce religious influences—argue instead that the Founding Fathers did not all believe in God and intended the separation of church and state to serve as a way of minimizing the power of both the church and the state, since the latter would gain from any implication of divine authority (Ehrenreich 1992b, 72).

Religious Belief and Secularization

Elite opinion in the United States confers respect on religion and its role in the public sphere. In recent American politics, Democrats and Republicans alike have supported "faith-based initiatives." There is no "culture war" at issue here, no dispute between advocates of moral absolutes and supporters of individual discretion. While policy disputes arise about how to implement faith-based initiatives—for example, whether churches should be required to employ nonmembers—most Americans appear to accept the basic principle. There are some dissenters, of course, just as there are a small number of commentators in our sample who are unhappy with the role of religion in American society and politics.

The culture wars are clearly related to the strength of religion among some Americans. For example, between 1984 and 1996, a dramatic increase occurred in the percentage of survey respondents who identified "family decline" as the "most important problem" facing the United States. The proportion of the population responding in this way rose from just under 2 percent to almost 10 percent, and the vast majority of those who responded this way were evangelical Protestants who attended church regularly (C. Brooks 2002, 198, 203).

American political campaigns also have been exceptional. Where else "could one find in the year 2000 a political campaign in which voters were obliged to choose between two more-Christian-than-thou candidates?" George W. Bush declared Jesus Christ to be his favorite philosopher, and Al Gore claimed to solve ethical questions by asking, "What would Jesus do?" (Hollinger 2001, 143).

The increased relevance of religion to American politics in the late twentieth century might appear to be anomalous in view of secularization and declines in religious participation. Yet perhaps the empirical reality does not match the cultural perceptions here. A majority of Americans believe that religious influence is in decline (Pew Research Center 2002), but those who study religion are not as certain.

In recent American politics, the Christian Right has mobilized voters for various causes and candidates. A study of the factors that make people susceptible to having their votes influenced by the Christian Right found that those who see themselves as "culturally embattled" are more likely than others to be so influenced. The sense of cultural embattlement was measured by questions asking whether or not the mass media, feminists, and the public schools "are hostile to your moral and spiritual values." To be sure, there are possible reciprocal influences involved: having a sense of being embattled makes one more receptive to the Christian Right, but being in the Christian Right constituency increases consciousness of such issues. The political involvement of the devoutly religious is motivated by a desire to protect the "private lifeworld" rather than for reasons of economics or status. "Those who 'vote their pocketbook' do not care to vote by the Christian Right's suggestions" (Regnerus, Sikkink, and Smith 1999, 1391, 1392, 1394).

Some analysts have speculated that the increased political involvement of committed white Christians might well be a reaction to the growth of a more secular and diverse society (Kohut et al. 2000, 123) or at least the perception thereof. Between the late 1980s and the late 1990s, increases occurred in the intensity of religious belief, in the number of people who "strongly agreed" that God exists, and in the number of people who believed that divine judgment is inevitable and that there are clear guidelines about good and evil (Kohut et al. 2000, 28). This increased intensity of belief occurred among all groups, including seculars. One may indeed wonder what *secular* means in American society when Pew Research Center data from 1997 show that 44 percent of those identified as secular "strongly agree" with the statement, "I never doubt the existence of God" (Kohut et al. 2000, 28–29).

What, then, is the status of religious belief and participation in contemporary American society? Ambiguities abound, despite the fact that Americans are notoriously more religious than citizens of other Western industrialized societies. In 1995, 50 percent of Americans rated the importance of God in their lives as a 10 on a ten-point scale; no other advanced industrial society even came close (Baker 2005, 40).

Analysts have long suggested that American religious strength is based on the absence of an established church, on the voluntary nature of American religion. More recently, this idea has been formulated in terms of an economic model: "an open market is conducive to religious vitality" (R. S. Warner 1993, 1057). However, religious pluralism in European societies does not seem to be conducive to individual religiosity. While government subsidies to established churches and government regulations might make the competition less open in European societies than in the United States, religious pluralism in Europe appears to undermine certainties and to increase religious tolerance. The result is less rather than more religiosity in the population (Halman and Draulans 2006, 268, 285).

It has also long been noted that immigrants to the United States have retained their religious practices while otherwise assimilating into American life. Famously, Herberg noted in the middle of the twentieth century that being Protestant, Catholic, or Jewish is a way "of being an American," that not to identify with a religion "is somehow not to be an American" (1956, 53, 274). Survey data from 2003 show that many Americans continue to believe that "affirming a religious identity is an important way of 'being American'" (Edgell, Gerteis, and Harmann 2006, 216). That migration to the United States increases one's religious belief is suggested by a study that attempts to account for the significant recent increases in belief in an afterlife among Catholics, Jews, and those with no religious affiliation: "immigrants are significantly less likely to believe in an afterlife than are their grandchildren" (Greeley and Hout 1999, 813). The authors suggest that "religious competition for the hearts and souls of the immigrants and their children led to a more vigorous religious socialization in the United States than that experienced by youth in most of the countries that sent emigrants to this country" (819–20). One of the authors of this study has also argued that in a pluralistic society without an official religion, religion plays more of a role in conferring identity and hence generates higher levels of devotion than it does in societies that have established churches. But within a society that has an established church, being a member of an alternative church or denomination would also have importance in conferring identity and should thus predict greater loyalty. By this logic, non-Anglicans in England should be as likely as Americans to believe in God and to attend church regularly, and the data support this hypothesis (Greeley 1991, 114–15).

Commentators have also noted that the cultural respect for religion in the United States and the social acceptability of religious participation have likely led to some exaggeration in the portraits that survey data reveal. For many Americans, expressions of belief in God and reported levels of religious participation may reveal more about "cultural expectations" than about the reality of their beliefs and practices (Demerath 2002, 17). If indeed it is true that the actual church attendance of Americans is approximately half of what they report, and if similar studies in other societies reveal less of this overreporting, then "a different sort of 'American exceptionalism' is at work. Americans may not differ much in terms of behavior, but rather in how they *report* that behavior" (Hadaway, Marler, and Chaves 1993, 749). While various methodological criticisms have been offered of the studies that show a gap between actual and reported church attendance (see Hout and Greeley 1998; Woodberry 1998), other research has demonstrated that the apparent misreporting is likely "caused mainly by social desirability pressures associated with interviewer-administration." Both self-administered questionnaires and time-use studies minimize such overreporting (Presser and Stinson 1998).

That norms of social desirability encourage Americans to overstate their religious participation—just as they similarly overstate their participation in voting—is itself a commentary on American attitudes toward religion. In addition, while young people in the United States are less religious than their elders, few "are *irreligious*—compared with young people in most wealthy industrialized nations, most are remarkably religious" (Zukin et al. 2006, 166), or at least they claim to be. It may well be true that in a religious society such as the United States, "irreligion . . . replicates itself across generations less effectively than active religious preference" because people "are surrounded more by religion than by irreligion" (R. S. Warner 1993, 1077). And the finding that the overwhelming majority of Americans believe people should arrive at their religious beliefs independently of any church or synagogue attests to the significance of the voluntary nature of American religion (1075, 1080).

While belief in God has remained remarkably stable, hovering around 95 percent for more than half a century, questions may be raised about this finding as well. For one thing, the proportion of the population that is absolutely certain of God's existence has declined, although the percentage remains quite high (Bishop 1999, 423). For another, the proportion that believes not in a personal God but rather in "a higher power of some sort" has slowly but steadily increased from 5 percent in 1964 to 10 percent at the end of the century (425). Perhaps, then, the addition of the phrase "or a universal spirit" to the "Do you believe in God?" question has masked trends in religious beliefs (426). Nevertheless, 87 percent of the population in a 2003 survey agreed with the statement, "I never doubt the existence of God." And while only 69 percent "completely agreed" with the statement (the equivalent to "absolute certainty" in other surveys), this number represented an increase from the 60 percent who completely agreed in 1987 (Pew Research Center 2003).

There is no doubt that since the late 1960s, increases have occurred in the number of people who never attend religious services and in the number who identify as seculars or religious "nones" (Kohut et al. 2000, 123; Layman 2001, 313). But it is difficult to understand the meaning of these figures in light of the fact that in 1998, for example, "almost 60 percent of 'nones' said that they believed 'that God watches over me,' and nearly 40 percent reported praying at least weekly" (Fischer and Hout 2006, 193). By contrast, among Europe's unchurched, 27 percent identify themselves as religious, while 57 percent say they are not religious and 16 percent identify themselves as atheists (Halman and Draulans 2006, 282).

Whether the importance of religion has declined in modern societies, as many sociologists and laypersons alike believe, has been a matter of considerable scholarly debate. The idea of secularization has long been one of the taken-for-granted elements of modernization. Like industrialization, urbanization, and bureaucratization, secularization was so well integrated into the modernization paradigm that few questioned the idea, and it "became sacralized" (Hadden 1987, 588). Yet some contemporary sociologists debate both the extent of secularization and its meaning. Does secularization simply indicate religious decline (that is, a decline in religious belief or participation)? If so, since belief and participation do not necessarily go together, which of the two is more essential? Or does secularization simply mean the separation of religion from all other social and cultural institutions, the differentiation between religious and other institutions? One sociologist has argued that if secularization just means the differentiation of religious from secular institutions, there is no basis for disagreement, since all can agree that the political power of Catholic bishops is less today than it was centuries ago (Stark 1999, 252). If differentiation is the central meaning of secularization, so that most public institutions no longer fall under the sway of religious institutions and values, has religion also become "privatized"? If so, has religion necessarily been weakened at the individual level? Or could private religious experiences flourish "even as public religious institutions flounder?" (Gorski 2000, 162). Perhaps secularization means competition or pluralism in defining the sacred. The competing institutions are not simply alternative religions but other institutions in which people place faith, such as education and science (Swatos and Christiano 1999, 225).

Those sociologists who take issue with the secularization hypothesis contend that it has exaggerated both the religiosity of people in past centuries and the irreligion in contemporary societies. There really was no golden age of faith, and even the most seemingly secular societies today have large numbers of believers in their midst. In Iceland, for example, only 2 percent of the population attends church services weekly, yet the 1990 World Values Survey found that 81 percent of Icelanders say they believe in life after death, 82 percent say that they sometimes pray, and only 2.4 percent describe themselves as "convinced atheists" (Stark 1999, 264).

Other sociologists, however, point to a decline in religious authority over both societies and individuals. To be sure, much variation exists among social groups in contemporary American society, with white Protestant Fundamentalists and African Americans showing lower levels of secularization than other religious groups. But, for example, by 1990, only 12 percent of American Catholics accepted the church's ban on artificial contraception (Chaves 1994, 768). The increase in religious intermarriage likewise suggests the decreased salience of religion. When religious authority is strong, religion significantly affects behavior, and religious endogamy is high. "If religious differences are increasingly irrelevant for marriage decisions, then religious authority's scope surely is narrowing" (768). Moreover, members of conservative Protestant denominations report having more sexual partners than do mainline Protestants, quite the opposite of what would one expect based on the beliefs of these denominations (Greeley and Hout 2006, 135).

While few doubt the significance of religion for those who are seriously committed to it, much less clarity exists about the significance of the kind of religious affiliation that is little more than nominal—identification with a religious tradition that does not translate into religious participation or agreement with its doctrines. This form of "cultural religion" may have public as well as personal significance because it may be activated during periods of crisis or conflict. "It is the stuff of civil religions," a "reservoir of meanings and values" tapped by religious and cultural leaders (Demerath 2002, 17–18). Tocqueville observed this sort of connection between religion and societal unity, noting, "I do not know whether all Americans have a sincere faith in their religion—for who can search the human heart?—but I am certain that they hold it to be indispensable to the maintenance of republican institutions. This opinion is not peculiar to a class of citizens or to a party, but it belongs to the whole nation and to every rank of society" (1848/1961, 1:316). More recent analysts see "strong beliefs in religion and God" as embedded in "America's traditional values" (Baker 2005, 54) and part of the "imagined community" on which American society rests.

Yet Americans' religiousness has long seemed to lack depth or seriousness. Even during the 1950s, large numbers of people were attending religious institutions and identifying themselves in religious terms while seeming disconnected from "matters central to the faiths they profess" (Herberg 1956, 14). Herberg's classic treatise on American religion detailed the "triple melting pot" of Catholics, Protestants, and Jews and noted that even people who valued the Bible as revelation were unable to name the first four Gospels (14). Almost half a century later, Chaves noted that "religious faith in the United States is more broad than deep," as only half of those who believe the Bible is the Word of God can name the first book, and even evangelical or born-again Christians simultaneously believe in "ideas foreign to traditional Christianity," such as reincarnation and astrology (2002, 20). Herberg characterized American "religiousness" as being "without serious commitment, without real inner conviction," although it generates "the sincere feeling of being religious" (1956, 276). Chaves similarly noted that although more than 90 percent of Americans believe in a higher power, "only one-third say they rely more on that power than on themselves in overcoming adversity" (2002, 20).

Religiosity in the United States may well be based more on the cultural encouragement that it receives than on deep personal convictions. Thus, there is more religious belief and practice among the nonchurchgoing public in the United States than in Canada, suggesting the pervasiveness of "American culture-religion," the sheer social desirability of religiosity in American society (Reimer 1995). This cultural religiosity is also manifest in the greater difference in Canada than in the United States between the beliefs and practices of those who attend church regularly and those who do not. And even secular Americans and those with weak religious ties believe that American society would be better off if religion's influence were on the rise (Pew Research Center 2002).

The secularization thesis has included the idea that in modern societies religion becomes privatized, confined to the realm of personal individual beliefs. But though the secularization thesis remains accurate insofar as the secular spheres are emancipated from religious institutions, religious decline and privatization do not necessarily follow. Indeed, it can be argued that a deprivatization of religion became widespread in the 1980s. Varieties of "public religion" now act as "normative critiques of dominant historical trends," raising questions about the moral norms or human considerations inherent in institutional activities (Casanova 1994, 43).

The belief that religious expression can contribute to American democracy has a long history, as does the belief that any religion is a good thing. Yet such ideas must "seem like a deplorable heresy to the European churchman" (Herberg 1956, 97) and may also deny the reality of tensions among religious groups. In the United States, Herberg suggested, "every tension between religious communities, however deep and complex it may actually be, tends to express itself as a conflict over church-state relations" (248). Disputes about the First Amendment often occur as conflicts between those who argue that there is not enough religion in the public square and those who think there is too much. Many of those in the latter camp see a continuing mainstream Protestant hegemony, so that diverse religions are marginalized and kept that way (Beaman 2003, 318).

The political salience of being an evangelical Christian appears to be greater in areas where there are higher proportions of secularists (religious nonadherents). In such areas, Evangelicals are more likely to vote Republican (Campbell 2006, 109). Observers suggest that Evangelicals feel threatened by larger number of secularists in their midst and that this tension is but the latest example of religious conflict in American politics, similar to earlier Catholic-Protestant conflicts (113). Perhaps, too, those who are anti-Fundamentalist feel threatened by the perceived increased political visibility of Christian Fundamentalists. They thus perceive Christian fundamentalist leaders as "too pushy" in asserting traditional values and exaggerate the degree to which they maintain ideologically "extreme" positions (Bolce and DeMaio 1999b, 514, 515).

Criticism of contemporary Fundamentalists comes from within as well. In *Beyond Culture Wars,* Michael S. Horton takes Christian Evangelicals and Fundamentalists to task for participating in culture wars that view "moral issues as ultimate instead of as effects of one's deeper theological and philosophical beliefs" (1994, 38). "It is a recovery of the Christian faith within the church itself, not the imposition of Christian values over a hostile society, that holds the only possibility for meaningful change" (281). Members of evangelical churches are just as worldly as liberals. Horton writes, "Our own people cannot name the Ten Commandments, and yet we are outraged that they are removed from the public halls" (123). "The 'testimony' ('what Jesus did for me') and personal experiences are often the most authoritative tests of truth in evangelical circles today" (67). Evangelical spirituality now contains the same "self-centered, self-deifying impulse" as secular humanism and New Age spirituality (63). Horton's view receives some confirmation in the work of a sociologist who analyzed the Lincoln-Douglas debates about slavery in comparison to the culture war discussions during the 1992 election. While the former legitimated arguments through the use of religion, the latter were largely therapeutic on both sides of the divide (J. L. Nolan 1996, 184).

The political behavior of Christian activists also receives criticism from within for negating the chief contribution that faith can make to politics: ensuring that the transcendent perspective of faith judges politics. When Christian "report cards" are issued, measuring how members of Congress vote on "key moral/family issues," the resulting anomalies are shameful. Members of Congress who have been involved in corruption and sex scandals may receive high scores, while highly moral Democrats get low scores. The problem is that "politics, not piety or ethics, was the ruling criterion" (Guinness 1993, 191).

Conclusions

When culture was understood to consist largely of values that were internalized and that shaped people's behavior, churches were seen as exercising a beneficial influence on the society by influencing individual members' values. When this view of culture began to come into question, churches began to exercise their power by attempting to influence the morality that was "lodged in the culture at large rather than in individuals" (Wuthnow 1988, 69). As the social movements of the 1960s—beginning with the civil rights movement—challenged churches to take a stand on social issues, a split arose between those that supported activism and those that maintained their role in guiding individual consciences (147–48).

Since that time, churches and their parishioners have wrestled with the question of their proper public role. Although religion undoubtedly "propelled some people into politics" during the 1990s, "the politicization of religion might have caused people who dissent from the conservative agenda of vocal Christian leaders to stop identifying with those religions." This phenomenon could account for the increase in "unchurched believers"—people with conventional religious beliefs who nevertheless express "no religious preference" because they are alienated from organized religion (Hout and Fischer 2002, 179). Fears of alienating parishioners by political activism have also led to the dismissal of several celebrated pastors, as their congregations' lay leaders saw activism as "getting in the way of the Gospel" (Kirkpatrick 2007, 39).

In the late 1990s, in a moment of despair about the progress of the Religious Right's causes, a leading spokesman for the movement, Paul Weyrich, suggested that Evangelicals needed "to get out of politics, go back to the churches and change hearts one at a time, in the belief that the culture will someday follow" (Gibbs 1999, 47). After the 2004 election, however, Weyrich was exultant. He issued a letter to Evangelicals that read, "God is indeed a Republican. He must be. His hand helped re-elect a president, with a popular mandate" (Rosin 2005, 120).

Cycles of increasing and decreasing separation of church and state and increasing and decreasing secularization are probably inevitable in a society that respects religion but lacks consensus about its public role. It is clear, however, that the very waging of the culture wars over the past few decades belies the claim that religion has been privatized. And this very public argumentation has produced internal dissension on all sides. Evangelicals debate their public involvement, while nonbelievers on the left contend with the majority who see religious influences as beneficial.

While most Americans maintain a "quiet faith" that entails respect for the beliefs of others, even nonbelievers (Wolfe 1998, 50–54), many churchgoing Protestants maintain the contradictory beliefs that "everyone should be free to live as they see fit" and that "Christian morality should be the primary authority for American culture and society" (C. Smith et al. 1997, 190). Reconciling these contradictory ideas has become more challenging as the non-Christian population in the United States has increased.

Increased religious diversity has also made consensus about American civil religion more difficult, although disputes about civil religion began during the Vietnam War, when arguments about America's role in the world were compounded by theological disputes about the meaning of God. Theologians no less than social scientists have shown a heightened "concern for the symbolically constructed character of reality" (Wuthnow 1988, 299).

CHAPTER 3

Moral but Not Moralistic

Observers since the time of Tocqueville have noted Americans' propensity to "see the world in moral terms" (Robin M. Williams 1957, 397). The dominant Protestant denominations have called on people to follow their consciences, and even agnostic and atheistic reformers have tended to be "utopian moralists who believe in the perfectibility of man and of civil society and in the immorality, if not specifically sinful character, of the opposition" (Lipset 1975, 144). Perhaps Americans share this view because the "founding myth" of the United States is that of the Pilgrims at Plymouth Bay Colony rather than merchants in Boston, planters in Virginia, or inventors in Philadelphia. American political discourse has often been a matter "not of tariffs and raw metals but of a Cross of Gold, not of a rival hegemonic power but of an Evil Empire" (Leege et al. 2002, 41). Contemporary Americans are more likely than Canadians to think that "raising moral standards" is a highly important goal (Hoover et al. 2002, 361). The language of morality so dominates discourse in the United States that even a writer decrying the "God-drunk society" in which 240 million of the 300 million Americans believe in the return of Jesus Christ contends that Americans have "a moral responsibility" to give up such "abject superstition" (S. Harris 2007, 44).

Far from one side advocating moral judgments while the other eschews them, all sides in the culture wars frame issues in the language of morality while speaking disparagingly of their opponents as either immoral or "moralistic." No one argues in favor of "moral relativism." Conservatives tend to lump together moral and cultural relativism (see Arkes 1989; J. Gray 1992; Lipman 1991b; Mansfield 2000) and to accuse the Left of espousing relativism, but progressives argue that the cultural relativism that they endorse does not imply that "there are no ultimate moral principles" (di Leonardo 1996, 29). And all agree in principle that it is foolish to attempt to legislate morality, even if such legislation might be the outcome of their preferred policies.

Through the Lenses of Morality

Although their understandings of morality may differ, both Left and Right clearly see their perspectives as moral. The Right speaks of the "moral foundations of capitalism" (Gilder 1986, 31) and suggests that capitalism breeds virtues such as honesty, achievement, and cooperativeness (Hyde 1990b, 53). The Left talks of the "moral principles" underlying progressive programs for economic democracy, antiracism, feminism, and gay rights (di Leonardo 1996, 29) and suggests that some immorality—such as the intolerance of social differences—is espoused by those "who claim the mantle of God" (Judis 1999, 56).

In the late nineteenth and early twentieth centuries, the progressive movement railed against the immorality of individual greed and wealth acquired through financial manipulation rather than hard labor (Rhys H. Williams and Alexander 1994, 10). In our more conservative era, a connection is often made between the free market and religious fundamentalism. Evangelicals share a conviction that "economic and spiritual freedoms go hand in hand" (J. D. Hunter 1991, 111). Regardless of the ideology, ideas "without explicit ethical support risk appearing individualistic to an immoral degree" (Hicks 2006, 508).

Well-known conservative and liberal commentators have long seen economics and morality as intertwined. Both sides see extramarket forces as important in shaping the economic system. Conservatives such as Francis Fukuyama (1999) argue against the frequently heard allegation that the amoral drive for profit and efficiency undermines the moral basis of capitalism. Rather, he suggests, people who repeatedly do business with each other establish norms to ensure trust. Self-interested individuals seek to acquire a reputation for honesty or fairness. Religion may help, but it is not required. In this view, contemporary conservatives hark back to the observations of Tocqueville, who saw "the principle of self-interest rightly understood" as disciplining people "in habits of regularity, temperance, moderation, foresight, self-command" (1848/1961, 2:131).

Liberals such as Paul Krugman, conversely, see an immorality in contemporary economic life because of the permissiveness that has altered earlier understandings of fair compensation. The norms of fairness that had been in place since the New Deal began to unravel in the 1980s and the 1990s. In their stead, a new "anything goes" ethic has arisen, allowing for soaring rates of executive compensation and generating extreme social inequality (Krugman 2002). While Fukuyama and other conservatives see the sexual revolution as the root of immorality, Krugman here appropriates the "anything goes" idea to explain financial rather than sexual licentiousness and self-indulgence.

If Krugman and other liberals decry the excesses of executive pay, conservatives, too, see moral failure in the absence of self-restraint. But their concern is a broad one about the decline of the work ethic, and their targets of criticism are lower down in the class hierarchy. Thus, a *National Review* editorial argues that our system is "in deep trouble because it lacks the traditional moral imperatives of self-restraint and delayed gratification." The result is "non-competitive shoddy workmanship, an underclass locked in dependency, and widespread cultural vulgarity" (Editorial 1988a, 21). To the contrary, says a more progressive analyst. Consumer hedonism has transformed the old Protestant Ethic values. But "what is at stake is not the decline of morality but its redefinition" (Judis 1999, 56).

Commentators on the right portray themselves as the defenders of "'bourgeois morality' (which is drawn in the main from classic Jewish and Christian morality)" while labeling the Left as devoted to "a radical and thoroughgoing moral relativism" (Hyde 1990a, 25). The Left has created an "upside-down moral world" in which free choice is all that matters (Chiusano 1996, 56). Individual freedom is the supreme concern, even among children. Thus, the sex education supported by liberals is "uninformed by any value base but the moral autonomy of the child and the purported objectivity of the educator" (Nadler 1997, 50). Children are taught "the value-free science of sex" and are "trusted to make sexual decisions all on their own, rationally, using the evaluative and normative criterion of personal comfort" (Mindus 2000, 46).

Conservatives in our sample of political commentary contend that the firm exercise of authority is required to make people good. One writer in *National Review* notes that this statement is perfectly obvious but must nevertheless be voiced because authority is currently on the "Index of Prohibited Concepts and Words" (Martin 1991, 26). For their part, those on the left characterize many conservatives as "authoritarian" (Ehrenreich 1993b; Hitchens 1985). The New Left that emerged in the 1960s, as progressives see it, was all about questioning authority. The New Right, in contrast, developed to defend authority—whether legal, familial, religious, or military—in distinction to the Old Right, which had an antiauthority streak, as represented by the likes of Ayn Rand (Ehrenreich 1993b, 74).

The Left rejects the accusation that its programs are based on "license or rebellion" (di Leonardo 1996, 29), just as the Right rejects the idea that an inherent opposition exists between the workings of the capitalist marketplace and adherence to traditional values. All agree that individuals can and do make moral choices. "Blaming 'the system' for the moral failures of individual Americans is a cop-out," says a well-known conservative (Hyde 1990b, 53). All of us "must subject our choices to moral criticism," says another (Lipman 1991b, 53). Both sides face difficulties here, however, as a writer in *Time* points out: "Just as conservatives think they can restore a moral center without making concessions to government activism, liberals think they can revive the language of morality without being judgmental" (R. Wright 1996, 45).

Writers on the left see themselves as espousing causes of benefit to all. Movements in support of women's rights or gay rights, for example, do not simply serve the interests of these groups. Ideally, "every outgroup carries with it a critical perspective, forged in the painful experiences of rejection and marginalization." The aim of the women's movement is "to improve an imperfect world," not just to have women exchange places with men (Ehrenreich 1990, 15; see also Gevisser 1988). Feminists are called on to reaffirm "the moral legitimacy of women's liberation" and to recognize that "a repressive sexual politics " makes people "feel guilty about aspiring to freedom and happiness, and thus more inclined to bow to corporate and governmental authority" (Willis 1981, 495).

Disputes over the university canon and political correctness have also been seen through the lens of morality. One conservative sees the debates as representing a "moral divide" where one side is wrong and the other is right (Teachout 1992, 54). Political correctness "in its purest forms is evil," and liberalism is unable to "supply the moral basis for effective resistance to evil." Liberalism entails radical tolerance of all competing values; it insists that "opponents of right reason are never evil but merely misinformed" (55). On the other side, a progressive criticizes "political correctness" for failing to support true diversity, though "morally, it may pose as a compliment to pluralism and 'diversity'" (Hitchens 1991, 472). Since critics on the right similarly note that the claim of "diversity" is often used to enforce conformity to certain ideas, a Left-Right consensus exists against the ills of political correctness.

Popular culture fare presents both moral issues and the difficulties of weighing considerations of morality against those of censorship. Media companies that do not censor rap artists' violent messages are accused of exhibiting "moral irresponsibility," but companies that restrict such messages are accused of "corporate censorship" (Kinsley 1992c, 88). Several commentators advocate media self-censorship regarding sex, violence, and drug use (C. P. Alexander 1990; Kinsley 1992c). Conversely, a progressive argues that given our culture's violence, obscenity, sexism, and racism, smothering the messages we do not want to hear with "morally bankrupt, politically self-serving Muzak" also is not desirable. Isn't it odd, he observes, that the free market reigns "except when rap music captures a lion's share of the multi-billion dollar music market. Then, in the name of decency and family values, we're duty bound to regulate it" (quoted in Sachs and Washburn 1995, 33). But *The New Republic* takes liberals to task for failing to recognize that "lives are ruined by the ethos of 'anything goes.'" Since licentiousness in popular culture harms children, and liberal activists support government intervention for the public good, why not here? (Editorial 1988b, 7). During the controversy surrounding rapper Ice-T's album, *Cop Killer,* a progressive argued that "our free market of ideas and images . . . shouldn't be any less free for a black man than for other purveyors of 'irresponsible' sentiments" (Ehrenreich 1992a, 89). And a writer in *Time* contended that "X-rated pop deserves its First Amendment cloak" because "it speaks from the gut of disenfranchised America." One cannot argue, he said, that the material offends "community standards" because its popularity means that "a lot of the community is laughing and singing along" (Corliss 1990, 99).

If those on the right decry the immorality and depravity of television talk shows, those on the left find it "morally repulsive" that the guests "for the most part . . . are so needy—of social support, of education, of material resources and self-esteem—that they mistake being the center of attention for being actually loved and respected" (Ehrenreich 1995, 92). Thus, the Right appears to criticize the immorality manifest in popular culture, while the Left focuses on the structural injustices that it sees as the underlying causes of immorality.

Aspects of the feminist movement are likewise fraught with issues of morality. A conservative attacks the feminist "gender sliming" that labels all men rapists or potential rapists (Morrow 1994a, 55). Such a contention is not only outrageous but also "a moral stupidity," since it eliminates the distinction between decent men and rapists (57–58). A progressive assails the "difference feminism" that seeks to portray men and women as having different needs and accuses it of selling women domestic labor "as a badge of moral worth" (Pollitt 1992b, 805). A conservative notes that feminist concerns about women's health issues that have the effect of portraying women as ill might reflect "a subconscious way of saying that they want their moral superiority back"—a superiority women had in the days when they used illness as "a protective coloration" (King 1992, 64). From the perspective of the Left, of course, this alleged moral superiority came at the cost of economic and social inequality. And "there is no moral justification for treating women as having lesser rights than men" (Etzioni 1993, 76). A critic of radical feminism, however, sees earlier "first wave" feminism, which had an equity agenda, as carrying a "moral authority" that is lacking in newer, more radical, feminism, which seeks to eliminate all hints of male dominance (Sommers 1992, 32).

For some conservatives, "the woman's morality is the ultimate basis of all morality." Most of what we define as humane and individual "originates in the mother's love for her children," and "the woman in the home with her child is the last bastion against the amorality of the technocratic marketplace when it strays from the moral foundations of capitalism" (Gilder 1986, 31). In the battles between the feminists and the traditionalists, women will decide what happens next, since "women transmit culture" (Charen 1984, 27).

Conservatives also assert that gender traits "make a tremendous difference in the way people can and will act. Any worldview that pretends otherwise is either dishonestly or maliciously inviting human misery" (Marshner 1988, 39). While feminists assert that the real differences between men and women are "merely cultural" and therefore are amenable to elimination, this idea is clearly false. No society really believes that women could be as aggressive as men or men as nurturing as women (S. Goldberg 1993, 34–35). The behavioral and emotional differences between men and women "are rooted in male and female physiologies," and "all social systems conform to the limits imposed by that reality" (S. Goldberg 1991, 30). An editorial in *National Review* that advocates single-sex schools because they boost girls' achievement notes that feminists view sex as a socially constructed category, like race. "But sex is not at all like race. Sex matters a whole lot, particularly for adolescent girls, who are wont to exchange concern over grades for concern over appearance in the presence of boys. That's not an artifact of sexism; it's a fact of life" (1998b, 17–18). In the dominant conservative view, biology trumps culture and has great significance for human behavior and morality.

Progressives are more likely to see behavior and morality as rooted in cultural realities, though at least one article on the progressive side cautions against the currently fashionable view that denies that "any biologically based commonalities . . . cut across cultural differences" (Ehrenreich and McIntosh 1997, 12). It is too simple, the authors contend, to see biology as deterministic while viewing culture "as a domain where power relations with other humans are the only obstacle to freedom." In truth, culture is not "a realm of perfect plasticity" (15). A similar concession is made on the other side, as a conservative writer concedes that however much the reality of male and female behavior is biologically based, cultural definitions matter: "the attitudes and values held by men and women do determine whether they live their lives on a dance floor or a battlefield, and this is not such a little thing" (S. Goldberg 1993, 36).

While liberal feminists early on sought to improve women's standing in the public spheres of business and politics, more radical feminists argued that one could not separate the public and private in this way. As one progressive writer in our sample has explained, radical feminists have always "emphasized the connection between women's exclusion from full participation in the public world and their subordination in the so-called private sphere of familial and sexual relations" (Willis 1981, 494). Of course, the idea that marriage is not a purely private matter is also endorsed by a conservative who sees "the increasing privatization of marriage" as "a key legal and cultural factor contributing to our current marriage crisis." Government must recognize, protect, and strengthen marriage in much the same way that government acts with respect to private property (Gallagher 1999, 40). To be sure, Left and Right have different perceptions about what marriage should look like.

Abortion and Homosexuality

On abortion and homosexuality, the issues most closely associated with morality in the public mind, a surprising degree of complexity exists. The arguments of both supporters and opponents are more nuanced and ambivalent than one might expect in a "culture war."

Unsurprisingly, those on the right see abortion as immoral and express grave concern about the "lack of moral revulsion" regarding abortions ("The America We Seek" 1996, 38), while those on the left question whether it can "ever be moral for a woman to be pregnant against her will" (Houppert 2000, 7). Yet the antiabortion side is willing to consider matters of personal interests and happiness, and the proabortion side is willing to engage with issues of morality and "sin."

Most Americans, suggests one writer in *National Review,* "deliberately refuse to face up to the moral character of abortion because morality no longer seems to serve our interests." But since the "new morality" of feminism has not made most women happy—"many of them are poorer and more lonely"—"the missing piece of the puzzle is the link between the moral life and the happy one. Life without abortion is often more difficult; life with abortion promises to be easier. But in the end it creates its own problems. And in a sense not meant by whoever coined the phrase, living well is the best revenge" (Cunningham 1992, 48). This statement represents a thoroughly American blend of moralism and pragmatism.

Supporters of abortion rights disagree internally on the issue of morality. Some feminists consider abortion to be essential to women's freedom and therefore view abortion as a moral demand. A "feminist moral vision proposes to extend to women—and to the entire realm of familial and sexual life—the democratic principles of self-determination, equality, and the right to pursuit of happiness." Feminists should therefore not accept the terms dictated by the Right but should "assert women's moral right to autonomy and sexual love, and therefore their moral right to kill an unwanted fetus" (Willis 1981, 494–95).

In contrast, another supporter of abortion rights argues that women are entitled to feel a "sense of sin" regarding their abortions (Wolf 1995, 34). We need to "mourn the evil—necessary evil though it may be—that is abortion" and to treat the decision to abort the fetus with the "moral gravity" that it deserves (28). The abortion decision is "a place of moral struggle, of self-interest mixed with selflessness" (32). Abortion rights should be defended "within a moral framework that admits that the death of a fetus is a real death." The failure to address the moral issues of abortion puts us in danger "of losing what can only be called our souls" (26). Another pro-choice writer proposes that abortion should be legal in the first two trimesters but banned in the third, when the fetus exhibits full brain activity. Banning third trimester abortions "would harm the rights of American women, but the harm would be small, while the moral foundation of abortion choice overall would be strengthened" (Easterbrook 2000, 25). A feminist responds with disdain to this suggestion, however, noting that abortion is "an issue of sexual politics and morality" and that the fetus is, after all, "being carried inside a woman's body" (Houppert 2000, 7).

Another attempt to support abortion as a moral right contends that abortion may be seen as a pro-family and pro-social act, since under some circumstances choosing to give birth "may be socially dysfunctional, morally irresponsible or even cruel." Whereas the right-to-lifers believe it is "a moral imperative" to keep an anencephalic infant alive, those who support middle-class family life believe fertility must be effectively and rationally controlled using all the technologies available, including prenatal screening and abortion. The issue is not the furtherance of individual freedom but the needs of the family (Muller 1995, 27). The idea that abortions might be necessary for the benefit of the family of course runs directly contrary to the assumptions of those in the pro-life movement who view the pro-choice arguments as a manifestation of excessive individualism. They see the rights of the autonomous individual, embedded in court decisions, as threatening "to give us an America in which the only actors of consequence are the individual and the state; no other community, including the community of husband and wife, or the community of parents and children, will have effective constitutional standing" ("The America We Seek" 1996, 38–39). Some abortion rights advocates contend that the issue is not individual privacy but rather the larger society's responsibility to help women with both child rearing and abortion (Petchesky 1990, 734).

Issues of class are pervasive in the culture wars, and advocates of abortion rights are mindful of class differences. One of them differentiates between the "middle-class vision of family life"—one that assumes that fertility is to be rationally controlled, with a repertoire that includes abortion—and those of other social classes. An "elite culture" emphasizes career advancement for both men and women while conceptions of family life among the lower-middle and working classes are more fatalistic (Muller 1995, 28). A conservative writer characterizes the abortion debates as a "class-based Kulturkampf" (Neuhaus 1989b, 42). And a progressive writer decries the use of individual privacy claims in abortion disputes as "a class-biased and racist concept" because it fails to provide the economic and social conditions under which poor and nonwhite women would be able to exercise their individual rights (Petchesky 1990, 734).

The Left also criticizes the moral stance of such "antichoice militants" as Operation Rescue, which commits violence to rescue the helpless "unborn." These groups see themselves as engaged in a moral protest akin to the antislavery or anti-Holocaust movements. Yet their targets, likened to slaveholders or Nazis, are women who enter abortion clinics. These women "are to be treated as being without rights or freedom from assault: that is the moral sensibility of Operation Rescue" (Green 1989, 178).

Some who see abortion as morally abhorrent greet with derision the idea that there can be any moral complexity attached to abortion. What, then, is "the source of the intellectual and moral difficulty?" one such critic asks. "Is a mortal assault on a fetus something on the order of assault and battery? Or is it no different from stuffing a tomato into a blender?" (Buckley 1990a, 62). Americans should "consider the possibility of a connection—cultural as well as legal—between the virtue deficit in contemporary American life and the abortion license" ("The America We Seek" 1996, 41).

Commentators of all persuasions recognize the ambivalences and hypocrisies attendant upon abortion decisions. Americans appear to favor both pragmatic and moral responses to the issue. As one commentator perceives, "Americans want to register their moral disapproval and keep the procedure available at the same time" (Caldwell 1999, 15). Most Americans say that they oppose abortions for lifestyle reasons, such as not wanting another baby now, not being able to afford one, and not being married. Yet they use abortion for precisely such reasons. Because abortion has become an "indispensable part of the normal middle-American toolkit," there is "a rock-solid, European-style support for abortion, with American moral posturing plastered on top" (16). "A pro-life regime is not really something Americans want—it's just something they feel they ought to want" (14). Most Americans see abortion as a "necessary evil" (Forsythe 1999, 42).

For many Americans, the way to resolve this dilemma is to avoid thinking or talking about abortion. We fear that "to voice any doubts might jeopardize our tenuous hold" on the issue "and could give aid and succor to the other side" (Carlson 1997, 40). "Not thinking about the issue is the way a majority of the public can say that abortion is 'murder,' but not feel obliged to do anything about it" (Ponnuru 1999, 43). Americans agree with the idea that the fetus is a human baby and killing it is wrong, but they also accept the idea that a woman has a right to choose (Mathewes-Green 1997). The abortion issue has made "hypocrites of us all" (Kinsley 1989, 96). The majority of Americans clearly want to keep abortion legal, but they are "passive and quiet." Shifting the debate to partial-birth abortions gave momentum to the pro-life movement. "By failing to acknowledge the moral questions raised, pro-choice leaders stilled the voices of many of their allies, ashamed to be on their side" (Carlson 1998, 60). Yet, a pro-choice pastor is quoted as saying, "as long as the bottom line is the protection of the conscience of the individual woman to do what she has to do, we're in our tradition" (M. P. Harris 1988, 44). There is clearly recognition here of the pulls of both moral and pragmatic considerations.

The existence of both pro-life feminists (see Gallagher 1987) and of a well-known "Jewish, atheist, civil libertarian, left-wing, pro-lifer," Nat Hentoff, offers further testimony to the complexities of moral argument regarding abortion. Hentoff argues that abortion is, in fact, inconsistent with "the liberal/left worldview," since "respect for human life demands opposition to abortion, capital punishment, euthanasia and war. . . . It is out of character for the left to neglect the weak and helpless" (1992, 24).

Antiabortion advocates who perceive "a war over the moral definition of American culture" nevertheless recognize the significance of law and practice in influencing moral sentiment. The "pedagogical force of law" is so great that popular attitudes toward abortion will change only when *Roe v. Wade* is overturned, says one conservative (Neuhaus 1989b, 39). Another conservative contends that only when abortions become much more rare will a broad consensus emerge in favor of the right to life (Forsythe 1999, 45). Progressive writers likewise see changing social conditions as influencing our views of morality. For example, a progressive argues that "as an increasing number of gay people live open and honest lives, the public view of the morality of gay conduct will continue to change, ultimately influencing both the courts and the legislatures" (Feldblum 2000, 25).

Some abortion rights advocates allege that the so-called moral opposition to abortion is really opposition either to female sexuality (Tax 1989, 632) or to the "empowerment" of the young and poor women who are the main users of abortion. The availability of abortion "symbolically threatens white patriarchal control over 'their' young women's sexual 'purity'" (Petchesky 1990, 733). "Feminists are the bearers of the only authentic family values" (Gordon 1998, 5). The "postpatriarchal family" is not only more loving but also "more moral" (Wolf 1992, 25).

Abortion opponents, by contrast, maintain that abortion hurts women by encouraging male irresponsibility and contributing to the marginalization of fatherhood. ("The America We Seek" 1996, 38; Editorial 1998a, 12). Many women have abortions because they are forced to do so by their irresponsible boyfriends (W. Shalit 1998, 29).

Even those opponents of abortion who view it as "the most serious moral question facing America" may still disapprove of the tactics of antiabortion crusaders such as Operation Rescue (Editorial 1991c, 13). Nevertheless, despite disagreements about tactics, abortion opponents generally seem more unified on questions of morality than its supporters do. On issues related to gays and lesbians, however, there appears to be more division among those who disapprove of homosexual activity.

The majority of those who oppose homosexual behavior view it as immoral. They therefore assume that "hostility" toward gays "proceeds in large part from sincerely held moral beliefs" (Klinghoffer 1989, 23). There is some contention, however, regarding whether homosexuals are morally responsible for their sexual proclivities. One conservative argues that homosexuals are "fundamentally unable to change their offensive ways"

(Teachout 1983, 1412). And a gay conservative takes offense at the many cruel things uttered by conservatives against "people who through no fault of their own happen to be different in their sexuality" (quoted in "Notes and Asides" 1990, 17).

Yet other conservatives balk at the idea of absolving homosexuals of moral responsibility. They argue that even if homosexuality is in some sense "natural," it is still not right. If we found a gene for arson, we would still expect people to exert self-control, and "we would hardly waive our moral reservations about arson" (Arkes 1993, 44). It is false to believe that when something is biological, there is no volitional element. Nor is it true that the degree of volition determines "the moral status of homosexuality" (Editorial 1993b, 16–17). Furthermore, "the precise mix of genetic and environmental influences is morally irrelevant. They can cause a predisposition toward homosexuality; they cannot cause homosexual conduct itself" (Editorial 1998c, 16).

How to translate a moral distaste for homosexual behavior into practice is unclear, however. The conservative movement is split between those who advocate "institutionalized repression of the homosexual community" and those who prefer what one writer considers "a more sensible and less strident way." Before the gay rights movement, a kind of "tolerance contract" was in effect whereby homosexuals agreed to be discreet and the law left them alone. Now that such is no longer the case, conservatives in some communities are taking repressive measures against what they perceive as subversive elements. The "sense of the community" must be respected (Teachout 1983, 1412).

Conservatives find the gay rights movement offensive because it is "an attack on privacy and on the very idea of sexual morality. It seeks public approval for every variant of sexual activity." Behaviors that are socially harmful may be tolerated in private life—a matter of discretion, not hypocrisy. Gay people who are conservative "neither hide nor proclaim what they are." Their friends know; others have no business knowing (Short 1990, 44). Many conservatives see the public acceptability of homosexuality as a challenge to the whole "moral tradition." God judges nations, says one conservative, "less on what the nation does in private than on what it sanctions in public" (Klinghoffer 1998, 26). "The demand for 'gay rights' is essentially a demand for respect and approval rather than for rights" (van den Haag 1991, 35).

But another conservative suggests that the gay rights movement is merely a rebellion against the persecution to which gays are subjected. Though such rebellions "are often childish and self-destructive, . . . they are also typically American reactions to moral hypocrisy and politicized lying. The persecutors of gays bear significant responsibility for gay militancy and have no right to cite it as an excuse for more persecution" (Woolman 1986, 29).

If many conservatives speak of tolerating behaviors practiced discreetly in private but not publicly flaunted, one conservative has argued precisely the reverse. The very idea of morality, John Gray contends, is that it is part of a common culture. If government must practice neutrality with respect to different ways of life, if it cannot encourage or support "some ways of life . . . deemed by . . . the moral common sense of society, to be undesirable or inferior," the consequence "is nothing less than the legal disestablishment of morality. As a result, morality becomes in theory a private habit of behavior rather than a common way of life" (1992, 20). For Gray, then, a common morality must be understood and endorsed by social policies. In a free society, those who do not conform to the accepted morality are to be tolerated but seen as inferior. People are imperfect and are not always perfectible. In their efforts to eliminate prejudice, movements for political correctness produce "a dissociation of private thought from public life and so undermine the freedom of their institutions" (35).

Gray's view thus differs substantially from Short's argument that "private life is a place where faults which it is best to tolerate, but inimical to society to approve, may be abided" (1990, 44) and Klinghoffer's notion that God judges nations more on what they publicly sanction than what they privately practice (1998, 26). Gray maintains that the gay rights movement has been brought into being by the actions of a government that does not, in fact, practice the radical neutrality that some contemporary liberals preach. In reality, the government favors and gives legal privileges to certain "fashionable" minorities. Policies of positive discrimination for members of certain cultural minority groups have meant that "some who may not hitherto have considered themselves members of a cultural minority—such as many homosexuals—are encouraged by such practices to constitute themselves as one" (J. Gray 1992, 30).

At least one progressive agrees that "the liberal neutrality rhetoric" is "disingenuous" with respect to antidiscrimination laws for homosexuals. It is not true, she argues, that such laws merely establish basic equality and are neutral with respect to the morality of being gay. Rather, they "effectively stand for the proposition that discrimination based on homosexuality is as reprehensible as discrimination based on race or gender." Moreover, judges who think homosexuality is immoral will continue to see discrimination against them as legitimate (Feldblum 2000, 24).

As conservatives view the matter, the law cannot and should not compel people to regard homosexuals as "morally equal" to heterosexuals (van den Haag 1991, 38). "The heterosexual community would flatly resist, and quite properly so, any demand for a modus vivendi the implications of which are that the difference between the two lifestyles is on the order of the difference between people who like Pepsi Cola and those who like Coca-Cola" (Buckley 1993a, 70). Most Americans are hostile to same-sex marriage precisely because it "constitutes the ultimate societal declaration of the moral equality of homosexuality and heterosexuality" (Krauthammer 1996, 102).

Charity and toleration toward homosexuals are desirable but should not come at the cost of "convictions rooted . . . in theological and moral truths" (quoted in "Notes and Asides" 1990, 18). There is concern that if required to interact with gay people in more intimate settings, such as in Boy Scout troops, people will be unable to express their moral views about homosexuals (Cloud 2000).

As a result of such concerns, some conservatives take a dim view of laws that compel association with gays. Such laws, one conservative argues, "redistribute rights from straights to those gays willing to use the power of the state to compel social acceptance." Landlords must rent to them, employers must hire them, and "nondiscriminatory" school curricula have given gays "the right to have the city proselytize on their behalf" (Sobran 1986, 24). But another conservative suggests that laws requiring nondiscrimination in housing and employment do not forbid anyone from disapproving of homosexual acts. Nor do "morally neutral" descriptions of homosexuality in school curricula constitute "proselytizing" (Woolman 1986, 30).

Yet another conservative maintains that although homosexuals should have the same civil rights as heterosexuals, laws should not prohibit private discrimination. Churches, for example, have a right to discriminate. And the law should not interfere with the right of parents not to have their children taught by "persons whose conduct they abhor and who they think will set a bad example for their children." This right should take precedence over anyone's right to be employed in a school (van den Haag 1991, 37). A well-known gay conservative, Andrew Sullivan, argues that while all public discrimination against gays should be eliminated, private discrimination is another matter. There should be "no political imposition of tolerance" (1993, 36). Indeed, argues another conservative, using state force to bar private discrimination is "immoral," and "state immorality is much more dangerous than personal immorality" (Woolman 1986, 58).

From a strictly libertarian perspective, neither gay rights laws nor antisodomy laws are good, since government should not be used for such purposes. The same libertarian logic should apply to both kinds of laws, argues one conservative. Nevertheless, conservatives have not called for the repeal of sodomy laws (Woolman 1986, 58). Others in the conservative camp argue that antisodomy laws represent a widely shared defense of a set of "binding norms." Thus, William F. Buckley Jr. takes Senator Barry Goldwater to task for calling the ban on gays in the military "just plain un-American." That, Buckley says, is a peculiar way to talk about banning a practice (sodomy) that until recently was outlawed by forty-seven states (1993a, 70).

Similarly, for one conservative writer "the conservative view, based as it is on the inherent rights of the individual over the state, is the logical political home of gay men and women" (quoted in "Notes and Asides" 1990, 17–18). Not so, says another, since conservatism recognizes that "freedom also depends on moral character—on habits of self-control" (Short 1990, 44). Yet another insists that a clash arises between the Judeo-Christian tradition as a "way of life" and homosexuality as "another way of life" (quoted in "Notes and Asides" 1990, 18). He cautions that conservatives should not abandon their belief that "the practice of homosexuality is a violation of an organic moral code. Those in favor of gay rights must guard against a kind of extortionate moral egalitarianism" that sees any opposition to gay practices as bigotry (Buckley 1992b, 71).

If those on the right fear falling into the definitions set by the Left, so that opposition to gay practices is seen as bigotry, an exquisite parallel to this sentiment exists on the left, where the concern is that gays might buy into the Christian Right's definition of acceptability. As gay images and gay culture have become increasingly visible, the national movement has become more conservative, say progressive critics. There is now the risk that gay leaders appear to be saying, "We're just as good as any Christian, white

American family" (Ireland 1999, 16). There is a danger that the Right has a "lock on the way gay issues are framed. . . . We present ourselves as 'just like heterosexuals,' when most people—straight and gay—believe we are in fact quite different. . . . We argue for civil rights at a moment when the entire paradigm of that phrase has been shifted by conservatives to be equated with special rights" (Vaid 1993, 28).

Gays now have the opportunity to change American values and politics, to subvert traditional gender and sexual roles and counter the oppressive uses of male power (Kopkind 1993, 592). Homosexuals must seek to "go beyond mere identity politics to bind equality for gay people with equality for all people" (Vaid 1993, 28). To seek only acceptance by the larger society means setting "narrowly self-serving goals" divorced from "the larger battle" (Gevisser 1988, 414). While the gay rights movement adopted the strategy and tactics of the civil rights movement or of identity politics—"How else do you get ahead in America except by banding together and hoisting a flag?"—the true significance of the movement lies in making everyone aware that sexuality is fluid, that our conventional categories may not be valid (Ehrenreich 1993a, 76). The struggle for gay rights is thus, like the struggle for women's rights, an issue with broader social and moral implications.

In disputes about same-sex marriage, both sides argue that morality is on their side. Those opposed to same-sex marriage consider homosexuality morally inferior to heterosexuality and hence see homosexuals as not entitled to the same privileges (Buckley 1992b; Krauthammer 1996). Supporters argue that legalizing gay marriage would provide a "long-overdue correction of a moral anomaly that dehumanizes and excludes a significant portion of the human race" (Editorial 2000a, 9). Marriage acts as both an incentive and a reward for "moral behavior" (Sullivan 1996, 12); "not to promote marriage would be to ask too much of human virtue" (Sullivan 1989, 20).

All in all, it is hard to fit the culture war rubric to issues regarding homosexuality. Conservatives disagree among themselves on the stance to be taken; gays are divided in their goals and the definition of their identity. There is no neat division between the "orthodox" and the "progressive." What is apparent, however, is that all sides share the tendency to frame issues in moral terms. And when "rights" rather than "morals" are the chosen framework, sympathetic onlookers suggest that such framing is insufficient. Thus, observers argue, if gay student organizations seek not just legal rights but "social and cultural acceptance," they need "to confront the issue of morality more directly. . . . The possibility exists here to define the action of protecting and supporting gay students as a moral imperative as well as a legal matter of civil rights" (Miceli 2005, 609).

Moral Decline and Relativism

While all sides use the language of morality, they do not agree about whether the prevailing situation is one of moral decline or moral progress. Differing opinions exist even within the conservative side. Thus, Paul Weyrich, who coined the term *moral majority,* is cited as arguing at the end of the 1990s that such an entity no longer exists. "Abortion is still legal; the NEA is still funded, the Greater Adulterer is still in office; the Republican establishment still thinks social issues are too thorny to embrace; and too many evangelical leaders have been seduced by their power at the expense of their principles" (Gibbs 1999, 47). Only a few months earlier, another conservative had suggested that conservatives could claim credit for turning the tide in the culture wars. The divorce rate had fallen; the marriage rate had stabilized; births to unmarried women had fallen somewhat; the teen birthrate had dropped; the number of abortions had dropped; fewer teenagers were sexually active; and suicide and violent crime rates were decreasing (Nadler 1998, 26).

For the most part, writers on the left do not speak of moral decline. For all the "hand-wringing about moral decline," says one, "there is surprisingly little evidence that Americans act more immorally today than they did a quarter-century ago. . . . Americans are less likely to drink too much, take drugs, cheat on taxes, drive drunk, rely on the dole. . . . They also give more to charity, volunteer more, and spend more time in church" (Whitman 1999, 18–19).

Progressives, of course, do not always accept the conservative designations of what is immoral behavior and sometimes look askance at some of the movements to improve morality. Thus, one liberal writer questions the motives of those involved in promoting "family values," suggesting that "most of the impulses that propel people toward the right-wing profamily movement" are "nasty ones: misogyny, racism, sexual repressiveness and a punitive attitude toward young people" (Ehrenreich 1982, 305). Another liberal argues that people "divorce for all kinds of reasons, not because they lack moral fiber." If what people want from family life is more intimacy, sexual pleasure, and shared goals, and if single women want to be mothers, "why shouldn't society adapt? Society is, after all, just us." Yes, such behavior has costs, but the reasons for the suffering "lie not in moral collapse but in our failure to acknowledge and adjust to changing social relations." Most of the harm associated with family dissolution is economic (Pollitt 1992a, 90, 92, 94). A writer in *Time* notes that the very idea of "family values" represents "an American warehouse of moral images, of inherited assumptions, of pseudo-memories of a golden age, of old class habits" (Morrow 1992b, 26). He also suggests that politicians and government cannot "have much to do with improving a society's values—family or otherwise. Surely the values if worth anything, must be more deeply embedded in the culture than the slogans of transient politicians" (25).

The one clear reference to moral decline in a liberal publication occurs in the context of an argument against the "cultural conservatives" who "would have us believe that government, politics, and public policy should be instruments through which to affect a moral revival." This writer argues that "cultural politics and the law" do not provide answers to moral problems. And "when thinking about moral decay in the inner city," it is important to remember that "we should be embracing these people, not demonizing them" (Loury 1998, 17).

The general thrust of conservative discussions of moral decline is that the culture has become exceedingly permissive. The "moral education" of children has been shaped by rock music, with only ineffectual efforts made to deal with it, argues Allan Bloom in his best-selling *The Closing of the American Mind* (1987). The Left "has in general given rock music a free ride" in part because liberals "regard it as a people's art" and enjoy its revolutionary potential (77–78). Moreover, "the uneasy bedfellowship of the sexual revolution and feminism produced an odd tension in which all the moral restraints governing nature disappeared" (105). With the help of secular liberals, the media, and Hollywood executives, an "anything goes" aura has been established.

For many conservatives, much of the moral decline in American society can be traced to the countercultural movements of the late 1960s and early 1970s. William F. Buckley Jr., for example, wrote a scathing piece attacking the *New York Times* for its praise of the counterculture. After the 1994 election brought Republican control of Congress, Speaker of the House Newt Gingrich expressed the hope that the country might finally be liberated from the counterculture. In response, the *Times* editorialized in favor of the counterculture, even praising its music. Buckley responded by suggesting that "the countercultural music is the perfect accompaniment for the culture of sexual self-indulgence, of exhibitionism, of crime and illegitimacy and ethnic rancor and victimology. We have to hope that the *Times* editor will one day grow up, like Jerry Rubin," a famed hippie who abandoned the counterculture for Wall Street (1995, 79).

In his book on how the counterculture changed America, Roger Kimball alleges that "it is now practically taken for granted that going to college involves not so much the 'questioning' as the repudiation of traditional moral and political values" (2000, 129–30). Our degraded popular culture, our addiction to sensation, and our inadequacies as citizens and "moral agents" all can be traced to the countercultural revolution. But the counterculture is so much "part of the air we breathe" that even conservatives sometimes seem to deny how bad things really are. "It is both ironical and dispiriting to realize that the counterculture may have won its most insidious victories not among its natural sympathizers on the Left but, on the contrary, among those putatively conservative opponents who can no longer distinguish between material affluence and the moral good" (Kimball 2000, 282).

Yet liberals, too, are "uneasy with a consumerist, individualistic culture that often violates their sense of community, decency, and mutual obligation" (Dionne 2006, 135). And both sides see remnants of the counterculture in the arts, universities, and the media. Even a supporter of government funding for novel or experimental art concedes that there is something irritating about "people wanting to be a counterculture on the majority's nickel" (Kinsley 1992a, 41). An opponent of such funding, conversely, argues that "countercultural crowds now gather to demand, not an end to war or the start of Revolution, but the right to a government grant" (Eichman 1990, 24).

The relativism of the multiculturalist intellectuals also comes under conservative attack as a contributor to the moral decline of American society. "The moral lesson of multiculturalism is a lazy, cynical relativism of 'nothing matters.'" We need "to return to simple right and wrong. . . . Not all moral questions are complex" (Mansfield 2000, 26). Furthermore, if there is really no way of distinguishing right from wrong, if there is "no rational ground for our moral judgments," then "the enterprise of moral judgment" is "dissolved" (Arkes 1989, 36). Almost all of the discussion of moral relativism appears in *National Review* (see Arkes 1989; J. Goldberg 2000; J. Gray 1992; Hyde 1990a; Lipman 1991b; Short 1990). There, Hollywood is seen as celebrating "the message of moral relativism" and "the idea that we are all our own priests" (J. Goldberg 2000, 62, 64). And conventional wisdom is seen as supporting relativistic and subjective approaches to issues that deny the existence of moral truths. That we harbor different ideas of ultimate good, one conservative argues, does not mean that we cannot distinguish between good and evil. Thus, "the goods expressed in the lives of Mother Teresa and Oscar Wilde are incommensurable," but we can "confidently assert that the life of a crack addict is a poor one" (J. Gray 1992, 36).

Yet for all their concerns with the evils of moral relativism, some conservatives acknowledge that views of what is moral are always changing, that moral absolutes are not always appropriate. Indeed, one conservative writer takes radical feminists to task for being "absolutists." Not so long ago, he notes, many people—including women—were indignant at the idea of giving spinster schoolteachers the same pay as men who were supporting families. "Lost in a dream of absoluteness, feminists are ill equipped to face the inevitable somersaults of modern moral pluralism" (Minogue 1991, 48).

As noted earlier, writers on the Left reject the assertion that their views amount to moral relativism. The "cultural relativism" that conservatives attack as meaning "moral relativism" is simply an attempt "to empathize with the moral logics of others" (di Leonardo 1996, 29). Some conservatives appear to understand the distinction, pointing out the dilemmas faced by liberals. According to O'Sullivan, some "principled" liberals are "equally hostile to all cultures, for instance overriding both Christianity and Islam without distinction where they conflict with sexual equality." Then there are "instinctive" liberals who are "equally friendly to all cultures, for instance embracing even those cultures that have no truck with individual rights." The two groups have fought "over whether clitoridectomy was a horrible violation of women's rights or a legitimate expression of Third World culture beyond our ken" (1994b, 39).

For all their disagreements, some commentators suggest that American society has more consensus than meets the eye. Writing in *National Review,* one analyst says, "we are mostly agreed about good and bad. . . . A consistent moral relativist is hard to find" (Martin 1991, 25). Another writer in *The New Republic* contends that all of the combatants in the culture war "stand for visions of the good society and not simply the good life" (Judis 1999, 56). In the early 1980s, a writer in *Time* suggested that the "right-wing insurgency in America today . . . may resonate in a certain moral harmony with large numbers of American citizens" because there is now a movement toward "the firmer, commonsense moral ground that radicalism and experimental youth abandoned years ago" (Morrow 1981, 74). Several years later, a writer in *The New Republic* pointed out that for people under the age of forty, a return to "traditional values" does not mean a return to the prevailing middle-class values of the 1950s. Even young conservatives now "avidly pursue extramarital sex, occasionally enjoying pornography, often listen to rock music, usually tolerate and sporadically use recreational drugs, typically regard abortion as a matter of personal choice. . . . These young conservatives share the American ethic of social permissiveness that holds many of these cultural innovations to be beyond the coercive reach of government" (Morley 1986, 12).

Moralizing and Legislating Morality

For all their moral consciousness, writers on all sides deride the "moralism" of their opponents. Neither side wishes to be seen as imposing its values or morals on the larger population. The Left may notoriously celebrate individuals' freedom to make their own moral and lifestyle decisions, but so does the Right: "as the party of liberty, conservatives find it hard to prescribe thought and behavior for others" (Lipman 1991b, 53).

Numerous commentators on the left take aim at the "moralistic images" of "the new family warriors" (Stacey 1994, 121, 119) and the "moralistic approaches" to family matters that conceal underlying economic realities (Pollitt 1992a, 92). These liberals consider "the packaging of sexual orientation as an issue of 'morality'" to be part of the repressive forces operating in contemporary society (LaMarche and Rubenstein 1990, 526). They deride "cultural feminists" (who believe that "female values" are superior to male values) as engaging in "moralistic attacks on women whose attitudes are deemed too aggressive, openly sexual or otherwise 'male-identified'" (Willis 1981, 495). Some progressives note that appearances to the contrary, television talk shows are in fact "moralistic"—preaching the middle-class virtues of responsibility and self-control (Ehrenreich 1995, 92). In any event, "the legions of outraged moralists have little enlightenment to offer" about why these shows are so popular (Willis 1996, 19). Those on the left denounce the "moralistic scheme" of some conservatives to fight AIDS by preaching chastity and monogamy (Fumento 1988, 21). A commentator on the left suggests that the dispute over the canon is moralistic because concerns about what students read are based on the idea that "the chief end of reading is to produce a desirable kind of person and a desirable kind of society. . . . How pragmatic, how moralistic, how American!" (Pollitt 1991, 331).

Meanwhile, the Right accuses liberals of being "moralizers and uplifters" because of their efforts to combat antigay feelings (Brookhiser 1993a, 74). New Left "intellectuals" are seen as "moralistic" actors who frame policy disputes as "moral assaults" (Bork 1989, 27). And a 1996 opinion piece in *Time* derides Republican and Democratic politicians alike for their "politics of virtue": "politicians have always been willing to go on the record as firmly pro-morality. But seldom have they done it so relentlessly" (R. Wright 1996, 43).

Some writers suggest that in American culture, sleaze and immorality go hand in hand with soul-searching and Puritanism. We worry about the "deterioration of American morals" but savor "every lurid manifestation of the decadence." Perhaps moralizing has become "just another variety of entertainment," suggests a writer in *Time* (Morrow 1994b, 158). Another *Time* writer similarly contends that tension has always existed in the United States between "the pursuit of individual liberty and the quest for Puritan righteousness." Thus, the "crusade to reassert family values" is "a reaction to the sexual revolution" (Stengel 1986, 17). Both the *Murphy Brown* debates and the Clarence Thomas–Anita Hill hearings represented a kind of "moral pageant," at once "amazingly stupid" and "somehow important at the same time" (Morrow 1992a, 29).

All sides are guilty of moralizing: "The rise of virtue-talk—which generally takes the form of communitarianism on the left and nostalgia for Victorianism on the right—has resulted in a striking re-moralization of public policy debates" (Kaminer 1996, 26). Both the "politically correct left" and "the right wing minions of moral correctness" have attacked the arts (Brustein 1997d, 31). Unlike Europe, in America, the arts "have always had to prove how moral they are" (Hughes 1995, 64). Our "New Puritanism," with its obsessive devotion to health and longevity, has meant that joggers and vegans have become "favored minorities" that can obtain legal privileges, while smokers and drinkers have become "unfashionable minorities . . . subjected to . . . moralistic intervention in their chosen styles of life" (J. Gray 1992, 30).

Perhaps this tendency to take some moral offenses seriously while overlooking others (and dubbing those who do manifest concern about those offenses as "moralists") is a long-standing American characteristic. Thus, Tocqueville noted that Americans treat certain vices differently than others. Those connected with the "love of wealth," for example, "are lightly reproved, sometimes even encouraged," whereas "all those vices that tend to impair the purity of morals and to destroy the conjugal tie are treated with a degree of severity unknown in the rest of the world" (1848/1961, 2:248–49). In the contemporary United States, sociologists characterize middle-class Americans as favoring "nonjudgmentalism" (Wolfe 1998), while a leading conservative writer decries this development in language usage: "to pass moral judgments is to be 'judgmental' and 'moralistic'" (Himmelfarb 1999, 118).

Ambivalences about morality and moralizing are well demonstrated in the popular response to the scandal involving President Bill Clinton's affair with Monica Lewinsky. While European allies mocked the Clinton impeachment as evidence of a peculiar American Puritanism, Americans reacted somewhat curiously. To the surprise of many analysts, "Clinton's job approval ratings climbed throughout the scandal." When asked about this increase, "65 percent said they had adopted a more 'realistic' view that presidents should be judged on their performance, not on their personal lives. Yet, in another twist, 56 percent said that Clinton's high approval ratings reflected a national decline in personal standards and morality" (White 2003, 30).

Whatever the desire to see one's view of morality ensconced in the culture, all agree that legislation is not the appropriate route for doing so. Attempting to legislate morality while behavior contradicts it leads only to cynicism, as Prohibition demonstrated (Loury 1998, 17). Moral disapproval or censure is a better technique. Most civilizations have expressed their moral values by mobilizing social opprobrium. Such opprobrium, rather than legislation, has changed the treatment of minorities in films and television, for example (Wills 1989, 71). A gay conservative argues against using the law "to legislate culture" (Sullivan 1993, 36). A *Time* article asserts that the state should legislate morality only if there is an overwhelming moral consensus and the behavior in question poses a serious threat to social order (Church 1995, 108). A conservative argues similarly that because of our diverse views of homosexuality—specifically, of its morality or even whether any moral question is involved—attempts to legislate in this area are likely to cause more fragmentation and provoke more intolerance (J. Gray 1992, 30). Both the Moral Majority and its liberal opponents must learn that "virtue cannot be enforced by law" (Morrow 1981, 74). Translating all of morality into law would only overburden the law and bring it into disrepute (Neuhaus 1989b, 39). Yet conservatives and liberals agree that advocates attempt to use the courts to try to impose a particular sense of morality (Bork 1989; Feldblum 2000). Perhaps, indeed, the general opposition to legislating morality accounts for Americans' ability to see homosexuality as immoral while still supporting the civil rights of gays and lesbians (Loftus 2001, 779).

Conclusions

Invoking moral criteria is a characteristically American pattern, by no means confined to the Right. While Left and Right may pursue different moral goals, both groups seek the moral course. And even if a misguided exit poll question in 2004 made it appear that predominantly conservatives were concerned with "moral values," considerable evidence shows that most Americans exhibit such concerns. Indeed, an August 2008 survey found relatively little difference in this area between McCain and Obama supporters. Among those voters who said they were certain to vote for McCain, 71 percent rated "moral values" as a very important issue; among those certain to vote for Obama, 55 percent did so (Pew Forum 2008b).

Neither the moral outlook nor its conflicts with pragmatism are new in American culture. Indeed, if one were to remove the culture war trappings, the critique of contemporary morals in 1980–2000 would appear remarkably similar to such a critique in the 1920s. Critics then as now attacked "the pursuit of personal liberation, especially sexual liberation" (J. Goldberg 2000, 64). Similarities abound between the cultural currents of the Roaring Twenties and the counterculture of the late 1960s and early 1970s. Both were hostile to "bourgeois morality" and celebrated personal liberation—or "narcissism," in critics' eyes. Perhaps the one difference here is that the Great Depression of the 1930s muted or repressed the cultural changes of the 1920s, whereas aspects of the later counterculture were absorbed into the larger culture. The "moral relativism" criticized by so many at the end of the twentieth century was likewise assailed in the 1920s. In the 1920s, sociology, anthropology, comparative religion, philosophy, and "higher criticism" were seen as undermining morality and conveying the idea that "right conduct depends . . . on conditions and not on any eternal rules" (Adams 1926, 581).

What is new, once again, is the greater self-consciousness about culture and heightened attention to those attempting to shape it. That young people in the 1960s were seen as advocating a counterculture rather than simply manifesting generational wildness (as in the Roaring Twenties) testifies to the truth of this statement, as do the exaggerated responses found among culture warriors who perceive every disliked program or piece of legislation as critical to the moral stature of the society. As an example, the Catholic Church in Boston saw the presence of a birth control clinic in or near a school as establishing an "official state philosophy of situation ethics and moral relativism" (Leo 1986, 63).

A greater sensitivity to cultural difference has brought with it a reluctance to be "judgmental" in some quarters and a reaction against such sensitivity in others. Is being "nonjudgmental" a virtue or a vice? But the fundamental moralism of American culture remains evident—even in attacks on the excesses of individualism.

CHAPTER 4

Individualism but Not to Excess

In the American cultural lexicon, individualism is always good. When it is "excessive," however, it becomes "selfishness," which is not good. Contrary to culture war stereotypes of individual licentiousness being advocated on the progressive side and deference to larger purposes on the orthodox side, elite opinion on both sides of the cultural divide supports individualism and individual rights while condemning their excesses. Both sides reject "selfish" individualism in favor of the "greater good"—whether that is defined in terms of justice, liberty, and the social welfare or of spirituality, human dignity, and the sanctity of life and family. All sides wish to support the "community," which is also a good in the American cultural vocabulary. Here too, however, excesses are likely to be criticized. In the past, the excesses of community were dubbed conformity; more recently, they have been called tribalism.

Regardless of the issue under discussion, all contenders in the culture wars seek to show respect for both individual rights and the welfare of the larger community. In the case of multiculturalism, however, much confusion arises about how it relates to individualism. Is multiculturalism an expression of individualism or a corrective to it? Are individuals empowered by their cultures or enslaved by them?

Celebrating Individualism and Community

Because individualism is perhaps the quintessential American value, commentators on all sides accuse their opponents of squashing individualism. As seen by a conservative, the Left attacks individualism by seeking to impose its own cultural views and by its devotion to class struggles. "The Left wishes to use culture to remold man and society on radical lines, with destruction of individual autonomy and reason" (Lipman 1991b, 38); it prefers "proletarian community" to "bourgeois individualism" (Lipman 1991a, 40). From the perspective of progressives, the Right seeks to crush individualism with its "attack on free expression" (Editorial 1995a, 152), its "distrust of creativity in all spheres of life other than those of corporate profitability" (Mattick 1990, 358), and its "discrediting of the idea of a pro-freedom, pro-pleasure revolution in everyday life" (Willis 1996, 22).

Yet attacks on "rank" or "radical" individualism appear across the political spectrum, too. Both opponents and supporters of abortion declare their cause to be a matter of more than individual rights. For opponents of abortion, those who support abortion rights represent a "radical individualism that recognizes no restraints such as family or community." They believe that "all relationships—family, church, community, as well as motherhood—are barriers to self-fulfillment, unless the individual actively chooses them" (Cunningham 1992, 46). The pro-choice forces, says another abortion opponent, have "seized the liberal banner for a radical individualism that, in the pursuit of self-actualization, acknowledges no bonds of community or duty to others" (Neuhaus 1989b, 40). But some abortion advocates argue that abortion rights should be viewed not as "a civil liberties struggle for individual privacy" but rather as a matter of social rights. Society has a responsibility to help women with abortion and child rearing, and "the bearers of this right are not so much isolated individuals as they are members of social groups with distinct needs" (Petchesky 1990, 734).

Conservative commentators see excessive individualism as fostered by an "elite" that must be displaced (Cunningham 1992, 47). The family, for example, is under attack from "the individualism and hedonism of much of our popular and elite culture" (Muller 1995, 28). But some progressives view contemporary portraits of selfish individualism as greatly exaggerated. They argue that "moralistic images of hedonistic adults who place selfish emotional, erotic and 'career' ambitions above the needs of neglected children" do not accord with the realities of working America (Stacey 1994, 121). The Right equates feminism with individualism, as in the idea that "feminism—and radical individualism generally—is a bust outside academia and the activist groups" (Cunningham 1992, 48). But all sides disavow the exercise of merely selfish pleasures.

Excessive individualism or selfishness in the economic sphere also comes under attack. The Left assails the conservative culture for its "possessive individualism, ideological narrowness, social meanness, and Social Darwinist arrogance" (Howe 1984, 29), while a leading conservative spokesman argues the need for "a new conversation about the common good," since self-aggrandizement alone is "empty, ignoble, and in the end, profoundly unsatisfying" (Hyde 1990b, 54). The latter idea is certainly shared by the Left, where one feminist warns that the women's movement must not lose its idealistic vision of reform lest it end up "degenerating into a scramble for personal advancement" (Ehrenreich 1990, 15).

Writers from across the political spectrum suggest that Americans need to cultivate more of "the sense of what the individual owes to his community." They need to remember that "in many other cultures, individual is a pejorative, suggesting an antisocial elevation of one's own welfare above the welfare of everyone else" (Morrow 1981, 74). Individualism alone is insufficient to hold a society together. Without a common sense of what is good, without a common culture, constant battles over policy will erupt (O'Sullivan 1994b, 41).

Conservatives and liberals alike feel discomfort when they must choose between protecting individual rights and freedoms on the one hand and protecting the social good and exercising moral judgment on the other. Such dilemmas arise in connection with censorship of offensive or morally suspect popular culture. As one conservative puts it, "We must recognize that in a free society, private choices in culture must be subject to minimum restraint. But we must also be careful not to confuse rights with virtues: the exercise of the right to free cultural choice is not a good in itself, but rather must be subject to moral criticism and judged by the content of the choice" (Lipman 1991b, 53). An editorial in *The New Republic* suggests that while songs such as "Cop Killer" should not be censored, liberals should be concerned with such lyrics just as they were justifiably upset by the Willie Horton ads (used by Republicans to convey racist notions of blacks as criminals). The message is that "the contents of American culture cannot be hidden behind the freedom of American culture. For culture brings news." Therefore, "we must hear the news that culture brings. But then we must engage it, and challenge it" (Editorial 1992, 7).

Whether one gives preference to individual rights or to the welfare of the community hinges on the specific issue at hand. For all their attachment to laissez-faire economics and to individual self-sufficiency, conservatives are likely to condemn individualism if it appears to be wreaking havoc with certain institutions. The family is, of course, a prime example. Yet even here, unanimity is not present, as one conservative writer points out. For all the conservative desire to strengthen and preserve marriages, the *Wall Street Journal* is leery of changes in the tax code that would constitute "a marriage bonus" (Gallagher 1999, 40).

Whether or not feminists are ultimately "pro-family" is a matter of some dispute among progressives—again largely because of the individualist/communitarian split. Thus, one progressive has argued that feminist-backed measures such as child care support, flexible work schedules, parental leave, health care, and housing assistance can only help the family (Connell 1986, 106). But another progressive contends that such measures may be pro-family but will not necessarily produce the family stability so valued by the Right. After all, socialized medicine and day care would make women less dependent on their husbands' benefits and thus might encourage some young mothers to stray. By the same token, cutting off legal aid for divorce is pro-family but not progressive (Ehrenreich 1982, 303–4). One should affirm "individual desire and imagination" because "they are not disruptive, or selfish, but prefigurative of a happier World." This idea means, among other things, that "spouses whose lives are depleted by sexual boredom ought to be able to consider alternatives to monogamy" (306). Americans' classic ambivalence about family issues—wanting to protect the family while guarding individual rights—is to some extent reflected in the "neoliberal" or communitarian arguments that emerged in the early 1990s. This movement sought to bolster the family, arguing that individuals were happier within intact families. As seen by one progressive, these arguments exploited a yearning for "simpler family times" while offering a "gesture toward gender equality" (Stacey 1994, 120).

In addition to the family, conservatives see the military as another institution whose well-being is more important than the rights of individuals. In writing about the controversy concerning gays in the military, one conservative bemoans the waning of the "old" military culture, which is of much greater significance than "the posturing by both sides in the controversy over gays." The old military culture was conservative and was committed to the supremacy of society over the individual, unlike the liberal orthodoxy and individualism of the surrounding culture. In the aftermath of the Vietnam War, the military sought to recruit new people and thus to become less "different" from the larger culture. That movement, unfortunately, continues (Bacevich 1993, 30–31). For many on the left, the military represents a rather different cultural institution, one that "stands entirely against the humanistic values behind the gay rights movement." Thus, while gays must fight to remove the ban on their presence, they must also oppose "militarism" (Editorial 1993c, 157).

American Individualism: Complexities and Controversies

If the idea of juggling individual versus collective rights and well-being often lies at the heart of culture wars issues, the question of just how individualistic Americans are is a contentious one. In one respect, the evidence is clear: Americans are more supportive of economic individualism than are citizens of any other nation and are more likely than others to believe that individuals' fates lie in their own hands. Beyond this, however, there is considerable room for debate. Survey data reveal ambivalences and inconsistencies. Historians and sociologists offer varying portraits of individualism and its relationship to American society, both past and present.

Americans have consistently and unambiguously supported the values of free enterprise and competition. More than 75 percent of Americans in four different national surveys during the 1970s and 1980s supported the value of free enterprise and endorsed "the right to one's own opinion" and the view that "what happens to me is my own doing" (Inkeles 1990–91, 109). Of the sixteen nations included in the 1990 European Values Study, the United States ranked highest in preferring personal freedom to equality, blaming the individual for being poor, and favoring jobs that encourage individual initiative over those in which everyone works together (van Elteren 1998). To be sure, if one asks Americans questions about "social responsibility" rather than "economic individualism"—that is, beliefs about the obligation to meet the basic needs of all people in society and to redress unfair levels of social inequality—one finds substantial agreement here as well. Using National Opinion Research Center data from 1984, Bobo found that 49 percent of Americans were ambivalent, scoring close to the mean on measures of both social responsibility and economic individualism, while 20 percent were individualists and 30 percent were collectivists (1991, 86).

Historians have debated the degree to which economic individualism (or Lockean liberalism) has been the dominant philosophy in the United States. In the middle of the twentieth century, observers generally assumed that the Lockean tradition prevailed, but by the 1970s, some historians argued that republicanism was a better description of the philosophy of the American revolutionary generation. Republicanism rests on the idea of the public good as opposed to the sway of individual interests. It entails a commitment to an active civic life rather than concentration on individual rights. By the end of the 1980s, the idea of republicanism "had passed into general intellectual currency" as one of the "core traditions of American culture itself" (Rodgers 1992, 32).

The issue is a contentious one, however, with both the prevalence and the merits of republicanism a matter of dispute. While the much-discussed *Habits of the Heart* (Bellah et al. 1985/1996) celebrated republicanism as a worthy competitor or complement to the more familiar individualism, some historians allege that it was a philosophy of the elite and not appropriate to the needs of ordinary Americans. One historian has pointed out that "although the Founding Fathers never self-consciously conceived of classical republicanism as the coherent tradition we've created, they at least talked about 'republicanism' and invoked 'republican principles,' " whereas they never used the term *liberalism* (Wood 1987, 634). Nevertheless, the eventual domination of American life by liberalism represented a victory for democracy, "since a leisured gentry and an aristocratic disdain for direct market interests and working for profit were at the heart of classical republicanism" (640). Another historian has suggested that while elite views permeated all classes, competing views were not excluded and "in time exercised greater interpretive powers for those differently positioned in society" (Appleby 1985, 468–69). It is thus plausible that as economic issues became more important, Americans embraced the need to be "industrious," and with industriousness came the emphasis on individualism and liberalism (Barkalow 2004, 498). If republicanism and liberalism coexisted in the days of the early republic without either attaining "ideological hegemony," there is probably a consensus among historians that liberalism had achieved the ascendancy by the Jacksonian era (1830s–40s) (Curry and Valois 1991, 26).

While Americans have long noted their devotion to individual advancement, they often fail to take note of the flip side: the respect for authority and morality that also characterizes American culture. Bellah has argued that from the days of early New England, "Calvinist 'individualism' only made sense within the collective context. Individual action outside the bounds of religious and moral norms was seen . . . as the very archetype of sin" (1975, 18). Another scholar has noted similarly that in "positing a direct relationship between God and each recipient of Christian grace," Evangelicals "created a powerful spiritual individualism." But mindful of the "sinful nature of individuals, they sought to encapsulate the heightened self-consciousness of individuals within a community of believers that constrained individualism" (Calhoon 1991, 53).

In American cultural lore, however, the ideal is an individualism that struggles against both the conformity imposed by groups and the unwarranted exercise of authority by government and other institutions. We have often been told that "Americans, from the days of the Revolution on, have resisted authority" (Lipset 1990, 44). Lipset repeatedly notes that Americans have reacted more strongly than have Canadians to the imposition of governmental authority. Yet he reproduces without comment survey results showing that Americans conform more than Canadians do to the authority exercised by their employers: 68 percent of Americans, 57 percent of English Canadians, and 45 percent of French Canadians reported that "they followed their 'superior's instructions on a job'" (1990, 128).

Americans see themselves as individualists in part because "the rights of the individual are balanced against the authority of the state. But there is no way to refer to the authority of the welter of intermediate groups between the individual and the state" (Fukuyama 1995, 278–79). With regard to the authority of such groups, comparative survey data reveal that Americans defer to family and church at least as much and often more than other Westerners do (Fischer 2000, 13–14). Americans are more supportive than are British, Canadian, and Australian respondents of established authority and are less likely to favor serious forms of civil disobedience, such as participating in unofficial strikes and occupying buildings (Baer et al.

1995, 184). Americans strongly favor following a supervisor's instructions even when they are perceived to lack merit and strongly believe in the existence of absolute standards of good and evil (Halman 1996).

More than any other nationality in the European Values Study, Americans view the family as very important and support the idea that more emphasis on the family would be a good thing (van Elteren 1998). Perhaps, as Gans has concluded, "many values of popular individualism are familistic" (1988, 3). In Gans's depiction, "middle American individualism"—the individualism of the lower-middle and working classes—blends personal freedom with commitments to family and friends. It is about freedom from unwelcome constraints but not about separation from groups or society. And it is not concerned with individual uniqueness.

Americans are not just more familistic than others but are also more likely to defer to church and to nation, and they are among the least likely of seventeen nationalities to reject the idea of "my country right or wrong" (Fischer 2000). Perhaps, as Fischer suggests, "voluntarism" might more appropriately characterize American responses than "individualism." Individuals join groups voluntarily, but defer to the group while they are members. One can choose to join or to leave, but while a member, one must be loyal, whether the group be a family, a church, or the nation (Fischer 2008, 368). One scholar goes so far as to suggest that "the United States, like Japan and Germany, has historically been a high-trust, group-oriented society, despite the fact that Americans believe themselves to be rugged individualists" (Fukuyama 1995, 10). Another observer maintains that a "persistent tension between authoritarianism and individualism" has always existed in American history (Kammen 1972, 292).

As Gans has suggested, differences may exist between popular and elite understandings of individualism. Individualism, either in its classically liberal form or as tempered by social responsibility, may have been a philosophy held by the national elite (Grabb, Baer, and Curtis 1999). In this view, the population at large was dominantly communal or familistic in orientation, even while the elites offered individualist or republican ideas.

The American literary canon endorses strong individualism, while popular or best-selling writing does not. A study of canonical and best-selling novels in the United States and Canada finds the best sellers to be quite similar in both countries, while the literary works are different. In the formation of the literary canon, national elites undertake a conscious effort to mold the nation's identity. American canonical novels focus on strong and autonomous self-definition. They "stress the dangers of social identity, the constraints of human connection." This "emphasis on individualism, the freedom of each man from his family, birthplace, and ancestry was one of the central myths" in the effort to construct an American nation. By contrast, in the development of Canadian identity, the need was rather to differentiate Canadian culture from those of the United States and Great Britain (Corse 1995, 1288).

Elite culture thus represents Americans as the highly individualistic beings they imagine themselves to be. International comparisons indicate that Americans place a high value on individual self-expression, although the United States does not lead the world in the self-expression dimension of Inglehart's postmaterialism scale, an honor that goes to Sweden and the Netherlands (Inglehart and Baker 2000, 31). Then, too, ambiguities and ambivalences exist in American attitudes toward self-expression. When asked about child rearing, Americans rank near the top among seventeen nations in endorsing the desirability of children's "independence." But they are simultaneously among the highest in approving of "obedience" (in separate questions) (Fischer 2000, 6).

Americans are also the "least likely among citizens of large Western nations to agree that 'right or wrong is a matter of personal conscience'" and are among "the most likely to agree that the church provides answers to moral problems" (Fischer 2008, 366). As Alan Wolfe has noted, there really are not two mutually exclusive categories of people: those devoted to God and those devoted to the self (2001, 12). Americans combine the two. They defer to authority and respect self-expression.

Indeed, one might ask why critics of American life have recently focused exclusively on the negative qualities of self-expression despite the fact that it coexists with traditional morality and obedience to authority. Wolfe has observed that in both the Victorian and the contemporary periods, American "moralists tend to think that self-discipline is a virtue and self-indulgence is a vice. Yet over and over again, Americans told us that they agreed with the first half of that sentiment—but not the second." Some forms of self-indulgence are seen as humanizing people (Wolfe 2001, 75–76). Are late-twentieth-century critics of American individualism such as Christopher Lasch (1979) and Robert Bellah et al. (1985/1996) who focus on the narcissistic self-indulgence of contemporary Americans also engaging in "moralism" (Goodhart and Curry 1991, 202)?

Critiquing Multiculturalism

The animus against expressive individualism often stems from an underlying assumption that strong individualism necessarily detracts from the collectivity, that there is an inherent conflict between the individual and the larger society. Much of the commentary about multiculturalism partakes of such conflict imagery. The individual and by extension the individual's intimate groups are often seen as harboring needs and desires that conflict with those of the society as a whole. But is conflict always or necessarily present? And are the ethnic and cultural groups that form the basis of multiculturalist arguments an asset or a detriment to the health of the larger society?

In the 1930s and 1940s, some analysts saw virtue in "the cultural vigor of different ethnic groups" because such cultural pluralism could counter the dangers of mass politics—dangers that arose from individual isolation and alienation (Gerstle 1994, 1072). As one mid-twentieth-century sociologist viewed it, "If we look at the city of the twenties from the perspective of the city of the fifties, the widespread 'marginality' caused by exposure to diverse sub-cultures appears almost attractive when compared with the superficial homogeneity of . . . modern city life" (M. Stein 1960, 43–44). At least one contemporary observer has also seen the search for distinct cultural identities as a response to standardization: "as people feel threatened by standardization, they search out and cultivate differences. This should not be disparaged, as if individual choice and commitment were irrelevant. Nor should it be fetishized" (R. Jacoby 1994, 159).

To be sure, the fraternal organizations of the late nineteenth and early twentieth centuries that appeared to represent fellowship and communal engagement may in fact have impeded members' ability to integrate into the larger society (Kaufman 2002). But perhaps the earlier communities were seen as but transitory—a way station on the road to eventual assimilation—whereas the cultural associations in a multiculturalist society appear to be more permanent and hence more threatening.

The newer cultural associations also seek public rather than merely private recognition. And to its critics, this public quality renders multiculturalism undesirable. Multiculturalism represents "not just an empirical description of culturally diverse societies, but also a normative claim that cultural difference is to be publicly recognized and instituted, and thus to be made the business of state rather than of private initiative" (Joppke 1996, 487).

If, in the early or mid–twentieth century, cultural groups were viewed as a healthy counterweight to standardization or "mass society," by the late twentieth century they were more likely to be seen as an undesirable form of "social capital." Putnam's "social capital"—the trust and reciprocity necessary for a healthy society—was divided into two categories, bonding and bridging social capital. "Bonding" entails strong in-group ties that may generate out-group hostility or lack of concern with the larger society, as compared with the societal involvements of "bridging" social capital. The examples of bonding social capital Putnam cites include "ethnic fraternal organizations, church-based women's reading groups, and fashionable country clubs"; examples of bridging social capital include "the civil rights movement, many youth service groups, and ecumenical religious organizations" (2000, 22).

Thus, ironically, while those commentators who fear the decline in social capital are concerned about individuals' withdrawal from participation in group life, they also fear the kind of intensely meaningful participation that binds individuals into tightly knit groups. Tight-knit groups are not as socially constructive as those that are less well integrated. It appears, then, that the fear of excessive individualism has come to include a fear of excessively individualistic—or "selfish"—groups (Thomson 2005). Hence the dominant concern in our sample of political commentary is to counter the antisocial or selfish tendencies of the groups that gather under the multiculturalist umbrella. In the words of one commentator, multiculturalism "promotes group loyalties at the expense of a larger national identity" (Steel 1998, 13).

That all groups do not have equal power makes the matter somewhat more complex, as the loyalties of dominant and subordinate groups to the larger society may differ. Indeed, some evidence suggests that high-status groups may more readily retain allegiance to both their ethnic groups and the larger society than do lower status groups. Perhaps unsurprisingly, one study has found that the patriotism and nationalism of Euro-Americans are significantly higher than those of African Americans (Sidanius et al. 1997, 114).

Because the rights of individuals generally have primacy over the claims of the collectivity in American society, multiculturalism is widely criticized for promoting group rights. In part for this reason and in part because of fears of social fragmentation, this sample of writings includes no defenders of multiculturalism per se. While essays in *The Nation* and *The New Republic* defend some aspects of "multicultural education" or changes in the university canon, no one in the sample supports the general idea of multiculturalism.

Of the thirty-eight articles devoted to a discussion of multiculturalism, twenty-seven assail multiculturalists for failing to appreciate that there *is* an American culture. Whether American society is a melting pot or a WASP culture, it is composed of individuals and based on individual rights; it is multiracial and multiethnic but also monocultural. Whether there is a "centrist consensus" at its core (Henry 1993, 75) or "mutual respect" among heterogeneous groups (Hughes 1992a, 44) or a "time-honored American mixture of assimilation and traditional allegiance" (F. Siegel 1991, 35), American culture is to be protected against the fragmentation or Balkanization that multiculturalism would bring.

Of the remaining eleven articles dealing with multiculturalism, seven deal with the internecine battle among conservatives about the wisdom of limiting immigration from Third World countries: five favor restricting immigration, while two oppose such restrictions. Two of the remaining four articles consist of progressive criticisms that oppose multiculturalism because it fails to help the groups it is intended to help (Daryl Michael Scott 1998; Walzer 1996). One article celebrates the "post-multiculturalism" that now flourishes among those in the arts whose bonds are based on aesthetic tastes (Breslauer 1995, 22). And the remaining article discusses the tension between "celebrations of difference" and a commitment to universal human rights (Elshtain 1998, 11), suggesting that sensitivity to cultural differences must not be used to undermine commitment to universal human rights (12).

Multiculturalism goes against the grain of American culture primarily through its failure to honor the ideals of individualism. According to a writer in *Time,* "Put bluntly: Do Americans still have faith in the vision of their country as a cradle of individual rights and liberties, or must they relinquish the teaching of some of these freedoms to further the goals of the ethnic and social groups to which they belong?" (P. Gray 1991, 13). The current "celebration of cultural diversity" entails an "insistence on group rights over individual rights" (Krauthammer 1995; see also Auster 1994; J. Gray 1992); it "emphasizes the betterment of the group" (Henry 1993, 74). It advocates a nation of "inviolable ethnic and racial groups" rather than a nation "of individuals making their own choices" (Schlesinger 1991, 21). "Imagine places where it is considered racist," says a critic of multicultural curricula in universities, "to speak of the rights of the individual when they conflict with the community's prevailing opinion" (Henry 1991, 66). Multiculturalism entails a "revolutionary" change from America as "a nation of individuals, voluntary associations, and ethnic groups to a confederation of diverse 'peoples' with separate worldviews and different 'cultures.'" This phenomenon represents a shift from individual citizens entering the public arena to groups entering the public arena, a change from a "multiethnic America" to a "multicultural America." (Fonte 1996, 48). Multiculturalism might be called "the socialist theory of American nationality, in contrast to the liberal theory that sees Americans as rights-bearing individuals" (O'Sullivan 1994a, 38). The dreaded result is Balkanization (Krauthammer 1990, 1995; O'Sullivan 1994b).

Multiculturalism "turns upside down" the principle on which America is based: "the freedom to create a new personal identity" and "to become part of a nation of people who have done the same thing" (P. Gray 1991, 17). Indeed, "the American achievement is not the multicultural society, it is the multicultural individual" (Wieseltier 1994, 30). Diversity does not mean simply the presence of different racial, ethnic, or sexual groups. "True diversity lies in acknowledging that every human being is an individual, and not simply a member of racial, ethnic or sexual groups. The variety of these individual differences is what bonds us all to each other." We must recognize that "we are individuals first, Americans second and tribalists third" (Brustein 1997a, 34). One writer cites Woodrow Wilson to the effect that "you cannot become thorough Americans if you think of yourselves in groups. America does not consist of groups" (Hart 1996, 52).

Furthermore, individuals can and do transcend their groups and subcultures. "The great artists and thinkers of every culture have always looked for what is individual in humanity rather than what is general" and have celebrated the capacity of people "to transcend externally imposed roles to achieve a richer individuality" (Brustein 1991, 34). Students' minds should not be made to conform to any of the "socially constructed group minds" but should instead be encouraged "to find their way to an individually achieved sense of culture" (Howe 1991, 47). The American experiment is about individuals pursuing their own private views of happiness (Crain 1993, 16).

By contrast, the "cult of multiculturalism" is seen as introducing a tension between individual uniqueness and group identity. "Blacks are forced either to deny their individuality by being made 'representatives of their race' . . . or to deny their race by insisting on their individual uniqueness" (F. Siegel 1991, 34). The tension between individual uniqueness and group identity is, of course, a classic sociological dilemma, well described by Georg Simmel at the beginning of the twentieth century. Simmel saw that for the group to maintain a unique identity, it must stifle individuals' proclivity to deviate from group norms. Either the group itself is unique, or the group enlarges to allow for more individual diversity at the expense of its own individuality (Simmel 1908/1971, 257). Some observers have argued that African Americans today face the dilemma of reducing their opportunities for individual advancement by adhering to "the culture blacks have built in opposition to oppression" or abandoning this culture and its attendant solidarity to seek individual success (Merelman 1994, 6).

Tensions between individualist ideals and group-based commitments exist in popular consciousness as well as scholarly and critical discussion. Thus, in-depth interviews with respondents who are "well-informed and articulate about diversity" reveal that some see the ideal of diversity as a matter of treating all individuals the same regardless of their social differences, while others believe that diversity means that group differences are "consciously valued, celebrated, and sustained." It is almost impossible to endorse both of these ideals at the same time because "they represent two fundamentally different conceptions of the proper role of the individual and the group in social life." Many respondents applauded the idea of accepting diverse individuals into the group and seeing their diversity as enriching the group. At the same time, however, respondents viewed collective representations of diversity as problematic. They thus found it hard or undesirable to incorporate literature from diverse groups into school or college reading lists and complained of the difficulties of communication among different groups in community settings (J. M. Bell and Hartmann 2007, 898, 903).

One commentator notes that American society has long harbored "a contradiction between . . . commands to be oneself while also being part of a common culture, a creative tension that has produced a literature populated by loners, rebels, and misfits." It has also produced much stress. "No one ever said it was easy to be an American, to learn the rules anew each day, every day" (P. Gray 1991, 17). Another observer suggests that the influx of Latin American immigrants might begin to subtly change this individualist culture: "The glamour of the United States is the Easter promise: you can be born again in your lifetime. You can separate yourself from your past. . . . Immigrants still come for that promise." But the more communal cultures of Latin America and Asia are now presenting alternatives that "beckon the American imagination." The Latin American culture offers "an undistressed leisure, a crowded kitchen table, even a full sorrow. . . . We will change America even as we will be changed" (Rodriguez 1988, 84).

According to one writer, Americans are currently so individualistic that U.S. society contains a new kind of "tribalism of conviction." People in the new tribes may live in the same towns or even in the same houses, "but their minds might as well be in separate countries." In their personal lives, Americans readily handle such differences, he suggests. But "Affirmative Action and ethnic politics, supposedly designed to bring people into the system, have the effect of turning people against each other." What is needed are "some myths of commonality, and some actual commonalities, to keep us from flying apart, . . . some notion of an American way of life" that goes beyond "diversity." The older American way of life, replete with republican virtue and *Poor Richard's Almanac,* can serve this purpose. "The tribes won't disappear. . . . But they will flourish a lot more harmoniously if the main lines of American civilization are a little more firmly drawn" (Brookhiser 1990, 65).

The sole article in *The Nation* that deals with the overall philosophy of multiculturalism is highly critical of it, not because of its threat to social unity but because contemporary multiculturalism—postmodern multiculturalism—insufficiently supports black identity groups. These multiculturalists "couple their celebration of group differences with a concerted effort to blur group borders. . . . They promote fluid notions of group identity, emphasizing cultural differences and fragmentation among African-Americans." They thus undermine the possibility of "a vibrant black community in which people have stable identities, grapple with internal differences," and are committed to a common culture (Daryl Michael Scott 1998, 26–27).

Progressives, the author argues, must recognize that "black politics should address economic inequities" and must therefore reject postmodern multiculturalism (27). For if it fails to maintain a vibrant group life, "the black community will continue to be vulnerable to AIDS and crack epidemics, and must await salvation from without or resort to rank individualism" (29). This piece demonstrates that social scientific discourses about culture have affected the thinking of some activists who are struggling to support a kind of multiculturalism that recognizes the looseness and fluidity of "culture."

Another liberal commentator in *The New Republic* shows some sympathy for those who assert multiculturalism but similarly suggests that their tactics are misguided. Michael Walzer argues that the groups involved are not well served by multiculturalism because it is "a symbolic politics" that "challenges dominant beliefs . . . where the emotional pull of oneness—flag and country, God and family—is most deeply felt" (1996, 39). Instead of cultural symbolism, he argues, political and economic power are needed.

Concern for preserving group identity is not confined to the Left, however. All sides recognize the need for groups or communities to maintain their own cultures and identities. Being open to others' ideas must not mean having no commitments to beliefs of our own. If we are "liberated from tradition and particularity," we will not have much to say to each other, says a conservative writer (Neuhaus 1988b, 24). When the mainline Protestant churches "persuaded people to embrace tolerance and inclusiveness," they "lost their internal sense of identity" (Ostling 1989, 95).

For all the ethos of the group and group rights that is embodied in multiculturalism, however, some commentators view multiculturalism as an outgrowth of individualism. It is seen as a form of "collective narcissism" (Brustein 1995, 30), a kind of "tribal solipsism" in which blacks, women, and the Moral Majority, for example, assume that true understanding is available only to their own membership (Morrow 1981, 73). If I love some work of art or music "because it is mine," says another critic, "properly translated, this means: I do not love it, I love me" (Wieseltier 1994, 32). For those who define the United States as "a nation almost like any other," reflecting a "sense of common nationhood in the European sense," multiculturalists' demands point up the fallacies of the liberal theory that Americans are united by their devotion to individual rights. This theory cannot resist the claims of multiculturalism because "if people believe they can find self-expression only in ethnic and linguistic enclaves, the theory of individual rights allows them to do so" (O'Sullivan 1994a, 43).

Multiculturalism in Relationship to the Individual, the Group, and the Society

A number of well-known sociologists also perceive a link between multiculturalism and individualism in American culture. James Davison Hunter, for example, argues that because multiculturalism assumes an "autonomous individual whose cultural identity is a matter of relatively unconstrained choice," it does not challenge "radical individualism, it only reinforces it" (2002, 44–45). Only "creedal communities" can resist "the excesses of radical individualism" (47–48). What is ultimately wrong with multiculturalism is its failure to appreciate the power of culture. Multiculturalism equates culture with "the ethic of individual choice," seeing religion as something one "can choose to embrace or choose to reject" and race and ethnicity as something one can "choose to feel good about or be ashamed of" (J. D. Hunter 1994, 201–2). As a result, multiculturalism does not provide a way of understanding difference; "it only acknowledges differences among individuals in the choices they make" (J. D. Hunter 2002, 45). Thus, ironically, a philosophy that officially celebrates diversity reduces all to sameness (200). Because "individualism is paradigmatic in America," it is powerful enough to "suppress innovation when innovation is subversive to the basic commitments of the paradigm. This is what you have in multiculturalism. . . . Alternatives are offered but only in ways that are consistent with the assumptions, rules, and social practices of individualism" (J. D. Hunter 2002, 47).

Robert N. Bellah argues similarly that the ideology of multiculturalism operates as an agent of the dominant American culture; "multiculturalism, which has become so widely accepted in America, is part of the process of assimilation into the dominant culture, . . . and thus not in any real sense the expression of a genuine cultural pluralism." Its underlying message is that we must respect the fact that "we're all different; we're all unique" (2002, 27).

In Bellah's understanding, as in Hunter's, "deep cultural codes," often derived from religion, operate beneath the level of conscious awareness. In

American society, Protestant religious individualism operates in this fashion. It is reinforced by economic individualism, and both the state and the marketplace inculcate the common American culture of individualism. As Bellah sees it, "something is wrong not on the surface of American life but deep in the core of our common culture" (2002, 28). "What economic individualism destroys and what our kind of religious individualism cannot restore is solidarity, a sense of being members of the same body" (20). American society needs "to recover an idea of the common good toward which we can aspire in the face of the disintegrative tendencies not of cultural pluralism but of radical individualism" (28).

While sharing Bellah's view of what ails American society, Michael Walzer places multiculturalism in a different frame. Like Bellah, Walzer sees individual withdrawal rather than "multicultural cacophony" as the worrying aspect of American society. But unlike Bellah, Walzer sees multiculturalism as an antidote to excessive individualism. Leaders of movements for multiculturalism, he argues, lack power over their membership and consequently "demand governmental programs (targeted entitlements, quota systems) that will help them press their own members into line. From their perspective, the real alternative to multiculturalism is not a strong and substantive Americanism, but an empty or randomly filled individualism. . . . The critical conflict in American life today is not between multiculturalism and some kind of cultural hegemony . . . but between the manyness of groups and of individuals, between communities and private men and women" (1994, 188). In Walzer's understanding, then, multiculturalism represents the collectivity against the individual, a way of righting the imbalance between "culture and selfhood" (191). Because of the need for balance between the individual and the group, we must not consistently defend either multiculturalism or individualism, he argues, but rather should support "now one, now the other, as the balance requires" (191).

While Walzer thus frames multiculturalism rather differently from Hunter and Bellah, he lumps together ethnic and racial groups, groups based on gender or sexual preference, unions, interest groups, and political parties. All need assistance in the face of individual withdrawal, he argues. He thus appears to give ammunition to those detractors of multiculturalism who assert that no genuine cultural differences are at stake, merely self-interested politics in a new guise.

The allegation that various cultural claims are false and simply self-interested has been framed by one anthropologist as a manifestation of the larger clash between what he calls "liberal theory" and "culture theory." Liberal theory, which is dominant politically, sees individuals as forming society based on their own self-interested concerns; culture theory, in contrast, assumes that culture is important in shaping individuals. Liberal theory does not "allow for persistent cultural difference" or for "the legitimacy of claims based on it." Thus, if Native Americans claim that a given location is a "cultural site," local non-Indians respond by suggesting that "today's Indians had lost their original cultures" and therefore cannot "claim legitimate traditional connections to it" (Boggs 2002, 604).

Multiculturalism can also be viewed as a different way of incorporating people into the larger society. Jeffrey C. Alexander sees multiculturalism as offering a more welcoming mode of "incorporation" into society for groups outside the mainstream. Unlike both the assimilation and hyphenation models, multiculturalism does not maintain a separation between one's public and one's private identity. It thus erases the suggestion of inferiority that is attached to difference in these other models. It celebrates difference and encourages the maintenance of these diverse cultural communities. Its aim is not separation but a "more democratic mode of civil integration" (2001, 238). In multiculturalism, the qualities that make one an outsider are to be understood by all, rather than relegated to the private realm. "It is the qualities of being woman, of being nonwhite, of being homosexual or lesbian, of being handicapped that core group and out-group members struggle to understand and experience. . . . Insofar as such understandings are achieved, rigid distinctions between core and out-group members break down, and notions of particularity and universality become much more thoroughly intertwined" (246). As the proponents of multiculturalism have long noted, they seek "cultural pluralism without hierarchy" (Asante 1992, 309).

In somewhat similar fashion, Richard M. Merelman argues that African Americans have developed their own culture in response to the larger society's racism. Indeed, multiculturalism claims that "racial domination has contributed to blacks and whites becoming *culturally different groups*. Symbols of commonality, such as 'individualism,' 'Americanism,' and 'citizenship' not only hide this fact, but also protect 'meritocratic' practices which impede real political and economic parity between the races" (1994, 17). Because blacks have been isolated and subordinated, whites have controlled "the definition and flow of cultural capital in most universities, in the media, and in primary and secondary schools. . . . Blacks are asked to absorb some types of knowledge and certain specific values which many in their own group suspect and which—being unfamiliar—are difficult to acquire" (5–6). As blacks and whites increasingly interact, and cultural capital becomes increasingly important for economic and political power, "a heightened awareness of culture *as such* may well develop," and conflict over culture emerges (6). Citing a study of student life at Rutgers University, Merelman notes that when confronted with racial realities on campus, "white students reluctantly are forced to acknowledge that race and culture do influence most [people's] choice of friends. In order to defend individualism in the face of this challenge, white students at Rutgers distinguish between spheres—such as friendship—where they think individualism should continue to apply—and other spheres—such as politics—where they think the group has the right to come first. In effect, students protect individualism by 'choosing' multiculturalism as a public norm and by 'choosing' individualism as a private norm." In this process, "multiculturalism transforms individualism itself," since the earlier idea was that racial group choice was to be confined to private life and proscribed in the public sphere. If this newer view were to take root in the larger society, "a public norm of racial, ethnic, and cultural diversity" would be erected "at the very time when the private, organic foundations of such diversity in 'ethnically pure' families, schools, neighborhoods, universities, and churches have substantially eroded" (16).

If advocates of multiculturalism celebrate it as a mode of incorporation into society, opponents see it as precisely the opposite. Spencer (1994), for example, characterizes it as a form of "minority nationalism" that competes with both American nationalism (white Christian supremacy) and cosmopolitan liberalism. The difference between American nationalism and African American nationalism, he argues, lies only in their power differentials; all nationalisms are essentially ethnocentric. Because it lacks power, African American nationalism must call for "diversity" and "inclusiveness," just as religious groups that are politically weak and the victims of repression call for toleration and religious freedom while those that are politically strong repress other religions "in the name of the 'one true faith'" (556). Other analysts, such as Ravitch, have talked of two different kinds of multiculturalism: pluralistic and particularistic. Whereas "the pluralists seek a richer common culture, the particularists insist that no common culture is possible or desirable" (1992, 276–77). Defenders of multiculturalism, by contrast, see a choice rather between the reigning Eurocentric hegemony and those who seek genuine cultural pluralism (Asante 1992, 309).

Multiculturalism thus appears as a kind of Rorschach test. Does it promote individualism or the collectivity? Does it promote social integration or separation? Is it beneficial for the larger society? Is multiculturalism undesirable because it is essentialist or ascriptive and thus violates the voluntarism of American society? Or does its very openness and choice violate traditional patterns of community allegiance?

As Hollinger and others have suggested, a tension exists within multiculturalism, between "cosmopolitan and pluralist programs for the defense of cultural diversity." Whereas pluralism defends and preserves existing groups, cosmopolitanism favors voluntary individual affiliations and views individuals simultaneously as members of multiple communities. Cosmopolitanism "is willing to put the future of every culture at risk through the sympathetic but critical scrutiny of other cultures" (Hollinger 1995, 85). Individuals may well be "eager to escape" their traditional cultures "through new out-group affiliations" (107).

If the individual is the ultimate basis for association in society, then cosmopolitanism is plausible, and so is assimilation. If, conversely, groups form the basis of social association, then pluralism results. The assimilationist model rests on a classically liberal view of democracy, whereas the pluralist perspective is based on a more communitarian view (Wuthnow 2006, 168–69). Hartmann and Gerteis (2005) present a more thorough typology of the ways in which individuals and groups are incorporated into society, noting that theorists differ not only about whether the social association is based on individuals or requires the mediation of groups but also about whether cultural cohesion requires strong substantive moral bonds ("thick" culture) or whether procedural norms and common legal codes ("thin" culture) suffice. Using these two distinctions, Hartmann and Gerteis produce a fourfold typology, with individuals as the basis of association producing either "assimilationism" (under thick culture) or cosmopolitanism (under thin culture) and groups as the basis of association producing either "interactive pluralism" (under thick culture) or "fragmented pluralism" (under thin culture) (224). In the assimilation model, the individual adheres to a cohesive culture, whereas the cosmopolitan individual gives basic loyalty to the larger society while choosing which group memberships to retain and which to abandon. In the fragmented pluralism model, allegiance to the larger society is minimal, as there is maximal attachment to the group. The groups have clear and strong boundaries, they are not freely chosen, and membership within a group is essential and ascriptive. The national order comes from respect for group rights. While groups remain the basis of association under interactive pluralism, they are subordinate to the larger society. Groups recognize and respect each other, and the larger societal order emerges via group interaction. The specter of fragmented pluralism clearly leads critics of multiculturalism to condemn it for social disunity and moral relativism (230). The political commentators in our sample supported assimilation, cosmopolitanism, and interactive pluralism but not fragmented pluralism, which relegates the larger society to lesser concern than the social groups composing it.

Fears of fragmented pluralism account for much of the hostility toward multiculturalism. Hostility toward multiculturalists is based not just on their favoring group rights over individual rights but also on their perceived unwillingness to join in a common or unitary American culture. Proponents of this view assert that the majority of multiculturalists are hard-liners who "damn as racism any attempt to draw the myriad of American groups into a common American culture" (F. Siegel 1991, 35). As a result, the melting pot ideal "that was universally celebrated until about twenty years ago" is being abandoned, and the "common American identity" is in danger of becoming a "diluted legal one" (O'Sullivan 2000, 22). Multiculturalists take seriously every culture except for "the traditional American culture, now given such epithets as hegemonic Euro-Americanism" (O'Sullivan 1994a, 40).

Some critics acknowledge that competing strands of multiculturalism exist, with the beneficial strand showing an appreciation of "transcultural blending," while the harmful one celebrates a single culture and seeks "the empowerment of disadvantaged people through the agency of culture" (Brustein 1991, 32). The latter is akin to Ravitch's distinction between pluralistic and particularistic multiculturalism.

Everyone opposes what is called separatism, tribalism, or balkanization.

In addition, a number of conservative commentators point out that real multiculturalism would pose insuperable difficulties: "What would it mean? The promotion of clitoridectomy among African-Americans? American volunteers to implement the fatwa against Salman Rushdie?" (O'Sullivan 1994a, 40). An "incompatibility" clearly exists between "our own culture and that of the fundamentalist Muhammadan" (Buckley 1993b, 71). A critic of multicultural education derisively speaks of the "liberating 'otherness' of diverse civilizations (suitably purged, of course, of castes, cannibals, and clitoridectomies)" (Melzer 1991, 10–11).

How one evaluates multiculturalism hinges on one's implicit models of how society and culture operate. Can one "exit" a culture? Are individuals autonomous agents or "determined as members of particular groups?" (Eller 1997, 250). Considerable disagreement has arisen within the liberal or progressive camp on the issue of multiculturalism because of such issues. On the one hand, the Left sympathizes with movements that speak for subordinate groups and cultures. On the other hand, there is much support for individual autonomy.

Despite some liberal misgivings about multiculturalism because of concerns that individuals might be oppressed in cultural communities, Joseph Raz has argued that a liberal case can be made in support of multiculturalism: "Only through being socialized in a culture can one tap the options that give life a meaning." The moral claim of cultural groups to receive respect thus "rests entirely on their importance to the prosperity of individual human beings" (1994, 71–72). To be sure, "opportunities of exit should be encouraged . . . for members who cannot develop and find adequate avenues for self-expression within their native culture" (77).

Raz's essay prompted David Bromwich to critique the "culturalist argument" that sees "a universal human need to belong to a culture." Bromwich contends that in the strong sense, culturalism means that " 'my culture' is a fact endowed with a dignity and deserving of a respect comparable to the dignity and respect I would claim for myself," and this "idea seems to me a lie" (1995, 89). The culturalist argument weakens the liberal commitment to individual artists and thinkers who choose "to cease to belong as reclaimable property to the culture that 'constitutes' them" (102).

In response to Bromwich's arguments, Michael Walzer has noted that the useful lives that individuals lead all differ and that "the differences are culturally determined." Furthermore, the "autonomous self-creating individual" that Bromwich celebrates "is a cultural ideal" too—"ours" (1995, 105). Liberal societies, to their credit, allow "ordinary people to live freely within more than one cultural community." And liberalism "protects its own competition—by tolerating, say, religious faith and practice. . . . Some of the protected groups are, no doubt, illiberal" (106).

Charles Taylor responds to Bromwich by suggesting that an argument about giving priority to the group or the individual can occur only in "a dissociated world of self-enclosed theory." In the real world, individuals and groups are intertwined. Taylor "realize[s] that we are still struggling to know what we mean by 'culture.' I know it has something to do with what has defined the important, the holy, the worthwhile for many people over time" (1995, 103–4).

Just as our understanding of culture has changed over time, so too has our image of the individual-society relationship. The dominant understanding of individualism within American culture has long been a kind of conflict model in which individualism and conformity are antagonistic to each other and individualism and social cooperation are at opposite ends of the continuum. But evidence indicates that Americans no longer define authentic selfhood as requiring conflict with the surrounding society. When mid-twentieth-century social critics and theorists perceived "conformity" to be the scourge of middle-class America, an implicit conflict model often became explicit. William Whyte, whose study of *The Organization Man* (1956) was a best-selling indictment of "groupthink" at the office and in suburbia, put it quite clearly. However benevolent the organization may seem, he argued, the organization man must not "hold before him the dream that ideally there need be no conflict between him and society. There always is; there always must be" (448). Half a century later, an article in the *New York Times Magazine* made "The Case for Fitting In" (Berreby 2008). Included here was a reinterpretation of classic psychological experiments in individual capitulation to the group or obedience to an authority figure. The article suggests that such experiments might reveal not "the evils of conformity" but the virtues of trust and social cooperation (25).

For many Americans in the late twentieth century and beyond, identification with groups and subcultures has become an essential aspect of the self. It is no longer necessary to renounce such ties in the name of "authenticity" or the "true self." Quite unlike the earlier self-help literature, advice books as early as the 1980s counseled readers to reject cultural images of a totally independent self. They also told readers to reject interpersonal manipulations of the kind taught by Dale Carnegie and Norman Vincent Peale. Survey data similarly reflect a heightened concern over time with the interpersonal dimensions of all roles and a more relational view of the self (Thomson 2000, 73–84). A self that is flexible, capable of change, and embedded within a variety of groups has become a more culturally approved model than one that is in conflict with the society.

This newer view of the individual self mirrors the change in paradigm that has taken place with regard to culture. Rather than seeing the self as an integrated, stable, and well-defined entity, newer understandings see the self as fluid rather than fixed, constantly in process of change and redefinition. This kind of self is nurtured as well as constrained by cultures and relationships (Gergen 1991; Leinberger and Tucker 1991; Thomson 2000). As one sociologist has described our current view of self, "whether we flee from it or embrace it—we know ourselves as a 'construction' of culture" (McCarthy 1996, 84).

Paradoxically, however, the decrease in conflict between the individual and the society may have generated greater levels of conflict—or at least the perception of conflict—among groups and between groups and the larger society. To the degree that Americans now embrace groups as vehicles for individual well-being, even reinventing themselves through groups of Fundamentalists or gays or Eastern mystics (FitzGerald 1986, 23), the groups come to be seen as selfish, perhaps particularly where the groups are defined in cultural rather than interest group terms, since interests can more readily be compromised than cultures.

Conclusions

In valuing individualism but not to excess, culture warriors replicate a long-standing American practice. Both major American political parties simultaneously endorse aspects of individualism and communitarianism. What is new here is the emergence of a multiculturalism that demands public recognition of subcultural differences. Culture war contentions notwithstanding, all seem opposed to this idea.

Multiculturalists are following in the tradition of feminists and others who recognized that "the personal is political." Confusions about whether multiculturalism represents a form of group supremacy or extreme individualism can be clarified by taking into account late-twentieth-century American conceptions of the self in society that allow for authentic individuality to emerge within group contexts.

In what is perhaps the dominant image of multiculturalism, multiculturalists worldwide appear to challenge the "cultural content" of their nations, reducing them to "civic communities committed to the same procedural rules" (Joppke 1996, 486). But the United States differs from other nations "because it alone has made the immigrant experience part of its national identity" (490). The question then becomes how it handles cultural pluralism.

CHAPTER 5

Pluralism within One Culture

Historical Perspectives

The debate about multiculturalism had a precursor in the much less contentious discussion of cultural pluralism beginning in the 1910s. In the early decades of the twentieth century, assimilation or Americanization was so much the dominant idea that cultural pluralism hardly received notice. While Horace Kallen claims to have first used the term during a class at Harvard in 1906 or 1907, half a century later he noted, "it has taken these two generations for the term to come into more general use and to figure in philosophical discourse" (1957, 119). Through the first decades of the century, cultural pluralism was opposed for much the same reasons that multiculturalism has been. Critics argued that it failed "to consider each individual personality as primary" and that it "made race a greater factor than it deserved to be" (Wacker 1979, 331).

Then as now, no unitary view on the issue prevailed. Even during the Progressive Era, some people adhered to the right-leaning view that sought to impose superior American ways on the immigrants, while others espoused a left-leaning perspective that saw immigrants' "heritages as cultural treasures too important to destroy" (Gerstle 1994, 1051). Unable to resolve this dispute, liberals abandoned the issue in favor of economic concerns. But Nazism brought a "shift in liberal sensibilities" in the United States as well as new concerns about racial and religious prejudices (1070). By the 1950s, Kallen suggested that Americanization as "a cultural monism" was "slowly and unevenly being displaced" by Americanization as "a cultural pluralism" based on "the American Idea" (1956, 97). In Kallen's understanding, the American Idea meant equality and freedom as enunciated in the Declaration of Independence and the Constitution. Pluralism within one culture is thus not a new idea.

Though lacking the language of multiculturalism, the United States may have been more multicultural in the past than it is today. In 1776, a greater proportion of the population consisted of racial and ethnic out-groups than is now the case. Today's immigrants learn English at least as quickly as those of the past and probably more quickly because of the mass media (Parrillo 1994, 525, 531, 543). "Too little remembered in the contemporary discussion, except by historians" are the widespread existence in the early twentieth century of bilingual public schools, teaching in English and German, and a Catholic school system that perpetuated French (Alba 1999, 8).

By the middle of the twentieth century, most Americans understood the term *pluralism* to mean a diversity of interest groups that contended for power and influence rather than a diversity of cultures that simultaneously gave allegiance to the American nation. The idea of pluralism largely focused on occupational groups and functional associations, with economic self-interest or advocacy of certain causes at the root of most contentions. Only toward the end of the century did the newer social movements based on cultural identity enter into discussions of political pluralism (Bickford 1999, 90).

Yet an earlier, more philosophical understanding of pluralism saw it as a matter of multiple perspectives based on the differing experiences and circumstances of diverse individuals and groups. In the writings of William James, for example, these different perspectives were justified and valid, and no unitary perspective was possible. Contemporary multiculturalists have returned, in essence, to this view of pluralism—to an understanding of multiple subjectivities or situated knowledge (Schlosberg 1998). But their views about diversity are complicated by concerns about inequality (Bickford 1999), since multiethnic or multiracial societies almost always entail the dominance of some groups over others. Because of their awareness of issues of dominance and subordination, many contemporary multiculturalists have maintained the internally contradictory views that there is no common standard by which cultures can be evaluated and that all cultures are of equal value (Barry 2001, 252).

Finding a way to incorporate differing opinions and perspectives has become more pressing in the face of what has been called deep pluralism, a pluralism that runs along a number of overlapping and intersecting dimensions (Bohman 2003). Arguments about pluralism have become more complex as they now address the nature of democratic inclusion as well as issues of cultural, ethnic, religious, political, and economic differences. Political commentators of all stripes struggle to define the kind of tolerance that is desirable under such circumstances.

The cultural pluralism enunciated by Kallen did not confront subcultures of feminists, Evangelicals, and homosexuals or the multiple complexities of white versus black and middle-class versus working-class feminists or gays. For the most part, too, manifestations of difference were assumed to be private rather than public matters. To be sure, earlier cultural pluralism was never as simple as myth would have it. Given the regional differences within the home country, Italian Americans, for example, existed more as an "imagined community" constructed after migration to the United States than as a cultural reality. Nevertheless, the sheer multiplicity of contemporary subcultures and their overlapping dimensions has made pluralism more complex and again raises the meaning of a "common" or "unitary" American culture. The disappearance of the communist enemy at the end of the Cold War might also have unleashed the centrifugal tendencies that multiculturalism and the culture wars embody (Gitlin 1995, 80).

Nevertheless, many analysts have argued that multiculturalism arose as a social movement at a time when real cultural differences were fading. Racial and ethnic group cultures within the United States have been getting weaker rather than stronger. When ethnic group consciousness began its resurgence in the late 1960s and early 1970s, one writer dubbed its adherents the "unmeltable ethnics" (Novak 1972). Yet even he acknowledged that "one belongs to an ethnic group in part involuntarily, in part by choice" (47). One chooses to identify with an ethnic group because of a desire to feel an ethnic identity. Such voluntary identification is the key to what Gans has dubbed "symbolic ethnicity," which coexists with assimilation and does not reflect strong "cultural practices or group relationships" (1979, 204). Rather, it is constructed by individuals and families, who are often unsure about "what constitutes ethnicity as opposed to idiosyncratic family values and practices" and who may need to learn ethnic behavior and beliefs from the mass media (Waters 1990, 115).

"Traditional group identity was largely unconscious and intuitive. . . . But as group isolation has receded, group identity must now be publicly declared. Rather than indicating the splintering of society, such declarations show how difficult it is to maintain old differences. . . . Subcultures that once manifested their identities locally . . . now look to television for verification of their existence. The clamoring for inclusion in the national television arena makes everyone in the culture much more aware of differences that have always existed—and once were much greater" (Meyrowitz and Maguire 1993, 42, 48). Ethnic group identity may thus have little "cultural content" (Barry 2001, 22). "The cultural differences invoked by multiculturalists are fundamentally identity markers or labels rather than ways of life or sets of values that contrast sharply with those of most native-born Americans" (Wrong 1997, 299).

If the reigning mid-twentieth-century image of immigrant and ethnic group behavior was that of assimilation to the dominant Anglo-American culture, the idea of assimilation lost favor after the turmoil of the 1960s and the accompanying rebellion against "Anglo-conformity." Yet by the late 1970s and early 1980s, new ideas of assimilation began to be considered, ideas in which American identity would be "contested terrain, fought over by ethnics with their own definitions of Americanism" (Kazal 1995, 461). The newer idea of an "American core" resembles more recent ideas of culture, "subject to change and contestation" (438). Furthermore, American culture influences its constituent ethnic group cultures, so that Irish Americans, for example, are culturally Irish American, not simply Irish (Walzer 1999, 612).

For all the contemporary discussion about multiculturalism, then, cultural pluralism today is arguably no greater than in the past and may well be weaker. The "myth of bygone cultural homogeneity" has made us unaware of the reality of cultural pluralism in the colonial and early national periods of American history (Parrillo 1994, 525). Yet culture is taken very seriously in contemporary American society, so that even if "the persistence of unique cultures within American society is increasingly questionable, . . . the debate assumes 'culture' is sacred, almost beyond discussion" (R. Jacoby 1994, 156).

The present situation may also differ from the past insofar as some groups are creating new identities rather than holding onto old ones. If ethnic groups previously hesitated to give up aspects of their native cultures, Latinos, African Americans, and Native Americans now construct their identities based on "the particular circumstances that these groups face in contemporary American society" (Spencer 1994, 564). If older white ethnic groups fought to hold onto their cultural characteristics, newer groups often must construct their own identities. As Appiah has suggested, "the new talk of 'identity' offers the promise of forms of recognition and of solidarity that could make up for the loss of the rich, old kitchen comforts of ethnicity" (1997, 33).

Curiously, however, the black middle class, which is larger and doing better than ever, has "led the fight for the recognition of a distinctive African-American cultural heritage" and has done so "at a moment when cultural differences are diminishing" (Appiah 1997, 32). The tensions that now exist with regard to race and gender are not really cultural ones. "Because on many occasions disrespect still flows from racism, sexism, and homophobia, we respond, in the name of all black people, all women, all gays. . . . But the truth is that what mostly irritates us in these moments is that we, as individuals, feel diminished. And the trouble with appeal to cultural difference is that it obscures rather than illuminates this situation. It is not black culture that the racist disdains, but blacks. . . . Culture is not the problem, and it is not the solution" (36). Talk of multiculturalism rather than structural obstacles may be harmful (Barry 2001, 307).

To the contrary, argues Henry Louis Gates Jr., it is important for African Americans to construct themselves culturally. "Self-identification proves a condition for agency, for social change. And to benefit from such collective agency, we need to construct ourselves, just as the nation was constructed" (1992, 37). "One must *learn* to be 'black' in this society, precisely because 'blackness' is a socially produced category" (101). Although some aspects of black culture are the products of encounters with white racism, "black culture . . . is radically underdetermined by the social dynamism of white racism" (103). "To say that ethnic identity is socially constructed is not to say that it is somehow unreal" (127). The differences matter. But blacks must not "resurrect our own version of the Thought Police, who would determine who, and what, is 'black'" (127).

"Whether a particular grouping of persons is or is not 'a culture' is not simply a fact" (Segal and Handler 1995, 396). Indeed, the current definitions have a certain circularity: "If a grouping of persons is perceived as 'a culture," then differences of power within it are masked; and if differences of power are perceived, then multiple cultures are said to exist" (397). The cultures that are a matter of concern in multiculturalism are based on race or perceived victimization. The particularities that differentiate the subcategories of Europeans are no longer discussed.

Contemporary Images of Pluralism

The assumption that the United States had a unitary culture into which immigrants would be assimilated remained dominant into the middle of the twentieth century. At that time, American culture was understood as having a set of overarching or mainstream beliefs and practices. Those who differed from these practices—groups that would now be seen as subcultures or as part of our multicultural society—were characterized as alienated. As one empirical sociologist of the time noted, "a high or moderate intensity of alienation" was to be expected among individuals in "religious, ethnic, political, educational, occupational, associational, status, 'residential,' and other minorities" (Hajda 1961, 761). Social commentators frequently characterized students, intellectuals, blacks, and poor whites as alienated (Finifter 1972, vii). By contrast, contemporary commentators rarely use the language of alienation.

It is of interest, therefore, that the term has reappeared in the writings of some conservative spokesmen who seek to portray contemporary American society as essentially unified except for the few dissidents. William J. Bennett, for example, asserts that a cultural split exists between "most Americans" and "a liberal elite" that is "marked by alienation" (1992, 27). He characterizes the (liberal) leaders of mainline churches as showing "a profound alienation from the American experiment" (223). Another conservative commentator sees both "the overclass" (or the "knowledge class") and the "underclass" as "profoundly alienated from the American experience" (Neuhaus 1995, 66). Still another observer argues that the Left is so mistrustful of American society and its institutions that it can be seen as in a "state of alienation" (Bork 1989, 27). And after arguing that Americans "should take pride . . . in the historic content of their culture," another conservative commentator suggests that "if there are Americans who feel as alienated as the Amish, let them live like the Amish—without harassment, but without subsidized proselytizing for their rejectionist world views" (Brookhiser 1992, 74). Implicit in such remarks are the ideas that there is one agreed-upon American culture and that those who depart from it are aberrant.

By contrast, the few progressive writers in our sample who talk of alienation use it in the Marxist sense of disconnection from one's fellows and lack of power to effect social change. One such writer argues that the negative and stereotypical portraits of the members of poor and minority groups who appear as guests on television talk shows eradicate any understanding of their plight. The audience "feeds off the misery and humiliation of others. Less obvious is the price we all pay . . . in increased alienation, contempt and hatred" (Nelson 1995, 801). Another notes that these talk show guests appear to the audience "as alien and unreal" (Willis 1996, 22). In this view, it is not the absence of mainstream characteristics that makes one alienated but the inability to understand the social conditions underlying individual behaviors.

Discussions of American culture during the last two decades of the twentieth century are fraught with concern about whether the United States retains a common culture. Within the conservative camp, a contingent of writers argues that American society "is not multi-cultural—at any rate, not at or near the top," where behavior conforms to the modern American version of the English gentleman (Hart 1996, 56). American culture is fundamentally Anglo-Saxon (Brookhiser 1992; Editorial 1991a; O'Sullivan 1994a, 1994b).

Other conservatives express concern that when "ethnic cultures thrive, the sense of national solidarity is weakened" and that if immigrants are introduced into a multicultural America, they may never become American (O'Sullivan 1994b, 45). Our "universalist immigration policy" has unleashed the "forces of cultural separatism and group rights" (Auster 1994, 54). If nations are "imagined communities," held together by shared culture, multiculturalism works against the creation of such communities (Custred 1997, 39). A multiethnic society will survive only if it becomes monocultural (O'Sullivan 1994a, 44).

But no unity exists within the conservative camp on the topic of immigration. For all the hostility that social conservatives bring to bear against unlimited immigration, some economic conservatives see immigration as beneficial. Moreover, as portrayed by a liberal, some neoconservatives have viewed Third World immigrants as "cannon fodder in the culture wars" because they have strong "family values," unlike the "aliens among us"—the black underclass, gays, writers and academics, and a significant proportion of American religious leaders (Lind 1993). Those conservatives who are hostile to unlimited immigration suggest that the neoconservatives and the Republican establishment have denied the connection between immigration from Third World countries and the multiculturalism that they abhor. These "pro-immigration conservatives subscribe to an organizing myth" that "America was built on universal principles of human rights, equality and open borders" and has an infinite capacity to absorb people of any race and culture (Auster 1994, 49). As a result, proponents of this view do not see the "prospect of cultural dispossession" when "citizens in New York or Los Angeles often feel like strangers in their own land" (50). Some members of this group, such as Francis Fukuyama, have argued that any group endowed with "family values" will fit into American society, but this idea is clearly absurd: stable Mexican or Cambodian families might "still not be American in any meaningful sense of the word" (54).

Those who favor immigration see things very differently. "The claim that America is 'a nation no different from any other,' far from being 'the conservative view,' is akin to national heresy. . . . The image of an 'immigrant nation' is not an idea imposed upon the lived experience of American culture; it is the lived experience of American culture" (Neuhaus 1995, 65). Furthermore, multiculturalism is generated not by immigrants but by left-wing academics and elites. Many Hispanic and Asian college students "'discovered' their ethnic identity after they arrived on campus" (Chavez 1994, 30).

Those conservatives who welcome immigration assume that new arrivals will assimilate to American ways, while those who are hostile see immigrants as triggering movements of multiculturalism. Liberals and conservatives alike see assimilation as real: the United States is not in fact "a congeries of ethnic and racial groups, and nothing more. Assimilation is a reality. . . . Millions . . . owe no allegiance to any identity other than America" (Glazer 1991, 22). Most people in the United States see themselves as Americans despite the "romantic ideologues" and "unscrupulous con men" whose claims to represent their people are "carelessly accepted by the media" (Schlesinger 1991, 21). Although the melting pot has been something of a "myth," it was an ideal that produced a "unified country" (Steel 1998, 13). Still others insist that "the melting pot never melted," as America continues to define and redefine itself (Hughes 1992a, 44).

One conservative notes that only those groups that strictly forbid intermarriage, such as Orthodox Jews and the Amish, have preserved "distinct, full-blown cultures within American society" (Chavez 1994, 30). Intermarriage is the ultimate form of assimilation, and at least one liberal commentator sees it as the likely future. He notes that the large number of Latin Americans currently in the United States "will disappear with you into a new miscegenation. . . . For generations, Latin America has been the place, the bed, of a confluence of so many races and cultures that Protestant North America shuddered to imagine it. The time has come to imagine it" (Rodriguez 1988, 84).

Some critics of multiculturalism contend that rather than representing truly differing cultures, multiculturalists often tend to conflate race and culture (Brustein 1991; Chavez 1994; Henry 1990). Treating race and ethnicity as synonymous with culture makes culture something genetic rather than acquired through experience (Chavez 1994, 26). Yet an editorial in *National Review* comes close to conflating the two in a way that all is too common. The piece chastises Harvard University for a committee report suggesting that minority students are isolated from the college mainstream and face the choice of "conforming to the cultural norm" or defending their "identity to the point where the benefits of a diversified student population are compromised." The university itself had sanctioned "social apartheid" in the late 1960s and 1970s—had indeed encouraged it "in the name of 'cultural identity' and 'racial pride'"—says the editorial (1981a, 140). The fact that the university's policies generated the current bitterness is not acknowledged. Moreover, the talk of conformity to the cultural norm makes it appear "as if grim Brahmins waited to corset the souls of their manservants' grandsons. . . . If Harvard is not tolerant of racial differences, who or what on the North American continent is?" (141). Is the issue one of "racial differences" or of "cultural norms," or are the two synonymous?

The tendency to use *multiculturalism* as a code word for race leads to another example of mirror images among the culture warriors, with each side accusing the other of using multiculturalism for political gain. Thus, a progressive commentator suggests that race is the real reason why President George H. W. Bush "turned his attention to P.C., with Willie Horton's equivalent in '92 being 'extremists' eroding Western values with their multiculturalism and contempt for Great Books" (Cockburn 1991, 704). In the eyes of another writer, "Republican attack politics turned on culture and suddenly both academe and the arts were full of potential 'Willie Hortons'" (Hughes 1992a, 46).

Conservatives view the connection between race and multiculturalism in a different but equally political way, arguing that proponents of multiculturalism have associated the common American culture with whiteness and have thus made opposition to "diversity" appear racist. As one conservative puts it, "The common American culture has been relativized as 'white' culture, [and this] lie serves to delegitimize assimilation, by characterizing it as the imposition of an alien culture on all non-Anglo Americans. . . . And once America is relativized as a 'white' construct, it can hardly be defended, let alone celebrated by whites with a guilty conscience about race. Hence the weakness of the opposition to diversity" (O'Sullivan 2000, 22). Once the "traditional reference points" such as "our Western heritage" or "our Founding Fathers" are ruled out because "a critical number of us are no longer from the West" or because Founding Fathers sounds racist, a "massive deculturation" takes place (Auster 1992 , 43).

A recent study that employs in-depth interviews suggests that the conflation of race and diversity is quite prevalent even among a sample of people active in urban organizational life. Respondents "typically define diversity in broad and inclusive terms, but when asked to describe personal experiences with difference, their responses are almost exclusively tied to race" (J. M. Bell and Hartmann 2007, 905). The language of both diversity and multiculturalism assumes a "white center" to which racial others "add flavor" (909).

While critics of multiculturalism see it as divisive, some liberals accuse the "monoculturalists" of being divisive. "Identity politics," says one liberal, is attacked as divisive "by people who cling to the vision of a singular America. . . . But perhaps their love of singularity also divides us" (Walzer 1996, 39). Perhaps, too, it is no longer possible to maintain a unified culture. For one thing, technology is now "dividing a culture once clustered around a common core into distant, discrete clumps, making it harder for any one preacher, however high the pulpit, to reach the whole nation" (R. Wright 1996, 44). For another, globalization creates an international class of managers whose "cultural and political loyalties" are no longer clear.

Their "primary allegiances are to themselves and their current employers." Globalization thus adds to the "divided loyalties" of various immigrant groups and "makes the very notion of a single national identity seem anachronistic" (Steel 1998, 14).

Class differences thus compound or intersect with those of race. One writer notes that black students in a multiracial seminar at an Ivy League university defined black identity largely in terms of class. One such student said, "I have relatives on welfare and others in prison. That means I see things differently." Another argued that "we've been robbed of our culture. . . . We have no culture . . . except the so-called culture of the ghetto" (T. Jacoby 1991, 29–30). Some progressives contend that "class is itself a cultural as well as an economic issue." A kind of cultural nationalism applies to class just as much as to race or sex, "which is why blue-collar unions have been reluctant to organize white-collar workers, and why in certain circles preference for beer and pretzels over wine and cheese is elevated to a political badge of honor" (Willis 1998, 19).

The complexities of multiple and intersecting subcultures have led numerous commentators to note the difficulties of maintaining any strong cultural attachments. One conservative critic argues that multiculturalists' demands appear to contradict the idea that their subcultures are strong and resilient. "Cultural identification" must be "fragile" if it needs to be "reinforced" in the schools "lest these youngsters be seduced by American culture" (Chavez 1994, 30). A writer on the left likewise contends that "homogeneous communities" are more myth than reality (Mattick 1990, 357).

There is one source of agreement among the commentators: all applaud pluralism. While it may be tempting to assume that pluralism, like morality, is merely a buzzword to which everyone can assent, evidence suggests a desire to retain subcultural variations. To be sure, differences exist among the specific groups that are the objects of concern. Liberals seek to protect the disadvantaged, while conservatives are more likely to concern themselves with "traditional" groups such as religious and rural communities. Yet both sides suggest that pluralism offers a solution to the culture wars.

Some critics suggest that if the multiculturalists were not such extremists, they would recognize that their goals are really those of American pluralists. Like American pluralism, multiculturalism rests on the idea that minority groups "can play a part in molding the larger culture even as they are molded by it" (F. Siegel 1991, 35). Our founders were European, but immigrants have come from all over the world, attracted by our democracy and our economy. "This blend produced a genuinely pluralist society—indeed, the very concept of pluralism is itself a product of the European (or 'Eurocentric') tradition" (McConnell and Breindel 1990, 21). The multiculturalists often fail to appreciate this idea as well as the many "American gains in cultural pluralism" (Sullivan 1990, 21).

Pluralism could not only replace the extremism of the multiculturalists but also defuse the culture wars. As opposed to the "bogus pluralism of multiculturalism," with its ethnic, religious, and sexual militias, true pluralism is bred by decentralization and consumer choice, says a conservative. School vouchers, for example, would allow parents to choose their children's curricula (Brookhiser 1993a, 74). In the past, this genuine form of pluralism was "based on the relative isolation of internally homogeneous communities" (Wagner 1986, 32).

As seen by conservatives, liberals have redefined pluralism as "mandatory exposure to conflicting viewpoints" (Wagner 1986, 52). The public schools and the mass media wield "tremendous cultural power" against the family, church, and small town. In the face of the ban on school prayer, the legalization of abortion, and sex education and "values clarification" curricula in the school, traditionalists attempted to take back their culture. As they did so, civil libertarians argued that they were blocking pluralism. Yet the "old-fashioned pluralism" of internally homogeneous communities can be restored via school vouchers and parental choice, cable television, greater local control of public schools, and generally through competition "in the various culture-making arenas" (52).

If some liberals oppose school choice because they see it as establishing "cultural, religious, or ethnic ghettoes" (Wagner 1986, 32), a conservative also acknowledges that parental control, school vouchers, and decentralization would yield so much diversity that "children of neighboring families would end up learning none of the same things." It would also be irrational to have public money financing the teaching of Satanism, for example. Yet opting for a centralized educational system brings the danger that professional educators will be able "to clarify your child's values, to tutor him in pacifism, multi-culturalism, and atheism" (Finn 1986, 35). The author, writing as an administrator in the U.S. Department of Education during the Reagan administration, finds a self-serving solution to this dilemma. Today, he argues, one can trust the federal government because it is "amplifying the voice of common sense," encouraging "the purposeful development of character, the primacy of parents, . . . the centrality of discipline" (37).

The American people are more likely to support national rather than state-level approaches to controversial issues. When asked whether the national or state governments should make decisions regarding gay marriage, abortion, stem cell research, and teaching creationism, majorities or pluralities favored national decision making in all cases. This preference is seen across all demographic groups and does not appear to reflect political strategy, since those who live in areas where their values are widely shared are no more likely to favor a state-by-state approach (Pew Research Center 2006b).

Conservatives argue that "true pluralism," resting on internally homogeneous communities and on mechanisms such as school choice, can offer a solution to the culture wars. In the eyes of some liberals, school choice is an easier solution than fighting the culture wars associated with "family values." While more militant culture warriors on the right, such as Patrick Buchanan and Gary Bauer, have continued to attack "liberal 'lifestyles'" and "to assert themselves as the moral guardians of the past," more moderate culture warriors such as Jack Kemp and William J. Bennett have turned to "parents' rights" issues such as school choice. "Once seen as a flaky libertarian crusade, school choice is rising to the top of the family values litany for conservatives who lack the stomach for the culture war" (R. Shalit 1993, 13).

Liberals, too, contend that pluralist institutions can provide "the right way out of the 'culture wars.'" They argue that many groups really need "resources and institutions, political and economic power, not flags of their own." "What distinguishes contemporary America is that multiculturalism is now asserted from below—by the very groups that once responded to accusations of difference with fearful denial." If we could help these historically disenfranchised groups build institutions, we "would have a more visibly diverse but also less divided society" (Walzer 1996, 39). Religious communities run their own schools, hospitals, and day care centers, sometimes with government assistance. These institutions are not seen as problematic in "provid[ing] space for a culture's enactment and reproduction. . . . Helping new groups provide similar services would produce a more egalitarian multiculturalism" with "less division." Such institutional realities as female-operated banks, black Baptist nursery schools, and gay men's health centers matter more than debates about feminism, homosexual organizing, or "sun people and ice people" (39). "Groups need a well-rooted institutional life to flourish. Pluralist theory accommodates both a shared civic culture and the room for private-sphere institutions to maintain a vibrant group life" (Daryl Michael Scott 1998, 29). Even in the matter of funding for the arts, one commentator suggests that if one believes all citizens should have access to art, what we need is not a National Endowment for the Arts but "art vouchers for the needy" (Chait 1997, 14).

Sociologists also have noted that pluralism defuses culture wars. Thus, even Christian Evangelicals in the United States who believe that Christian morality should dominate in the culture have a commitment to freedom of religious belief that neutralizes cultural warring. Historically, this "pluralism-versus-Christendom dilemma" was fairly readily resolved, since Protestantism dominated American public discourse. Today, individuals manage the dissonance by compartmentalizing their beliefs (C. Smith et al. 1997, 189–91).

In addition to this convergence about the desirability of pluralist communities, both sides agree that indifference to values or to cultural differences is a form of false pluralism. A number of conservative writers make this point. Pluralism, says one, is not to be confused with "moral indifferentism." "It is sad to see so many college students who think that pluralism means moral relativism. . . . Such relativism reduces genuine pluralism to molasses. It is powerless before ugly passions" (Novak 1984, 48). Nor does pluralism require one "to transcend the particular in order to embrace the universal." Such a response really represents a "denial of pluralism" because it rests on "pretending that our deepest differences make no difference. Genuine pluralism is the vibrant engagement of differences." We need to have strong beliefs to discuss with others; it is hard "to suppose that we have much to say to one another unless we have internalized the tradition that distinguishes our contribution to the conversation" (Neuhaus 1988b, 24).

A writer in *The New Republic* similarly argues that the absence of strong beliefs does not produce pluralism and tolerance. Unfortunately, he maintains, it is all too easy for "people who grow up in a world of great skepticism and diversity" to become complacent and not self-critical. "The danger that people will arrogantly impose their beliefs on others is happily diminished," but people who "do not believe in anything strongly enough to engage in systematic persecution . . . also lack the strength of principle that would lead them to stand up to the intolerance of others, and the intolerance within themselves. Students today . . . are too morally mellowed out to object to racist jokes" or to "mock slave auctions at a fraternity party." The loss of certainty that arises in a diverse or multicultural society generates the danger of dogmatism and closed-mindedness (Melzer 1991, 11). Another writer in *The New Republic* expresses concern that modern life has destroyed many of the traditional channels for transmitting the culture to new generations. As a result, there is the threat of a "hitherto unknown infirmity: deculturation." For this reason, Americans should learn American traditions—the institutions or concepts of public life, not just the original cultures of individual inhabitants, many of whom are recent immigrants (Todorov 1989, 29).

Nor does pluralism require us to challenge all of our own sincere beliefs. One conservative alleges that the people who today run the schools include liberals who appear to define pluralism in this way. "So 'pluralist' are we that we cannot allow traditional moral norms to be propounded to the next generation without a challenge" (Wagner 1986, 32). By the same token, those academics who proclaim "cognitive and moral relativism" to be a matter of expert consensus and exclude those who view truth as "neither a dogma nor a chimera" fail to manifest the "pluralism" of which they boast (Todorov 1989, 29). One commentator on the left argues similarly, attacking "the P.C. felons" whose "emaciated terminology leads in the direction of a mini-consensus that does not welcome dissent" (Hitchens 1991, 472). Efforts to do away with ethnic humor in the name of political correctness not only may backfire but also do little to deal with real power differentials. That ethnic humor "is often deployed by the powerful against the powerless is best answered not by silencing the powerful (that hardly takes away their power) but by unleashing the humorous abilities of the powerless." Let blacks make fun of whites, gays mock straights, women deride men (David Segal 1992, 10).

For all the self-consciousness about cultural pluralism, some old-fashioned ethnocentrism appears in the writings of both conservatives and liberals, although agreement does not always exist about precisely which aspect of "our culture" makes us superior. One liberal takes offense at the notion that multiculturalists sometimes portray "Europe—the unique source of the liberating ideas of democracy, civil liberties and human rights" as "the root of all evil" (Schlesinger 1991, 21), while a conservative argues that "Americans should take pride in the historic content of their culture," which is "clearly superior to Europe" (Brookhiser 1992, 74). Another argues more stridently that for all the scorn heaped on Eurocentrism and the legacy of Columbus, the culture that developed on American soil is far superior to that, say, of the Incas, who lived "beehive-like," lacking in individual freedom. "Is it Eurocentric to believe the life of liberty is superior to the life of the beehive?" (Krauthammer 1991, 74).

How, then, can one maintain pluralism within one culture? For all the hostility directed toward multiculturalism, questions of how to provide education for a diverse society loom large, and more support exists for multicultural education than for the philosophy of multiculturalism.

Multicultural Education and the Canon Wars

Much debate was generated by questions of whether schools should include more instruction about other cultures and whether the university canon might be expanded to include the works of those previously excluded. While the response to multicultural education was dominantly negative, it was not entirely so. Of the twenty-seven articles devoted to multicultural education, sixteen are mostly hostile, eight are largely supportive, and three are neutral or mixed. Among those hostile to multicultural education, the specter of balkanization looms large. Of concern, too, is the idea that multicultural education provides therapy, cheerleading, or an attempt to raise the self-esteem of minority students rather than genuine education. One conservative critic captures several of these ideas simultaneously: "the fixation on feeling is leading to the Balkanization of American education. The battle cry is 'inclusion' in the teaching curriculum for every politically situated minority. . . . This is ideology masquerading as education and aspiring to psychotherapy" (Krauthammer 1990, 78; see also John J. Miller 1993; F. Siegel 1991; Tifft 1990). Critics also suggest that school curricula are increasingly "fragmented" (J. S. Siegel and Delattre 1981) and promote "interethnic strife" (McConnell and Breindel 1990, 21).

An editorial in *National Review* connects programs of multicultural education to the need for school vouchers and parental choice: "Diversity through choice would certainly be less disruptive than having the myths of multiculturalism fed to all school children by a state monopoly" (1991b, 16).

The population at large did not appear to share in these commentators' negative assessments. National survey data from 1994 found that only 26 percent of the population believed that "ethnic history is getting too much attention," 50 percent agreed that "there's now about the right amount of attention to ethnic minorities in history classes," and 24 percent believed there should be more such material (Citrin et al. 2001, 259–60). Moreover, while 92 percent of the sample agreed that we should "choose teachers based on ability, not ethnicity," only 44 percent agreed that we should "choose history teachers based on ability, not ethnicity" (258). The difference in the two numbers presumably indicates sensitivity to ethnicity in the teaching of history, an indirect suggestion of support for multicultural education.

Defenders of multicultural education suggest that it benefits not just oppressed minorities but all of us, since we all need "to navigate a society that truly is multicultural and is becoming more so everyday" (Ehrenreich 1991, 84). All students need "to learn how to develop multiple perspectives" (quoted in "What Do We Have in Common?" 1991, 19); acknowledging the contributions made by different groups is a way of "strengthening our unity" (20); "America has always been a study of different cultures operating on one continent" (20). Conversely, a critic notes that two- and three-year-old children in nursery school are now being taught about "cultural differences." Families that have been American for generations are required to produce some other heritage for show-and-tell. The result is that children are now "talking about things that separate rather than connect" them (Konig 1997, 46).

If support for Afrocentric curricular changes in the schools amounts to "the politicizing of history," says one supportive commentator, so be it: "teaching the young is necessarily and inevitably political. It entails the authoritative promulgation of values as well as information" (Loury 1997, 25). But a more right-wing commentator argues that it is absurd to consider every choice of college textbooks a political one: "what makes it political? That it is a choice? . . . Would the choice of textbooks in a course in mathematics be political too?" (Hook 1989, 32). To claim that all texts have political dimensions, says another, that "politics or ideology is everything," is to diminish both politics and literature (Howe 1991, 46).

Despite a strong hostility to curricular revision in the pages of *National Review,* some of its commentators' views converge with those of writers in *The Nation.* For example, from the left, Elizabeth Pochoda endorses the idea that we should teach Shakespeare and Darwin as well as the excellence of Pygmy bushcraft and of Fuegian survival in the world's harshest climate (1991, 615). Similarly, from the right, Harvey Mansfield comments that "multiculturalism can be saved if it is improved—in courses of world history that focus on the excellence of each nation and its contribution to progress. Here is genuine pluralism without flatness, unafraid to pass judgment and eager to teach respect" (2000, 26). Thomas Sobol argues that "there is no inconsistency between teaching the common democratic values and traditions that unite us and teaching more about our differences" (quoted in Russell 1991, 20).

A more challenging defense of multiculturalism about which there is less agreement suggests that minority students benefit from feeling a sense of identification with great figures of their own tradition who are included in the curriculum. "A wonderful thing happens when you encounter images of your cultural self in a book at an early age," says Henry Louis Gates Jr. Therefore, it makes sense to "change the curriculum so that the experience of identification can occur for people who are not Anglo-Saxon" (quoted in Clarke and Durham 1991, 18). Exposing ghetto children to Shakespeare is not "what 'culture' should mean. . . . The educational event we call empowerment . . . replaces fetishized respect for culture as a stagnant secular religion with respect for culture as a living historical process, in which one's own experience is seen as an authentic part" (Robinson 1989, 321). While serving as New York's state education commissioner, Sobol suggested that one can get "otherwise alienated blacks to feel comfortable with a larger tradition in which they had a role" (quoted in Russell 1991, 20). And Glenn Loury compares inner-city black students who seek an Afrocentric curriculum to Christian Fundamentalists who advocate the teaching of "creation science." Both are responses to the stresses and anxieties of modern life; both exude "an aura of defensiveness and tragic folly—and yet, ultimately a certain dignity." The desire to use school curricula to give black students "a strong, positive sense of racial identity" should be "accommodated rather than denounced." After all, "it makes little sense to tell blacks in the Oakland ghetto that they should drop their racial fixation and get on with the job of integration" (Loury 1997, 25).

If conservatives rail against the new history curricula as representing the tendency of previously excluded groups to "turn to remaking the past in the image of their desires" (Henry 1990, 30), some progressives also criticize "a sanitized, feel-good history, whether inspired by the desperate plight of inner-city youth or by the passion for conformity" in patriotic self-celebration (Foner 1995, 302).

Various commentators attack the idea that revising the school curriculum to include works by and about previously excluded groups can enhance the self-esteem of minority students. They argue that such programs do not work (John J. Miller 1993) or are unrelated to academic success (Glazer 1988; Krauthammer 1990). But, Sobol argues, "Our goal is intellectual honesty. . . . [I]f it happens to promote self-esteem along the way, why would anyone object?" (quoted in Russell 1991, 20).

In the discussions about the university curriculum—the canon wars—the commentary is more evenly split and more given to nuance. Observers on all sides agree that adding works to the curriculum based solely on the race, sex, or class of their authors rather than their merit is patronizing and wrong (see Brustein 1997b, 1997c; Hook 1989; Howe 1991). Irving Howe, for example, maintains that it is "grossly patronizing" to suggest that middle-class white students can read diverse literary works but that students from minority groups should be given literature that is "racially determined" (1991, 47). There is also broad agreement that it is wrong to evaluate the truth content of a work based on the race, class, or gender of its author (Hart 1989a; Howe 1991; Pollitt 1991; Todorov 1989). Furthermore, art "works to transcend differences of race and gender. . . . We do not attend a performance of *Hamlet* as whites or blacks, males or females, but as human beings" (Hart 1989a, 45). Another commentator suggests that if I as a white man listen to the music of Duke Ellington, "I am certain that I don't hear these pieces the way a black man hears them. But I am also certain that I hear them rightly, that I hear them as music" (Wieseltier 1994, 32). Defenders of curricular change, of course, maintain that the added works are of high artistic or literary merit. They also mock the idea that modifying the curriculum is tantamount to the "destruction of Western civilization" (Robinson 1989, 319).

Indeed, the defenders of curricular change contend that much of the criticism directed at it has this quality of exaggeration. The Left is not dominant in academe (D. A. Bell 1986); there is no "radical hegemony" on campus (Robinson 1989, 319); free expression is not being stifled (Kinsley 1991). Traditional classics are still being taught (G. Graff and Cain 1989), and students can still take many courses about "dead white males" (Kinsley 1991). Debate and change are healthy, and curricular change always accompanies continuity (Bowen 1988; Howe 1991; Todorov 1989). Furthermore, only 20 percent of college students actually take core courses in Western civilization (Cockburn 1991, 691). And books neither determine behavior nor "mold a common national purpose" (Pollitt 1991, 331).

Supporters of curricular change note that all too often, "a different aesthetic is presumed to be no aesthetic. And the female, black, working-class or homosexual experience is uncritically assumed to be, at best, an unlikely candidate for canonization, precisely because it is the marked variant, whereas the experience of straight white men has a unique claim to universality." The idea is not to eliminate the canon but rather to add to it. The whole tradition can then be read "from a perspective informed by our sense of what is usually omitted and what that omission itself teaches" (Robinson 1989, 319). We must learn to see ourselves from the outside: "it is crucial to study not only our own history, but also other cultures . . . in order to convince ourselves there is more than one way of being human" (Todorov 1989, 30). History and philosophy necessarily subsume "forms of inquiry into the strange and unsettling." Therefore, adding gay studies, for example, to the university curriculum makes sense (Nussbaum 1992, 35).

Critics of curricular revision, however, see the changes as wrongheaded, silly, or pernicious. "Eccentric reading lists" accompany "a combative political agenda" (Henry 1991, 66); "fad is king" as 1960s radicals continue to "promote their own progeny" (Hart 1988, 32). The "multicultural fads" on campus promote student ignorance of history (Giesea 1997, 64). Academic freedom is threatened (Roche 1989); assaults take place on both free speech and common sense (Teachout 1992, 54); and diversity becomes "an excuse for suppressing real intellectual differences" (Sykes and Miner 1991, 31). Most of these criticisms come from the Right, but at least one progressive joins in, suggesting that much nonsense has entered cultural life as progressives in academe have littered the curriculum with courses in the humanities that are manifestations of race, ethnicity, regionalism, or class (Kriegel 1984–85, 714).

In a critique that harks back to the idea of multiculturalism as a form of individualism, one conservative argues that "the gravest fault of our education today is that its content gives us nothing to aspire to." The goal of education should be to produce citizens who "can love, admire, respect something or someone above themselves" (Mansfield 2000, 26). Rather than fostering diversity, the prevalence of multicultural curricula may end up encouraging solipsism. "The future may well lie with the Stanford student who, when asked about studying important non-Western trends such as Islamic fundamentalism and Japanese capitalism, responded, 'Who gives a damn about those things? I want to study myself' " (F. Siegel 1991, 40).

Just as some conservatives have expressed their acceptance of an earlier accommodation with homosexuals that rested on their sexual practices remaining private, so too a conservative writer has suggested that the literature of blacks, females, Jews, and others had long been taught within universities but only to "insiders"—everyone studied the traditional classics, while blacks also studied what blacks had done, women learned about what women had done, and so forth. This "benign consensus" of the 1970s later fell apart when the curriculum became a matter of contention and the "new humanities" were "promoted for parochial purposes (to give blacks self-confidence, to persuade Jews to remain Jewish)." Their promoters thus "turned themselves into mere pressure groups on the campus, extensions of political forces deriving from outside the campus" (Neusner 1984, 44).

Much of the animus against revisions of the curriculum, whether in schools or universities, is based on the idea that these changes seek to deny the existence of objectivity or truth. An editorial in *The New Republic,* for example, objects to "a curriculum geared primarily to attack the notion of objectivity itself." Yet the editorial writers, like many other contemporary commentators, are simultaneously wedded to the idea that reality is socially constructed. The dilemma is nicely captured here: "Nobody, least of all this magazine, is recommending a smug return to a naïve positivism. But . . . the facts (even at this late date, we insist, the term may be used without embarrassment) are far less contestable—and contested in American society today—than the multiculturalists claim." The editorial acknowledges, however, that "objectivity is often a mask for interests" (Editorial 1991d, 5–6). Others, too, make that connection, arguing that we need to distinguish between the power of an idea and its rightness. Nevertheless, works created by particular people with particular political concerns can contain universal truths (Todorov 1989, 30).

A fairly wide consensus holds that objectivity and truth do exist and that the truth of a statement is independent of who proclaims it. On the one hand, all disagreements are not related to power, and to reinterpret culture in this way is "tantamount to denying the distinction between fiction and history" (Hook 1989, 33). On the other hand, it is not unreasonable to analyze the politics of culture: "The notion that all political interpretation of Shakespeare is invalid—because it offends against 'the autonomy of culture'—is surely more philistine than any theory academic Marxists have cooked up" (Kinsley1991, 8). "Any large group with a common purpose . . . has difficulty tolerating those nuances and subtleties and complications that characterize the search for truth" (Brustein 1997a, 31—-32).

Whatever their differences, most commentators reject the extremes of postmodernist arguments that posit the impossibility of objective truths. This is important, as Barry has pointed out, because "democratic politics rests on the assumption that it is possible to give reasons for taking one course of action or another that are good or bad reasons—not just my reasons or your reasons." The minority cannot accept decisions reached by the majority "unless both sides occupy a common universe in at least this minimal sense" (2001, 236). This is akin to the idea that religious beliefs must be translated into secular reasons for presentation in the public square.

Because many critics maintain that the reigning academic orthodoxy questions the possibility of objective truth by asserting that all knowledge is political or socially constructed, there is much room for derision. One critic notes, for example, that "the same faculty who once demanded that religion be excluded from the curriculum now teach that objectivity is just another Western myth" (Hudson 1996, 40). Conversely, defenders of newer scholarship are pushed to argue that not all scholars of female studies or gay studies, for example, are "politically motivated"; nor are the scholars themselves gay or lesbian or deconstructionists or Foucauldians (Nussbaum 1992, 35).

Among progressives and centrists alike, the canon wars represent "a conflict over a society's vision of itself," since what is included in the curriculum constitutes "an index of what the culture deems important." When disagreement arises, it "becomes part of what is important" and should be examined within university curricula. Traditions within democratic societies are not simply fixed; they are critiqued and renegotiated (G. Graff and Cain 1989, 312). What exactly constitutes the "classical heritage" is "composed and fought over by cultivated men and women" (Howe 1991,

43). American culture has always been open to new regions, new oppressed classes, and immigrant communities. Democratic cultures move along through internal conflicts—of classes, ethnic groups, literary schools, and popular audiences (Howe 1984, 26). The debate about the canon "may be the healthiest thing to have happened around academe in years" (Bowen 1988, 67). Efforts to suppress hurtful words and ideas to bring peace to a racially diverse America are wrongheaded. "Up to now, . . . America's genius has not been in its civility, but in its raucous barroom brawl in search of truth" (Henry 1993, 75).

One writer sympathetic to the idea of curricular changes suggests that the concept of a canon, of the Great Books of Western Civilization, is itself something of a myth. He argues that anything resembling such a canon was ascendant only in the period from shortly after World War I through the decades just after World War II. The inclusion of writers such as Shakespeare and Walt Whitman had previously occasioned intense battles (Levine 1996, 15). And even a conservative critic of contemporary trends acknowledges that "conflicting cultural traditions" have "shaped the present." The curriculum should not be fixed; the texts selected "can be varied from time to time" (Hook 1989, 30). Another conservative commentator argued against a "reversion to the old world of institutionalized prejudice and cultural snobbery" and in favor of previously neglected works by blacks, Jews, and women that should be taught for "what is general and accessible, suggestive beyond itself" (Neusner 1984, 44, 61).

Yet by far the dominant stance among writers in *National Review* is to mock the idea of beneficial conflict about the canon. Thus, Arthur Schlesinger's assertion that debates over beliefs and values in schools and colleges are beneficial is derided as being "dismally squishy." At stake in the canon war are not simply "different styles of intellectual discourse" but rather a struggle over "the power to teach the young and shape the culture." And because the beliefs of the current curriculum revisers are "Leninist" or "totalitarian" in nature, it is not possible to compromise with them (Teachout 1992, 55). In contemporary academe, left-wing fads are so dominant that graffiti is studied as literature (Hart 1989b, 39), and serious intellectual life will move outside the university (Hart 1988, 32).

One of the major conservative books against the revision of the curriculum, Dinesh D'Souza's *Illiberal Education* (1991), similarly argues that the revisionists seek not so much to include diverse materials as to represent a point of view. The "multicultural project" smacks of "its own paradoxical provincialism" (75), since those who promote "diversity" actually seek to spread conformity to their own ideological thinking. Thus, "to be 'for diversity' you must believe that homosexuality as a sexual preference is morally neutral, or that women have been victims of domestic incarceration through history" (214). *National Review* editorializes against multicultural education because of its lack of true diversity and its failure to provide the kind of knowledge that children should have. "Most parents, whatever their ethnic background, want their kids to master the English language, and to learn that Washington prayed at Valley Forge. This kind of knowledge is . . . increasingly rare in the feverish and artificial world of public education" (Editorial 1991b, 16).

From the perspective of the revisionists—as represented, for example, in Henry Louis Gates Jr.'s book on the subject, *Loose Canons* (1992)—there has long been a tendency to depict anything outside of Anglo-American culture as "tribal" or "parochial" (175). The real challenge will be to shape "a truly common public culture, one responsive to the long-silenced cultures of color." Multiculturalism exists; the curriculum merely follows it. Ethnicity, class, and gender have long fragmented American society. To make multiculturalism "the culprit for this fragmentation is to mistake effect for cause" (176).

A variety of commentators see compromise in the canon wars as quite feasible. Not only can one teach about "current challenges to the established classics from the popular media and non-Western cultures," one could examine why *Moby Dick* became a classic and *Uncle Tom's Cabin* did not (G. Graff and Cain 1989, 312). And rather than removing *Huck Finn* from the curriculum, one could teach it and understand why it is racist (Todorov 1989, 30).

Because the revisionists argue that the criteria for making judgments of value "are socially constructed in ways tied up with political interests and consequences," their critics often accuse them of being either totalitarian or nihilistic. But their defenders say that by raising questions about the meaning of "good" and "bad," they are reviving rather than debasing the issue of value (G. Graff and Cain 1989, 310). Though concerns about the excesses of curriculum revision can be found on both the right (see, for example, Hart 1988, 1989a; Sykes and Miner 1991) and the left (see, for example, Howe 1991; Kriegel 1984–85), there is also a fair amount of agreement that adding works to the standard curriculum is permissible and even admirable as long as the number added is not so great as to "dilute" the traditional curriculum. There is, after all, "more to culture than Western culture, and one might well explore the standard list of classics for expansion and replacement" (Glazer 1988, 21). Stanford University's compromise is a recognition of "the essential pluralism of Western civilization" (Bowen 1988, 66).

Critics of multicultural education and of changes in the university canon allege that the underlying motivation for these program alterations is to improve the employment opportunities of various minority group members. Thus, it is argued, support for bilingual programs is high among Hispanics even though such programs do not help students academically. The benefits of such efforts lie in providing "employment and political opportunities, as schools are forced to hire Hispanics without regular teaching credentials" (Thernstrom 1981, 16). Another critic contends that matching professors' ethnic or gender identities with the fields in which they work is not a good idea: "The whole idea of history involves putting yourself in the shoes of someone else." Moreover, one could argue that minority students "feel empowered" when they see a black female English professor teaching the Shakespeare course (Barnett 1991, 26). And the idea that only blacks and Asians can and should play black and Asian theater roles means "turning theater into an arena of entitlement" and promoting "racial exclusionism" (Brustein 1991, 33). Some progressives take a more benign view of such matters but acknowledge this role of multicultural programs. Thus, Katha Pollitt suggests that when academic feminists define women as having a separate culture, they are carving out a safe space for themselves: "It works much like multiculturalism, making an end-run around a static and discriminatory employment structure by creating an intellectual niche that can be filled only by members of the discriminated-against group" (1992b, 806).

If pluralism within one culture is to mean more than separate enclaves replete with their own special employment opportunities, how is it to occur? If it means the coexistence of internally homogeneous communities, how are they to be created?

The Difficulties of Tolerance

The liberal solution to the problem of pluralism within one culture lies in promoting tolerance, though all liberals do not agree on how to define it. Conservatives exhibit even less consensus on the issue. Thus, one conservative derides multiculturalists' tendency to place the "normative rights of the community" above those of individuals (Henry 1993, 74), while another suggests that such rights may be more important than pluralistic tolerance. During the struggles over homosexuality in the early 1980s, this second commentator had suggested that "the community has a right to preserve its conception of the American consensus by repressing those whose actions would tend to undermine it" (Teachout 1983, 1433).

Yet another conservative maintains that only conservatives are capable of "genuine tolerance." Because the Left sees humans as perfectible and wishes to use state power to root out imperfection, leftists are intolerant of anything of which they disapprove. But since tolerance is an American principle, the American Left has had to redefine it as approval, and the result has been moral relativism. "Genuine tolerance, which is tolerance of those with whom one disagrees or of whose behavior one does not wholly approve, thus becomes uniquely a conservative virtue. A practicing homosexual can remain on the Left only as long as the Left decides that homosexuality is just as good as heterosexuality, but he can join the Right even if conservatism condemns homosexual acts" (Short 1990, 44). A conservative gay commentator clearly distinguishes between tolerance and approval, noting that the struggles of the gay rights movement have gone along a road from intolerance to tolerance to acceptance, with the last stage not yet having been reached (Bawer 1994, 26).

The idea that tolerance serves as a cover for moral relativism begins with the observation that liberals tolerate all sorts of lifestyles and are unwilling to attach sanctions or stigma to misbehavior (R. Wright 1996, 44). Liberals view all faiths and philosophies in our culture "not as objects of respect in their own right" but rather as the "the raw material for construction of a society whose only absolute is tolerance" (Wagner 1986, 32). In redefining "tolerance as approval," the American Left has sanctioned moral relativism (Short 1990, 44).

The relationship between tolerance and moral relativism is, in actuality, not a simple one. On the one hand, those Americans who believe in granting civil rights and liberties to groups of whom they disapprove—whether homosexuals, atheists, or communists—have done so on the grounds of tolerance. On the other hand, sociologists concede that some of the items in standard scales that supposedly measure tolerance may actually measure "attitudinal 'moral relativism' rather than actual behavioral graciousness towards those with whom one disagrees" (Woodberry and Smith 1998, 41).

The distinction between tolerance and social approval is significant. In the eyes of many conservatives, homosexuals deserve our tolerance but not our "coerced approval" (Editorial 1998c, 16). School curricula that include books such as *Heather Has Two Mommies* are seen as "going beyond toleration to approbation" (Brookhiser 1993a, 74). "Moral failure" is increasingly "rationalized" by convincing oneself that one's previously illegitimate wishes are now acceptable. But for the rationalizations to succeed, everyone must agree with them. Hence "the necessity for self-justification requires the complicity of the whole culture." Gays and supporters of abortion, for example, thus "moved naturally from a plea for tolerance to cultural conquest" (Reilly 1996, 61). An article in *Time* cautions, however, that social conservatism must be accompanied by tolerance because "in every era when moral fervor held sway, a counterreaction began to build when the community became intolerant of individual liberties" (Stengel 1986, 18).

Some conservatives express concern about the deleterious effects of tolerance on the unity of American culture, contending that "even the most tolerant American culture" could not "incorporate other cultures wholesale" (O'Sullivan 1994a, 40), that Americans should take pride in "the historic content of their culture" rather than in "empty formulas of tolerance and diversity" (Brookhiser 1992, 74). These conservatives decry liberals who rank all philosophies and faiths as subservient to the all-important value of tolerance (Wagner 1986, 32). And they argue that the "gratuitous insults to the religious sensibilities of fellow citizens by artists . . . are damaging to democratic tolerance" (Hyde 1990a, 27), quite in contrast to the assumption of many supporters of the National Endowment for the Arts that their side represented the virtues of "reasonableness and toleration against narrow-minded Philistinism" (Chait 1997, 14).

But if some conservatives portray tolerance as a prime liberal value, at least one liberal characterizes it as a basic American cultural theme. American society, he argues, was founded on the ideal of an "open society"—tolerant, heterogeneous, and pluralistic. Though tolerance is a difficult ideal, it is "not only a good idea but also particularly our own idea, our heritage as Americans" (Melzer 1991, 12). In contrast, a progressive writer attacks those liberal intellectuals who have moved rightward in their zeal to support unity and patriotism. Cockburn alleges that these liberal intellectuals condemn their fellow liberals for supporting "an overpermissiveness arising from the fear of being considered intolerant" (1985, 70).

Neither conservatives nor liberals can agree among themselves about the kind of tolerance that is required in a pluralistic society that retains a common culture. Many but not all conservatives see clear dangers attached to tolerance in a period of significant immigration. Because culture is essentially the "common sense of the community," when large numbers of immigrants from different cultures enter the United States, the status of the American culture is reduced. "It becomes merely the 'Anglo culture,' whose rules, standards, and conventions are thought to be alien to non-Anglo citizens and hence cannot be 'imposed' on them. And, paradoxically, because tolerance is such a strong component of Anglo-American culture, Americans are much more vulnerable to this cultural sapping than, say, the French" (O'Sullivan 1994b, 41). In a similar vein, another conservative critic takes Arthur Schlesinger to task for suggesting that the alternative to multiculturalism is "an open society founded on tolerance of differences. . . . If the toleration of differences is the be-all and end-all of America, then why not tolerate multiculturalism?" (Brookhiser 1992, 74).

The difficulties in negotiating differences of opinion within a pluralistic society are apparent in the case of parental objections to educational materials used in the public schools. In one example of "pluralistic democracy at work," numerous full-fledged battles take place among groups endeavoring to shape the school curriculum. Public education in the United States "can work well only in a pseudo-democracy or a pre-democracy where citizens are reluctant to exercise their right to protest against government decisions. . . . As more parents and taxpayers begin to feel their democratic oats—and become more empowered in their children's education—the number of these disputes will multiply. . . . The public schools are being driven toward extinction by the flowering of democracy itself" (Payne 1995, 60, 62).

The question of whether Americans are truly tolerant of others is a matter of some dispute. One writer notes that "while polls show that many Americans have a renewed appreciation for traditional values, their tolerance of their neighbor's right to reject these values has not declined at all" (Stengel 1986, 17). Yet critics on all sides see their opponents as producing a less tolerant nation. Opponents of multiculturalism and political correctness argue that they foster intolerance rather than tolerance. The new thinking in academe, which sees most of American history as racist, sexist, and classist, is "fostering a decline in tolerance and a rise in intellectual intimidation" (Henry 1991, 66). Those who advocate an Afrocentric curriculum do not seek interracial tolerance; rather, their spirit of racial pride is "synonymous with racial intolerance" (Sullivan 1990, 21). And an increase in "diversity" in the newsroom is seen as "driven by truly totalitarian impulses" that promote "cheerleading" rather than newsgathering and work "to suppress ideas and information" (Seligman 1993, 28, 34, 32). On the other side, a liberal accuses the Religious Right of preaching a "rabid intolerance of social differences (yes, lifestyles!)" (Judis 1999, 56). And right-wing PC, no less than its left-wing counterpart, is seen as representing "an intolerance of opposing views that verges on censorship" (Kinsley 1993, 66). Another progressive notes that although pressure groups on the right frequently demand political correctness, the term is never applied to them (Elson 1994, 64). And in a more humorous formulation: "Criticizing gangsta rap for demeaning women is defending 'American values.' Criticizing right-wing talk radio for doing the same is 'politically correct'" (quoted in Sachs and Washburn 1995, 34).

The issue of how tolerant Americans truly are is a complicated one. On the one hand, survey respondents say that all persons should be free to think and believe as they see fit; on the other hand, respondents are quite willing to see unpopular views being censored. If one asks people whether their most disliked groups (for example, atheists, homosexuals, racists, militants, communists) should be allowed to give speeches, run for office, or even legally exist as a group, surprisingly few Americans say yes (Gibson 1992). While some evidence indicates that Americans are becoming more tolerant, in part because of higher levels of education (see, for example, T. C. Wilson 1994), the use of a more stringent measure of tolerance—putting up with views that one finds objectionable—produces evidence of only very minor improvements in tolerance. An analysis of survey data from 1976 through 1998 found that "strong majorities of Americans were willing to limit civil liberties for members of unpopular groups"; in 1998, more than 79 percent took this position (Mondak and Sanders 2003, 501).

Questions of how to reconcile tolerance with strong beliefs and with cultural unity bedevil all sides. Are we a society based on "enlightened self-interest" or on shared moral beliefs? Can a deeply pluralistic society be held together on the basis of tolerance, or is tolerance to be sacrificed for the larger good of communal cohesion? Does republican civic virtue require the curtailment of some individual freedoms?

The liberal understanding has often included the idea that the United States is an association of citizens in which pluralism applies culturally but not politically. "The people are Americans only by virtue of having come together," and they may retain "whatever identity they had before becoming Americans." Politically, however, Americans are one, not many. The symbols of American citizenship are "culturally anonymous, invented rather than inherited, voluntaristic in style, narrowly political in content: the flag, the Pledge, the Fourth, the Constitution" (Walzer 1999, 595, 602). This idea is, in essence, a recapitulation of Kallen's earlier idea of cultural pluralism lodged within the American Idea. The "essence of the American identity" here "rests on democratic political values," and instead of cultural nationalism, there is tolerance (Spencer 1994, 562). One liberal commentator has suggested that it is easier to live in a society of shared moral and religious beliefs, and thus "all traditional societies and all pre-modern philosophers of society have been hostile to the mixing of religions, mores, and cultures in one society." But the modern liberal state is premised on the idea that people can be tied together "through an alliance of enlightened self-interest rather than through shared moral and religious beliefs" (Melzer 1991, 11).

In practice, of course, the United States has a long history of nativist movements that seems to suggest the difficulties of maintaining a heterogeneous society based on self-interest and tolerance. As Lipset has pointed out, "The crusade to keep America Protestant by barring massive non-Protestant immigration is actually almost as old as the United States itself." Conservative politics from Thomas Jefferson's time to Woodrow Wilson's included "efforts to impose ascetic Protestant morality on the lower classes—often viewed as largely immigrant in composition—and attempts to limit immigration or to withhold equal rights from the foreign-born." Through much of American history, such movements came into conflict with "more culturally cosmopolitan and egalitarian opponents" (1990, 184). This conflict continues unabated into the twenty-first century. That nativist upsurges did not result purely from the high proportion of immigrants in the United States can be demonstrated by the experiences of other nations. In South America, some nations received more immigrants than did the United States without generating nativist movements. Italian immigrants were more readily accepted in Argentina at the turn of the twentieth century than was the case in the United States (Degler 1987, 10).

In an era of large-scale immigration from non-European societies and the propounding of philosophies of multiculturalism, renewed debate has occurred about the very nature of American society. If liberals can unite around the idea of a society that combines cultural pluralism with political unity, conservatives argue among themselves about the essence of American society. Several conservative commentators argue against the "official rhetoric" of the United States as "a nation of immigrants, an idea rather than a nation," instead seeing America as "a common culture evolving into an ethnicity that encompasses other ethnicities" (O'Sullivan 1994b, 40). They are concerned that current immigration policies are "bringing in cultures and peoples too diverse to be incorporated within a single national and civilizational identity" (Auster 1994, 54). They fear that "precipitately changing an historically European-majority country into a multiracial, white-minority country must result in a breakdown of the common culture" (Auster 1992, 43). What emerges here is the idea of an American ethnicity. Conservative opponents, however, argue that ethnic homogeneity does not make sense in the American context. Rather, "one might say that the homogeneity of America is in the shared recognition that there are many ethnic identities that, for limited public purposes, are subordinated to a common enterprise" (Neuhaus 1995, 65).

Those conservatives who insist that shared moral beliefs are essential to the maintenance of a society reject the notion that a society can be politically united but culturally pluralistic. In their eyes, the idea of "a 'multicultural' nation" constitutes "an oxymoron if ever there was one." The "rationalist" idea that America can be reduced "to nothing more than a set of abstract principles (freedom! opportunity! pluralism!)" does not work. "A civic bond cannot long endure in the absence of an experienced cultural bond" (Auster 1994, 49, 51, 54). "If America consists of very different peoples, with very different understandings of what is virtuous, sensible, noble, or merely comfortable, and united only in their allegiance to liberty, equality, and prosperity, then they will eventually wage wars over the proper definition of the first two terms, and over the proper allocation of the third" (O'Sullivan 1994b, 37). Moreover, if being American means giving allegiance to certain political principles, then one ceases to be an American when one does not endorse these principles. By contrast, if being an American is a matter of "ethno-cultural solidarity," then one is free to dissent (O'Sullivan 1994a, 45).

In this conservative perspective, "a stable liberal civil society" obviously depends on "an undergirding common culture." Though such a culture does not need a shared religion or ethnic homogeneity, it does require "more than subscription to legal or constitutional rules—it requires commonality in moral outlook. . . . We can live together in deep disagreement about abortion, but not if we also disagree about the propriety of using force on our opponents." In contemporary society, disagreements arise even about what constitutes a moral issue. For example, is homosexuality a matter of morality? What is required is therefore a "radical tolerance of indifference," so that others' sexual habits are not a matter of concern. But a different form of tolerance is also required: toleration, which implies judgments. To tolerate a practice or belief means to allow something inferior or undesirable to exist. If we are to have a common culture, toleration is required. "A common culture—even if one defined thinly in terms of the practices and virtues that make up a liberal civil society—is essential if we are not to drift into chaos; and even such an attenuated common culture will be renewed across the generations only if it is animated by a shared sense of history and nationality." Such a culture requires the "inescapably judgmental" form of tolerance that can be called toleration (J. Gray 1992, 36). As expressed by another conservative, what is required is "censure" rather than "censoring." Rather than prohibiting certain forms of expression (for example, hate speech), we need to censure it; "censure is the free expression of moral disapproval." We have not been using censure because "a false ideal of tolerance has not only outlawed censorship but discouraged censoriousness (another word for censure)" (Wills 1989, 71).

Scholars have noted that in an earlier era, liberal communities tolerated all kinds of pursuits in private—that is, at home, in churches, in voluntary associations. This kind of tolerance provided a "safety valve," enabling "natural enemies to live together in peace" (Kautz 1993, 620). More recently, however, being left alone no longer seems sufficient, as numerous commentators on both the right and the left have noted.

Democratic societies in an era of multiculturalism must constantly examine the bases of their decisions. If all are to participate equally in the formulation of democratic decisions, then "cultural minorities may challenge the regime of toleration because they cannot accept it without subordination" (Bohman 2003, 772). A case in point might be some religious Fundamentalists' desire to ban some reading material in the public schools because it violates their sense of what is moral and true. From the perspective of liberal tolerance, it has seemed reasonable to reject the requests of parents who will not allow their children to be exposed to diverse literature. That is, "liberal toleration . . . defends diversity by not tolerating the intolerant." But if one wishes to treat all parties as "members of the same open and inclusive deliberative community," alternative modes of solving the problem could be found. Thus, school officials could exempt the children from the offensive material or could generate lists of books that are acceptable to all (769).

Put somewhat differently, "toleration can be manifest either in the blindness and indifference of the state to diversity, or in a more equalizing respect for the representatives of varied positions," and the latter position has been more characteristic of contemporary pluralists. Thus, color-blind hiring policies have been replaced by a conscious effort to produce a diverse workforce (Schlosberg 1998, 603). Similarly, observers have argued that greater sensitivity rather than blindness to differences is required in the religious sphere as well. "Religious cultures and identities are not treated fairly by declaring that religion is a private matter or by excluding religious arguments from political or constitutional debate." Equal treatment of different religious groups and of religious and nonreligious people requires taking into account "structural inequalities between majority religions and minority ones" (Bader 1999, 608). The recognition of such structural and political realities has meant that many groups are no longer content with merely private tolerance, that for all kinds of groups, "the personal is political." Perhaps, too, the recognition of selves as cultural constructions existing within cultural groups makes the demand for recognition so much greater. Tolerance thus means more than indifference; it means recognition. Given deep pluralism, the result is a kind of "agonistic respect" (Schlosberg 1998, 606).

For most commentators, "agonistic respect" among competing viewpoints does not mean that the United States is "merely a container of cultures that come and go rather than a cultural entity in itself" (Hollinger 1995, 160). Rather, the common culture continually emerges from the interaction of subgroups (Hartmann and Gerteis 2005). And relations among groups continue to evolve so that there is no final "consensus on identity, truth, or a social order. . . . The ongoing generation of different antagonisms, and the discourses among them, keep us from finally constituting ourselves" (Schlosberg 1998, 608).

Conclusions

However much most mainstream writers reject multiculturalism as a philosophy, it is nevertheless correct that "we are all multiculturalists now, " as Glazer's (1997) book title suggests. In Glazer's account, multiculturalism has "won" despite being "strongly denounced" by "powerful voices in American life" and being "at odds with the course of American culture, society, and education" (4). Glazer makes clear that his title signifies not an endorsement of multiculturalism but rather a recognition that it is "unavoidable"—much in the way that Sir William Harcourt, after the passage of a progressive tax on estates in 1889, declared that "we are all socialists now" (160). Whereas public education had long functioned to integrate immigrants into American life, school curricula now pay attention to minority groups and their distinctiveness as well as to "the oppression of the minority culture by the majority" (11). The demands for multicultural curricula arose, Glazer argues, because of American society's failure to integrate African Americans. While contemporary immigrants generally seek to assimilate to American ways, African Americans have been excluded. Their rates of intermarriage remain low, and residential segregation remains high. Educators supported multiculturalism in the hope that the incorporation of black themes would improve black students' achievement. Most blacks embrace multiculturalism because "they want . . . to become more like other Americans—for example, in educational achievement—not different from them, and believe that the way to becoming more like them is to take more account of difference, and yes, of ill-treatment, of past and current achievement, even if exaggerated" (Glazer 1991, 22).

In Glazer's version of multiculturalism, then, there really is but one American culture. And, indeed, from the perspective of at least some observers from other societies, the cultural differences subsumed under the umbrella of multiculturalism are not profound. Thus, one British philosopher has argued that true multiculturalism is a matter of "deep moral diversity." Therefore, he says, "when I refer to multiculturalism I do not mean the trifling local debate on American national identity that has occupied many in the USA" (J. Gray 2000, 325). In addition, the overwhelming majority of the population, regardless of educational attainment, does not support the kind of proportional representation that some more ardent multiculturalists advocate. Thus, 87 percent of the most educated and 89 percent of those without high school degrees disapprove of having Congress mirror the country's ethnic makeup (Citrin et al. 2001, 263).

If both "multiculturalism" and "culture wars" in American society are new in their labels but not in their essence, some aspects of the struggles over cultural pluralism clearly are novel. For one thing, the sheer extent of diversity has grown as people from all continents and numerous religious and racial groups have arrived in substantial numbers in the United States. Globalization has meant a more radical interpenetration of very different cultures and cultural ideas than was previously the case. Another new element is that the definition of what constitutes a cultural group has been broadened. No longer confined to race and ethnicity, cultural groups are now based on gender, sexuality, disability, religion, and other shared systems of meaning. Thus, even if the United States as a "nation of immigrants" had long been accustomed to dealing with cultural differences, the differences are now more numerous and cut across more aspects of daily life, both public and private. Perhaps, too, self-consciousness about culture presents new issues. Debates about multicultural education and the canon wars represent deliberate efforts by all sides to shape the culture via educational change.

CHAPTER 6

Antielitist but Respecting Achievement

One staple of American political discourse is defining one's opponents as elitist while portraying one's own side as reflecting the will of the people. All sides in the culture wars manifest this tendency. What is unusual here is only the number of elites at issue, since every sphere of culture wars contention is characterized by splits between the leadership and the grass roots—in the churches as in the arts world, among gays as among feminists. Yet as with all the polarities under discussion, ambivalence and a willingness to praise or emulate the elites also exist.

Who Are the Elites, and What Is Elite Culture?

While conservatives may eschew the language of cultural politics, the two sides nevertheless converge in recognizing that some actors are more powerful than others in influencing the culture. Conservatives clearly see power in the hands of an "establishment" or "new class" or "knowledge class" whose tastes and values conservatives dislike. Sometime during the 1960s, says one conservative commentator, "the power of explaining America to Americans fell to a liberal, sometimes radical 'new class'—academics, elitists, journalists—which, although accurate up to a point, somehow got the story wrong or told it from a vantage point of supercilious and frequently privileged hostility" (Morrow 1981, 73). The "Woodstock Generation elites" are very powerful now, says another conservative, though their views are not widely shared. But one must distinguish between such elites and a "true cultural elite" that "stands by enduring values" (Buckley 1992a, 54). "The traditional moral imperatives of self-restraint and delayed gratification" are currently absent because culture-transmitting institutions—mainline churches and universities—have "almost entirely gone over to liberationism" (Editorial 1988a, 22).

Media elites are an obvious target of attack from all sides. The Right asserts that media elites are less religious and more socially liberal than the population at large and are therefore "out of touch with the public" (Editorial 1981b, 533). As the Right sees it, parents are left struggling to inculcate values that the media ignore, attack, or "aloofly patronize." The media do not praise marital fidelity, for example, or appreciate the struggles of wedlock (Novak 1984, 48). When the "Don't ask, don't tell" policy regarding gays in the military was not eliminated, a *National Review* editorial noted that "conventional sexual behavior and morality was shown to have stronger social roots than the media normally allow" (1993a, 14). Since many media people are remnants of the 1960s counterculture, they "remain cultural revolutionaries" who exert their influence on the general culture despite their "alienated" and mistrustful stance toward American society (Bork 1989, 27). Liberals have an inside track with such cultural institutions as book publishers, a position that allows liberals to engage in behind-the-scenes censorship of school textbooks by lobbying sympathetic publishers, rather than by launching public challenges and court cases such as those brought by conservatives. In the eyes of sympathetic people in the book publishing industry, "critics who wanted books to feature more working women were a 'positive pressure group,' those who wanted more homemakers were 'censors'" (Bates, 1993, 69).

By contrast, the Left is concerned about the "rise of a veritable Culture Trust" that controls the major media, seemingly with little popular concern or opposition. Amazingly, the population has bought into the "great Myth of the Culture Trust" that there are many channels from which to choose (Tom Frank 1996, 16). People fail to see how fundamentally similar all of the channels are and fail to recognize that although capitalists themselves promulgate messages that appear to be against the system, being "hip" is no longer an oppositional stance. To resist "puritanism, homogeneity and conformity" is no longer a means of dissenting from the system. Capitalists endorse such resistance, thereby sidetracking popular discontent (18).

It is not entirely clear who is a part of the cultural elite. Are Hollywood and TV writers to be included? The Right appears to think so, but the Left is uncertain. Thus, Michael Kinsley noted that Vice President Dan Quayle's attack on *Murphy Brown* represented in part an attempt to blame the "cultural elite" for what ails our society (Kinsley 1992b, 6), but Katha Pollitt found it strange that Quayle thinks of TV writers as part of a cultural elite rather than as "crowd-pleasing lowbrows" (1992a, 88).

In the eyes of some culture warriors, the culture war itself is provoked by errant elites. Thus, William J. Bennett defines the culture war as a battle between "elite" and "mainstream" America, where the elites are liberals who "belittle mainstream American values." The public, he argues, "has been too quiescent and too accepting about what has been inflicted on them from the upper strata of society," though they "are regaining the confidence to express publicly the common sense sentiments they hold privately" (1992, 13, 256).

If those on the right characterize cultural elites—whether in the media, the arts, or schools and universities—as subscribing to liberal ideas, those on the left suggest that the contents of popular culture depend largely on the profit motive that drives economic elites. Commentators in *Time* take note of the economic realities that underlie television content. Thus, the 1997 television season contained an unprecedented number of shows with religious themes, as "people have begun to seek out the comfort of religion in all aspects of their lives—even on TV." Nevertheless, "the young and the reckless still rule. Sinners, after all, have killer demographics" (J. Stein 1997, 98, 100).

By contrast, a writer in *National Review* during that same year suggested that television shows about religion remained scarce relative to the interest of the American population. He also noted that the viewing population had succeeded in giving high ranking to *Touched by an Angel,* a show panned by critics, while making a flop of *Nothing Sacred,* a show about a with-it Catholic priest who saw the Bible as irrelevant to abortion, homosexuality, and premarital sex (Gahr 1997, 44, 45). In this version of reality, the good sense of the people may override the foolish liberalism of the elites who construct the media content. While this populist sentiment appears on both the left and the right, the audiences in question appear to differ.

While crediting the intelligence of average Americans over that of the critics, conservatives may also suggest that lower-class populations are all too easily influenced by the images they receive from the liberal media elite. As one conservative commentator notes, "common sense suggests that the pictures of the world disseminated by cultural elites would have an impact over time." Justifying their actions on the basis of white indifference and failure to provide jobs to ghetto residents, black and Hispanic gang members are echoing TV commentators, whose statements are picked up from the culture elites (Rothman 1992, 35). In contrast, a liberal commentator remarks that "young African Americans are not so naïve and suggestible that they have to depend on a compact disc for their sociology lessons." They know that police stereotype and arrest blacks more than whites for the same offenses. Critics of rap music imagine "empty-headed, suggestible black kids, crouching by their boom boxes, waiting for the word." This view is clearly false (Ehrenreich 1992a, 89). An editorial in *The Nation* similarly contends that the "culture war" propagated by the 2000 Democratic presidential and vice presidential nominees"implicitly portrays American teens as empty vessels at the mercy of corrupting entertainment" (Editorial 2000c, 3). And a writer in *The Nation* notes that those who wish to censor certain publicly funded artists manifest a "faith in the power of images" that "appears to involve a deep suspicion that seemingly decent Americans will be overwhelmed by dark forces within them that such images might unleash" (Mattick 1990, 356).

It is easy to see that the interests of various groups influence their perception of media influences. Thus, a conservative writer who decries the influences of Hollywood points out that "liberal activists who denounce Joe Camel as a pied piper of social coercion swear that screen idols have no influence on human behavior. Television executives who make billions of dollars off the persuasive power of 30-second commercials declare that the 26- and 54-minute programs those ads punctuate have no net impact on their views" (Goldberg 2000, 62).

If media elites have undue influence, those on the left see this phenomenon as a consequence of the economic interests represented by the major media. The media, they contend, are necessarily biased in a conservative direction. As a result, they find political correctness on the left to be newsworthy while ignoring that on the right. No attention is paid, for example, to the removal of a painting commemorating a 1912 strike from a congressional hearing room (Pollitt 1998a, 10). Nor is any notice given to what really destroys our language and thinking: the "everyday lying and jargon," the newscaster babble, that is "sanctioned and promulgated at the highest levels of media and politics"—terms such as *business community* and *peace process* (Hitchens 1991, 472).

The media's conservative bias is also evident in portrayals of contemporary social movements. The "conservative counterrevolution" against feminism leads to "a mediawide misimpression that young women are marching back into the kitchen with virginity intact" (Alterman 1999, 10), that women are rejecting feminism (Pollitt 1994a, 224). And the gay movement is dominantly represented by conservatives, as a small number of gay writers appear in all the media and promote ideas that "range from right to far right" (M. Warner 1997, 15).

During the 1980s and 1990s, Right and Left converged in their attacks on the media for being run by elites or elitists who are out of touch with the people. In a 1950s incarnation of a similar convergence, the attack was on mass or popular culture itself. At that time, the Left feared media manipulation of the masses and the dumbing down of the population through market-based entertainment, while the Right feared that mass culture would drive out high culture and diminish or trivialize cultural standards. By the end of the century, both sides disowned the earlier critique of mass culture, with portions of the Left now seeing the populace as smart enough to resist manipulation and portions of the Right disavowing cultural elites that produce immoral, antibourgeois art. At the same time, well-educated segments of the population appeared to have shifted from being "highbrow snobs" to being cultural "omnivores," with 95 percent of college graduates in one survey agreeing that "excellence is just as likely to be found in folk culture or popular culture as in traditional high culture" (Peterson 2002, 36).

The degree to which antielitism has grown since the middle of the twentieth century can be illustrated by examining almost any critic of mass or popular culture during that era. For example, a well-known sociologist of popular culture wrote in the *American Journal of Sociology* in 1950, "We wish to know whether the consumption of popular culture really presupposes a human being with preadult traits or whether modern man has a split personality: half mutilated child and half standardized adult" (Lowenthal 1950, 332). It is hard to imagine any of today's culture warriors on the right or the left subscribing to such sentiments.

Distinctions between popular and high culture had become suspect by the late twentieth century as observers recognized that what merits elite status in the cultural realm is a matter of social construction and the power to confer it. In an era when a major art museum (the Guggenheim) presented an exhibition titled The Art of the Motorcycle, the older distinctions made no sense. Yet what exactly belongs in the mainstream remains a matter of dispute.

One writer looks at contemporary American popular culture and declares that whereas a mainstream culture once existed, there are now "two streams: one traditional and tranquil, the other torrential and caustic." At midcentury, "there was a single official pop culture: white middle class, mid-cult, status quo." Today, this group remains tranquil, but there is a large pop culture that is based on the rage of those who are ignored: the homeless, the junkies, the insane, the ghetto underclass, and "the young white working class, in tattered towns and trailer parks, who feel left out of bland, sitcom America" (Corliss 1990, 97). Another commentator in the late 1990s suggested the presence of a new countercultural trend. Unlike that of the 1960s, however, it is "inchoate" and neither united nor political. Growing up around alternative music and the Internet, its members seek original identities and are "far more sophisticated and authentically nonconformist than Woodstock Nation ever was." But theirs is an "apolitical tribalism. . . . The belief in a singular 'system,' and a 'counterculture' in opposition to it, comes from a time when there was a consensus reality constructed of centralized media, personified by the three TV networks" (Sirius 1998, 88–89).

A liberal defender of middlebrow culture suggests that "it provides some unity in a culture where political, social, and intellectual fragmentation is now the norm." Highbrow culture, he argues, "has never been so high—so removed from daily discourse. And lowbrow has never so mesmerized the masses or carried such highbrow chic. . . . We have lost appreciation for the art that was once the mainstay of American culture and the unguilty delight of intelligent readers, listeners, and viewers." Middlebrow art "appeals across barriers of age or station" because it offers both amusement and instruction. It also engages with the world and can produce social change, as novels such as *Uncle Tom's Cabin* and *The Jungle* illustrate (Friend 1992, 24, 27). A writer in *The Nation* applauds this defense of middlebrow culture and reinforces the suggestion that accessible art can change minds and hearts (Pochoda 1992, 344).

Another progressive writer contends that a "democratization of culture" has taken place, so that the barriers between high and low culture have broken down, much to the displeasure of social conservatives (Willis 1996, 22). And indeed, one noted conservative art critic decries the fact that "all distinctions between high and low culture, including outright trash, are considered too invidious to be given a hearing." In fact, he argues, the priority given to "the lowest forms of popular culture and media entertainment at the expense of literature and the fine arts in the 'quality' press is now so advanced that it amounts to a cultural revolution. So does the politicization of reviewing, where the tenets of political correctness and multiculturalism are now regularly substituted for criteria of aesthetic judgment" (Kramer 1993, 37). Another critic agrees that "high art in America is dying" (Brustein 1992, 38).

A commentator on the left suggests that the "sleaze and moral degradation" of contemporary popular culture is less worrying than the "brutality and emptiness of our political culture." The excesses of TV talk shows demonstrate the problem. "Pop-bashing is the humanism of fools: In the name of defending people's dignity it attacks their pleasures and their meager store of power. On talk shows, whatever their drawbacks, the proles get to talk. The rest of the time they're told in a thousand ways to shut up" (Willis 1996, 23).

To be sure, even this supporter of the "proles" who "get to talk" on television talk shows notes that they are often subjected to "the manipulative condescension of their producers and hosts" (Willis 1996, 23). And as noted earlier, some progressives suggest that these programs merely exploit the poor and minority groups. In addition, not all progressives see cultural democratization as a good thing. Thus, what some progressives perceive as the "democratization" of culture others see as "a consequence of the left's inability to make distinctions. Because we tend to see all cultural expression as a manifestation of political ideology, ideology itself has ceased to serve any definable purpose, except as a leveler of distinctions. As a result, cultural life is overwhelmed by nonsense. . . . It was the left that favored education in the humanities for all; it was the left that wanted to make cultural life widely available. . . . When those of us on the left called for cultural diversity, we questioned, justifiably at the time, the obeisance to Western culture that pervaded American colleges and universities." But this "cultural politics . . . was disastrous. . . . Courses in the humanities became manifestations of race, of ethnicity, of regionalism or of class. And by allowing all values, all opinions, all feelings, all ideas—no matter how ridiculous or ill-conceived—to be considered equally, we made humanistic education a minor branch of what might be called 'arts for living'" (Kriegel 1984–85, 714). Irving Howe has noted similarly that "the deep suspicion of the making of distinctions of value"—long part of American populism—has "found a prominent place in the universities" since the counterculture of the 1960s (1991, 42).

The debates about the university canon appear to pit academics against their critics. This situation is unfortunate, says one liberal commentator, because there is clearly something wrong "if society no longer wants to listen to its intellectuals, and if intellectuals cannot bear to hear how they are judged by society." Academics argue that specialization of knowledge is required and even that it makes thought possible. "This is an outrageous claim. It implies, among other things, that outside of universities people do not think." This goes along with the elitism that sees "popular" books as inevitably being too simple (Todorov 1989, 26, 28).

While writers on the left and the right share an undertone of populist distaste for elites, the attacks on elites for behaving in a self-serving fashion appear more prominently from conservatives. The elites in question are those whose work is seen to influence the culture. Not just artists, intellectuals, and academics, but experts in the school system and supporters of multiculturalism come under such suspicion. The Right sees those who support multiculturalism as part of an establishment that is out of touch with reality. "It is only the political class and the intelligentsia" who do not know that there is a common American national identity (O'Sullivan 1994a, 45). "Multiculturalism is not a grassroots movement"; it would die without government support (Chavez 1994, 32). And immigrants themselves are not the problem. They are here because they believe in American values. The problem lies in an indigenous overclass intent on balkanizing American society and exploiting immigrants and the poor to that end (Neuhaus 1995, 66). Elites either "acquiesce in" or "actively promote" balkanization (Custred 1997, 40). Immigrants do not seek bilingual education; indeed, the gap between the advocates of such education and their "putative beneficiaries" is widening (Editorial 1990b, 14).

Those who promote multicultural education and design sex education curricula are particularly vulnerable to the Right's accusations of elitism. Thus, "multicultural professionals . . . often earn exorbitant incomes peddling identity. Thousands of consultants with little or no real experience sell feel-good programs to school systems across the nation" (Chavez 1994, 30). And mainstream sex educators advocate "the kind of anti-majoritarianism conservatives fear most: a group of experts who use the power of government to reinvent the culture" (Mindus 2000, 46). "Just as the cigarette makers wanted to get the kids hooked on their product, so the sexologists want to get the kids hooked on theirs" (Bethell 1997, 36).

In the eyes of conservatives, both secular and religious elites are guilty of "cowardice and silence" in response to the assault on family and religious values in the schools and the media. The leadership of the mainline Protestant, Catholic, and Jewish religions as well as of the Republican and Democratic Parties is chastised for seeming to acquiesce to current politically correct fashions (Simon 1993, 21). While "feminism and sexual liberation are the religion of the intellectual class in America," only the elite wants feminism; the people do not (quoted in Gibbs 1992, 54). The increasingly dumbed-down nature of American masculinity—where men's culture is defined in terms of sex, sports, beer, gadgets, clothing, and fitness—is also to some degree a function of the cultural elite's response to feminism. As areas of public life such as business and politics that once "inculcated a form of refined masculinity" have become "unsexed," and as men's clubs and schools have been "de-gendered," men need to find something in common beyond beer and gadgetry. While the reestablishment of single-sex schools and colleges and all-male clubs could help, "a decent amount could be accomplished simply by stopping the intolerance of such things that now passes for civilized consensus among American elites" (Sullivan 2000, 6).

Before *Roe v. Wade,* abortion was supported by the "elite culture" of the "knowledge class." The "democratic culture" has subsequently organized its response (Neuhaus 1989b, 42), and mainline churches are reconsidering their proabortion positions because of grassroots pressures (M. P. Harris 1988, 44). Decisions about abortion "must not be imposed by elites, or by institutions subservient to elites, or in the obscurity and mists, penumbras and prejudices of elites" (Novak 1997, 48). Those fighting to outlaw abortion must "unseat the social ideal of radical individualism" by "persuading or displacing the elite that fostered that ideal" (Cunningham 1992, 46–47). The population is more religious and more conservative than its leaders and has begun to express discontent. While the media focus on the Moral Majority and "the wilder manifestations of the emerging reality," they have ignored "the deeper and broader social currents, thereby proving again that they are out of touch with the public" (Editorial 1981b, 533).

Some on the right see the establishment as having engineered its own downfall by attempting to co-opt the 1960s counterculture. Instead, these "primitive forces" have taken over; the new elites prefer "primitive authenticity" to "learned sincerity" (Lipman 1991a, 40). The "Mapplethorpe Wing of American culture" now dominates "elite cultural opinion" (Buckley 1992a, 55).

Elitism and Funding for the Arts

To many conservatives, artist Robert Mapplethorpe became a symbol of the distasteful art that was being supported by cultural elites and subsidized by unwilling taxpayers. But the very definition of what constitutes elitism in the arts is a matter of considerable contention. Is the National Endowment for the Arts (NEA) elitist because it supports "an irresponsible avant-garde" or "snobbish un-American homosexuals" or insufficient numbers of minority grantees (Brustein 1997c, 30)? Or is it elitist to assume that ordinary Americans are not interested in the humanities and that culture should be the private property of those who can pay for it (Hughes 1995, 65)?

While opponents view the NEA as elitist because it takes tax dollars from lower-income Americans and benefits wealthy patrons of the arts, supporters counter that the NEA helps nonestablished artists and minorities, the young, the poor, and the "provincial." Without the NEA, American public culture would depend wholly on corporate support and thus would reflect the interests of one class, one race, and one mentality (Hughes 1990, 47). Defenders of the arts also note that political leaders such as Vice President Quayle, who beat "the populist drum on cultural and moral matters" and attacked the "cultural elite" for undermining American values, are themselves part of the elite. Quayle is the millionaire son of media millionaires (Hughes 1992b, 43). Observers have also suggested that conservative Republicans were free to criticize the "cultural elites" in the arts and humanities because these audiences were no longer so dominantly Republican (Jensen 1995, 28).

The controversy surrounding federal funding for the arts drew such high-level political figures as Republican speaker of the house Newt Gingrich and Senator Henry Hyde into writing articles against the NEA. Gingrich argued that Americans should not be forced to pay for "political statements masquerading as art," should not be required to support views that contribute to our "cultural fraying" instead of our unity, and should not be "forced to underwrite cultural dependents who add to our decay and undermine our values" (1995, 70, 71). Hyde similarly proclaimed that the public need not pay for offensive art or art that reflects merely the narcissistic self-expression of the artist rather than a quest for the good, the true, and the beautiful. Yet the two disagreed about the desirable outcome. Whereas Gingrich thought that removing cultural funding from the federal budget was the solution, Hyde hoped that such a drastic measure would not be necessary since it would mean that "we simply can't reach agreement on a reasonable approach to issues at the intersection of politics and culture," a result that would be "deeply saddening" (Hyde 1990a, 26).

Some on the left, by contrast, have no problem endorsing art that is "overtly political." "The demand that art must be representative of the whole community or must be universally accepted . . . is reminiscent of that used in totalitarian states to condemn any work of art that does not represent the whole community or that breaks with convention" (Neier 1980, 376). Some traditional art critics' animus against the "misdeeds of the NEA" may reflect their sense that it reflects a loss of their own power (Mattick 1990, 356). And in the climate of the culture wars, the arts have become "scapegoats, grotesquely politicized culture-war stereotypes," so that many people now believe that preserving the NEA means preserving "sodomy, blasphemy, and child abuse" (Hughes 1995, 66). Conversely, at least one liberal who disapproves of the NEA is concerned that it offers little money to the arts while wielding lots of power as a consequence of the prestige associated with its grants. This combination of little money and lots of control "is the worst of all possible worlds" (Chait 1997, 16).

All sides are concerned about the incompatibility between the interests of the art establishment and those of ordinary citizens. Some on the right argue that given this incompatibility, a libertarian argument is the best solution: let artists do what they want, but don't make taxpayers fund it (Ferguson 1989, 21). An editorial in *The New Republic* similarly contends that "taxpayers ought not to be expected to support displays that do violence to deeply held community values" (Editorial 1989, 6).

Both the Left and the Right accuse the art world of remaining aloof from the world of ordinary people. Some liberal commentators suggest that the lower classes' concerns and tastes are excluded. Arts producers and consumers display a "broad condescension" toward working people, who "sense that their lives and opinions are uninteresting to arts-world decision makers" and whose "rage was there long before it was tapped by . . . right-wing churches" (Spillane 1990, 739). In controversies regarding the placement of art in public squares, the rights and interests of those who use those spaces must be considered more important than the aesthetic value of the art. A commentator on the left thus argues against placing Richard Serra's large sculpture, *Tilted Arc,* in New York's Federal Plaza. Despite his personal admiration for the sculpture as a work of art, this commentator opposed such a placement because the public "has an interest in not having all of its open spaces treated as though they were museums" (Danto 1985, 776).

Observers on the right perceive that the art world has deliberately chosen to distance itself from the respectable world of the middle classes. Because the members of the bourgeoisie are afraid to look bourgeois, they are no longer shocked by art and are willing to pay high prices for Andy Warhol's soup cans. The NEA funds whatever the arts community produces because it too is afraid to look bourgeois, with the result that artists have become more violent and lewd and the public taste is further corrupted (Berns 1990, 35–36). Some on the right question whether offensive art—such as Mapplethorpe's photography and Serrano's *Piss Christ*—is indeed art as opposed to political statement (Buckley 1990b, 62).

Yet some commentators on the left defend the arts and art institutions against the charges of elitism. Unlike so many other institutions, "American art institutions are among the most zealous in reaching out. . . . How else explain the preoccupation with multiculturalism, the debate over quality, the effort, with whatever success, to dismantle the barriers of race and gender? (The contradictory fallback position of those who can't get the label 'elitist' to stick is that arts institutions are too 'politically correct'!)" (Danto 1997, 6). Those who condemn the excesses of multiculturalism and political correctness indeed suggest that being politically correct means being "deeply skeptical toward the very idea of a 'masterpiece,' because it implies that one idea, culture or human being can actually be better than another" (Henry 1993, 74).

Those concerned about the fate of art fear that the very controversies about artistic merit have been detrimental because the effort to avoid political controversies has made public art increasingly bland. Artists increasingly must fend off criticisms from all sides of the political spectrum—from "religious and cultural conservatism" as well as "identity politics" and "ordinary philistinism" (Grant 1999, 47). And the increased pressure against subsidizing provocative art may lead some theater producers, for example, to "decide that survival is more important than social commentary" (Yeoman 1998, 33).

Ambivalence toward Elites

While elites in many areas of American life may be seen as out of touch with popular sentiment, they nevertheless remain objects of respect and emulation. Indeed, the conflict between elitism and democratic populism plays itself out in a variety of spheres, with commentators from both conservative and liberal perspectives siding with the elites. Thus, a conservative commentator has argued that "the idea of the gentleman has been part of American culture from the earliest days" (Hart 1996, 52). Though it emanates from the English model, its American form is characterized by "self-control, subordination of the ego, understatement, respect for solid achievement, courtesy (especially to social inferiors), respect for women, family responsibility, professional obligation, respect for education, regard for athletics" (55). To be sure, "the whole idea of the gentleman is an offense against the idea of social equality." But then the extreme individualism of the American literary canon also "constitutes a polemic against the leveling tendencies of democratic culture." Despite the leveling pull of democracy, "the idea of the gentleman has been a powerful presence in America," and it "operates within, and is not in radical opposition to, society itself" (54). A liberal defender of high culture likewise suggests that the leveling tendencies of American culture make it difficult to sustain high culture. He speculates about whether Tocqueville has "been confirmed in his belief that a meritocratic art cannot survive in a democratic society" and suggests that "the serious artist finds it harder and harder to resist the pressures of popular taste" (Brustein 1997d, 32).

Conservatives are nevertheless careful to insist that their support of traditional university curricula and their revulsion at the revisionists are neither elitist nor undemocratic. Kimball, for example, assails the "pernicious" idea that establishing a canon in humanistic studies is "undemocratic." This "common" notion, he argues, incorrectly sees democracy as "inimical to authority, tradition, and rigor in its cultural institutions" (1990, 6). Indeed, suggests Bloom, the average student suffers from lack of familiarity with great literature. "As the awareness that we owed almost exclusively to literary genius falters, people become more alike, for want of knowing they can be otherwise. . . . Instead of being overwhelmed by Cyrus, Theseus, Moses or Romulus, [students] unconsciously act out the roles of the doctors, lawyers, businessmen or TV personalities around them" (1987, 64, 67).

Another conservative commentator asks if the classic texts of Western civilization were written by the elite for the elite. Of course they were, he maintains, but why does that matter? The origins of art and literature have little to do with their quality. And Karl Marx, after all, did not seek slave art or proletarian literature. Rather, he wanted the best of art and culture to be "part of the cultural birthright of the working classes" (Hook 1989, 31). Similarly, that most authors of the Western tradition are white males of high social class does not mean that their works are elitist or racist or sexist. Indeed, to believe that is itself racist, sexist, or elitist, "since it implies that the color of your skin decides the content of your thought" (Todorov 1989, 30).

The classic American ambivalence toward elites is strikingly manifest in the conservative literature, where conservatives accuse each other of pandering to the elites. Thus, many Americans, including corporate leaders and the Republican establishment, are seen as "chronic appeasers who know they are viewed with contempt by the cultural elite" (quoted in Scully 1993, 27). There's "social-class anxiety" among conservatives that makes them unwilling to cite Scripture or speak of gay sex as a sin because this puts them in the "ranks of hillbillies" (Klinghoffer 1998, 24). Because "society's leaders" are pro-choice, the status climbers feel a need to acquiesce to it: "acceptance of abortion is necessary for the approval of our betters" (Cunningham 1992, 44). In "elite circles," supporting abortion rights is "de rigueur," and politicians and the media therefore assume that since everyone they know favors abortion, everyone does (Editorial 1998a, 12). An "oppressive assumption" holds "that no one of any learning or sophistication could possibly be a religious believer," and "social penalties" are "meted out to those who nonetheless are" (Krauthammer 1998, 92). Catholics who mute their abortion views to make themselves appear more socially respectable are "social climbers aspiring to be accepted by a Protestant establishment already in eclipse" (Neuhaus 1986, 46). As the Left takes over more of the culture, what develops is "a subtle paternalism that regards moral conservatives as intellectual and social infants who have to be educated out of their backward ways" (Wagner 1986, 52). Conservatives have been charged with philistinism for so long that "they have accepted the characterization invented for them by their enemies. Instead of realizing that the accusation of philistinism is merely a way of smearing their defense of traditional standards and values, they have assumed that the realm of mental culture was a liberal preserve" (Lipman 1991b, 53).

The status anxieties within the conservative camp may be exacerbated by evidence suggesting that the most distinguished faculty and the brightest students tend to show greater affinity for leftward causes. While liberals may dominate all college campuses, they are strongest at the most prestigious ones (Lipset 1996, 180, 183). Cultural conservatives tend to have degrees from less prestigious institutions than do cultural liberals, and the grassroots membership of progressive causes is more educated and likely to be upper middle class, while conservatives are dominated by members of the lower middle class (Hunter 1998, 9). Nevertheless, evidence shows that Evangelicals have become increasingly prominent within elite circles in the United States since the late 1970s, even though their numbers within the population have not greatly changed. This development belies the conventional wisdom that people become more secular as their wealth and status improve (Lindsay 2008, 68, 79).

One Christian critic of the way in which the culture wars have been waged suggests that conservatives have blundered in identifying "the enemy as the 'cultural elite.' What does that make conservatives? The 'culturally impaired'? The 'backward fundamentalists'?" All too often, he argues, Evangelicals are so much a part of the culture that they believe that the cultural elite is evil simply because they are part of a cultural elite rather than because of their positions (Horton 1994, 31, 44). Yet this critique may be missing the intended irony in the use of the term *cultural elite.* According to Lakoff, conservatives subordinate culture to morality so that "the idea of a real cultural superiority that isn't moral superiority makes no sense. . . . For this reason, the term 'cultural elite' can only be ironic, referring to a self-sustaining influential group with false claims to superiority" (2002, 240).

The Right aligns itself with elites insofar as it defends WASP culture but characterizes WASP culture as little more than the traditional American culture. WASP ideals—of industry and success, of conscience and civic-mindedness—have continued to dominate American society even as WASPS themselves have slipped to minority status because "being a WASP was a game anyone could play. Over the years, everyone has, including descendants of the people Lincoln freed" (Brookhiser 1993b, 79). Attachment to this elite is thus acceptable because it represents the democratic potential of American society. Or does it?

Conservatives have reached no consensus here. One commentator argues that despite cultural myths of universalism and of the United States as an immigrant nation, "in real life what was important was the assimilation to a WASP norm" (O'Sullivan 1994b, 36). But another conservative contends that "there is no Anglo copyright on the characteristics that make for assimilation and success in America: hard work, thrift, civic-mindedness, devotion to faith, family, and freedom. The successful third-generation Polish-American is not a WASP but a successful third-generation Polish-American" (Neuhaus 1995, 64). Yet a third conservative writer suggests that whatever the ethnicities and cultures of those at the lower levels of the social pyramid, the culture at the top remains Anglo-American (Hart 1996, 52, 56). An editorial in *National Review* argues that not just the top of the social hierarchy remains WASP-like but rather pretty much everything above the bottom. "The important social divisions in American life are those between the Knickerbocker Club, the Nashville Kiwanis, and Teamsters Local 137—but to a foreign eye they all look WASPish." (1991a, 18). As seen by the Left, of course, the WASP nature of the hierarchy is offensive. That is, those at the top are always "indisputably American," seemingly without culture or race. White ethnic groups and then nonwhite ethnic groups follow the elite. These "hierarchies of worth" are "perpetuated by dominant groups" (Chock 1995, 317).

If some conservatives align themselves with WASP elites, other commentators are willing to align themselves with an elite by defending the cause of high art. The idea of "elitist" as meaning exclusionary rather than excellent is helping to kill the idea of high art in American society, one writer argues. He points out that "the charge of 'elitism' was hurled not only against the wealthy consumers of art but also against its often penniless creators. . . . You were elitist if you created works of art and you were elitist if you bought them. No wonder so few people were willing to come to the defense of elitism" (Brustein 1997d, 30). Another defender of the arts argues that if the NEA funds established institutions in the major cities, it is accused of "upper-class elitism," but if it funds "a suburban orchestra in Ohio or a young, unfamous poet in Oregon, that's subsidizing the second-rate." Why does no one complain about funding the space program when few people care "what kind of rocks Mars has"? (Pollitt 1997, 10). And some liberals perceive the "realm of mental culture" as a "liberal preserve." The Right began its attack on culture, the arts, and academe in the 1980s, at precisely the time when the Left had disappeared as a political force but not as a cultural one (Hughes 1992a, 46).

It is probably not accidental that the Right appears to defend the elite at the top of the class scale, while the Left primarily defends the elite in the arts. Yet in both cases, the argument suggests that elites are either holding out ideals to which all can aspire (as in the case of the gentleman or the WASP) or producing goods of direct benefit to the people. Thus, one liberal suggests that if one can find race, class, or gender bias in both Louis L'Amour and a classical Greek play, rejecting elitism might mean teaching the L'Amour. Doing so, however, would do violence to the ideal of democracy, which is to bring true education to the people (Howe 1991, 42). Hence, elitism and democracy are reconciled in the need to bring the best of the culture to the masses.

Both the Left and the Right are mindful of the pitfalls of "antielitism." While "elitism" is in disfavor, all applaud "standards" and "quality." All assert the need to make distinctions of literary or artistic merit. If antielitism means rejecting classic works of literature, no one is for it. Indeed, one commentator suggests that the survival of the NEA may be a kind of Pyrrhic victory, since the agency now avoids any discussion of what constitutes "excellence in the arts" and thus does not fulfill its mission (McCarter 1999, 17).

Writers on the left do not comment on experiences of being patronized by a cultural elite, but they, too, distance themselves from such elites—often as defenders of popular culture and of what they call the democratization of culture. Thus, one writer notes that "social conservatives have been notably unsuccessful at stemming the democratization of culture, the breakdown of those class, sex, and race-bound conventions that once reliably separated high from low, 'news' from 'gossip,' public from unspeakably private, respectable from deviant" (Willis 1996, 22). But critics including Thomas Frank have pointed out that little of substance has been accomplished by those in the Academic Left who have celebrated the "democratization" of culture. During the 1990s, he argues, academic specialists who engage in cultural studies proclaimed "a populist celebration of the power and 'agency' of audiences and fans, . . . and of their talent for transforming just about any bit of cultural detritus into an implement of rebellion." They studied these "lowbrow" samples of popular culture and "turned their attention from the narrow canon of 'highbrow' texts" as an "assault on the powers that be" (2001, 282–83). Yet their studies of resistance were not far from the "stuff of market populism." Rather than being "daringly counterhegemonic," their ideas seemed like an "apologia for existing economic arrangements" (295); "our newfound faith in active, intelligent audiences made criticism of the market philosophically untenable" (303). In a more conventional and old-fashioned vein, Robert Brustein bemoans the fact that "criticism is largely left to the mass media, which arbitrates . . . literary and cultural approval." This situation differs substantially from the earlier time of little magazines and small publishers, of avant-garde theaters, adventurous galleries, and listener-supported radio—a time when respected critics helped to develop new tastes and identify new talent (1992, 37).

A progressive writer cites TV talk shows as a product of cultural democratization and suggests that they are "anathema to social conservatives, for whom the only legitimate function of popular culture is instructing the masses in the moral values of their betters." Because it "would be a breach of American democratic etiquette" for critics to suggest that their cultural tastes are superior, they blame either money-hungry media corporations or "a perverse New York and Hollywood cultural elite" for such popular fare (Willis 1996, 19).

The Right is not alone, however, in deriding "Hollywood liberals." Frank, for example, paints an ugly portrait of this genre as seen in the pages of *People* magazine: "Here you read about movie stars who go to charity balls for causes like animal rights and the 'underprivileged.' . . . Minor TV personalities instruct the world to stop saying mean things about the overweight or the handicapped. . . . Here liberalism *is* a matter of shallow appearance, of fatuous self-righteousness; it *is* arrogant and condescending, a politics in which the beautiful and the wellborn tell the unwashed and the beaten-down and the funny-looking how they ought to behave, how they should stop being racist or homophobic" (2005, 240–41).

Division exists within the Left about the significance of television talk shows. Not all leftist commentators believe that these programs constitute a genuine expression of the people. Indeed, one observer suggests that such shows "take lives bent out of shape by poverty and hold them as entertaining exhibits. . . . This is class exploitation, pure and simple" (Ehrenreich 1995, 92). Another writer is concerned that these shows "intentionally or not, have become storm troopers for the right" because "they focus attention on the individual, aberrant behavior of a small number of citizens and declare them representative of a group." In exploiting and solidifying stereotypes about young, mostly black and Latino poor people, such shows destroy "any sense of understanding, connectedness, collective responsibility and the potential for redemption" (Nelson 1995, 801). As if to prove this writer correct, *National Review* editorializes that TV talk shows "offer a window on the future of diversity-dominated America. [They] are the only national forum in which blacks, Hispanics, and trailer-park WASPS freely join together with the ground rules drawn from Diversity Theory. No thought or desire is ruled out as unacceptably perverse" (Editorial 1995b, 18).

There is derision on the left about the Right's tendency to see "dangerous elites" in many places. Thus, liberal observers note that historians have been added to the list of such elites because of proposed national history curriculum standards. Historians have thus joined the "internal enemies," along with media executives who promote rap and eggheads who watch PBS and support government funding for the arts (Foner 1995, 302).

Some commentators on the left engage in criticism of elitist tendencies within their camp. Critics complain, for example, about the "cultural nose-thumbing" that is "common in the writings of feminists and leftists who speak about things that concern everyone in language interesting and available to few but themselves" (Pochoda 1992, 344). And some observers are concerned that the "cultural left" has given a bad name to leftist politics because of "its arcane 'elitist' battles over curriculum . . . and its aversion to the socially and sexually conservative values that most Americans uphold" (Willis 1998, 18).

Elitism in the Feminist and Gay Rights Movements

In the area of contemporary feminism, the Left offers a hint of the kind of status anxieties that conservatives discuss. One progressive feminist suggests that "the current attack on 'victim feminism' is partly a class phenomenon, a kind of status anxiety. It represents the wish of educated female professionals to distance themselves from stereotypes of women as passive, dependent, helpless and irrational" (Pollitt 1994a, 224). The helplessness and irrationality of those such as Lorena Bobbitt (who cut off her husband's penis) must be punished, lest all women are tainted by her characteristics. The Bobbitt affair revealed a gap between feminist intellectuals and the average woman, since Bobbitt garnered "grass-roots female backing" despite women's studies professors' reluctance to support such militancy (Ehrenreich 1994, 74). "Maybe the troops are more militant than the generals" (Pollitt 1994a, 224).

The Left and the Right converge in a way on the issue of feminist elitism, as commentators from the right and center also criticize American feminism for its detachment from the concerns of "average" women. Thus, a writer in *Time* notes feminism's "upper-middle-class intellectual elite" origins and suggests that feminism "remains suspect to those who have never ventured onto a college campus" (Bellafante 1998, 57). Those on the left are concerned about poor and minority women whose concerns are often ignored, suggesting that "what's missing is a grassroots, militant, political movement" (Pollitt 1998c, 10).

For many commentators on the right, feminist leaders have failed to appreciate most women's desire for marriage and families. These pundits argue that much of what has happened in the name of women's liberation hurts "all but an elite minority of career-oriented childless women professionals" (Gallagher 1987, 39). And they do not view the supposed backlash against feminism during the 1980s as an attempt to sow doubts in women's minds about feminist goals. Rather, they suggest that the media might simply have been picking up on existing concerns and touching "a nerve that had been rubbed raw by a generation of out-of-touch feminist leaders" (Gibbs 1992, 51). Some liberals express irritation with those academic "consciousness-raisers" who are attempting to transform the curriculum to eliminate "androcentric" materials. The women's studies crowd does not represent most American women, who subscribe to an older feminism that seeks equity, fair treatment, and an end to discrimination (Sommers 1992, 30).

The perception of a gap between leadership elites and members arises in connection with the movement for gay rights as well. More conservative gay commentators suggest that the gay leaders who align themselves with progressive causes and seek a "culture war" are clearly out of step with most gays, who want acceptance and assimilation into the larger population (Bawer 1994; Sullivan 1989). "Much of the gay leadership clings to notions of gay life as essentially outsider, anti-bourgeois, radical. Marriage, for them, is co-optation into straight society," says a gay conservative. "But for many other gays—my guess, a majority . . . a need to rebel has quietly ceded to a desire to belong" (Sullivan 1989, 22). Other gay commentators note that ordinary gays and lesbians have pressed for the adoption of same-sex marriage, while their leaders have retained "a powerful antipathy to 'heterosexist norms'" (Rotello 1996, 15). Some progressive gays suggest that the movement lacks a national activist group akin to those of the civil rights and women's rights movements (Kopkind 1993, 600) and that the national leadership too often operates "on a top-down and elitist corporate model" (Ireland 1999, 11).

Conclusions

Though populism and antielitism have long been part of American culture and politics, the unleashing of the culture wars brought new attention to otherwise arcane aspects of elite culture—the curricula offered at elite universities, the grants awarded by the NEA. A hyperconsciousness of how ideas in the arts and the academy might influence the larger society appeared to make culture war antagonists feel obliged to attend to aspects of the culture that might heretofore have received little notice. Defenders of the traditional culture on the right now had to distinguish between the "true" or traditional culture and that which passes for it in contemporary arts and academia. On the left, struggles took place between the desire to applaud the "democratization of culture" and the desire to maintain standards.

An increased self-consciousness about the cultural dimensions of status might also have caused concern among economic and political elites who have generally maintained a distance from cultural matters. Heightened insecurities about one's status in the social hierarchy might have led to attacks against cultural products that were unfamiliar or were perceived to be alien or challenging to their positions.

CHAPTER 7

Moderation, Plain and Simple

Unlike the other American cultural themes that occupy the culture warriors, moderation is seen as an uncomplicated good. The American admiration for it contains no ambivalences or ambiguities. In his 1979 study of American journalism, Herbert Gans suggested that "moderatism" or distaste for "excess or extremism" was among the "enduring values in the news" (51). Americans, he suggested, tend to question polar opposites and uphold moderate solutions. Both atheists and religious fanatics are frowned upon. Both conspicuous consumers and hippies who renounce consumer goods are condemned; "political ideologists are suspect, but so are completely unprincipled politicians." Being immoderate is not good, "whether it involves excess or abstention" (52).

Moderation is basic to American middle-class morality: "Americans instinctively try to find the centrist position between extremes" (Wolfe 1998, 72). They support seeking the "middle ground" even on such highly contentious issues as abortion (Pew Research Center 2006b). More than one-fifth of Americans have a highly unfavorable opinion of both anti-abortion activists and strong advocates of abortion rights, seeing both as intolerant and extremist (Dillon 1996, 120). In national surveys of religious attitudes, the majority of Americans identify themselves as being in the middle; only approximately a quarter of the population self-identifies as religious conservatives or liberals (Wuthnow 1996, 326). Seen in a cross-cultural perspective, "in America 'middle'—as in Middletown, middle class, and Middle America—is not a matter of mediocrity but centrality. Far from a question of being average (as in the verbal associations of middling, middle-brow, and middle-income to the British), it has everything to do with being American" (Guinness 1993, 42). To be sure, the well-known American fondness for moderation has occasioned some famous rhetorical flourishes. Accepting the 1964 presidential nomination, Barry Goldwater announced, "Extremism in the defense of liberty is no vice . . . and moderation in the pursuit of justice is no virtue." But Goldwater was resoundingly defeated in the ensuing election.

In the context of culture wars, moderation is often translated as "a plague on both your houses"—or indeed, on "all your houses." Partisans in the culture wars attack their opponents by derisively treating them as "extremists." Nowhere is this more evident than in the case of the canon wars.

One writer, for example, "agrees with all sides" in the debate about the academic canon. Conservatives are correct in seeing some books as more profound and more essential to our culture than others, even though dead white Western men wrote them. Liberals are correct in suggesting that the canon can be amended to include those—such as women and members of minority groups—who were previously excluded for the wrong reasons. Radicals who assume that one cannot have one reading list for all students are clearly wrong, however, since it is "foolish to argue that Chekhov has nothing to say to a black woman." This commentator rejects the extreme views of both the radicals who would have all students read material reflecting their own subcultures and the "ultraradicals" who attack "the 'privileging' of 'texts' . . . and think one might as well spend one's college years deconstructing *Leave It to Beaver.*" However, she ultimately sees the whole enterprise as foolish, a phenomenon that would not occur in a country of real readers. In such a country, the "top-ten list" would represent only a fraction of what people would read in a lifetime and would therefore be inconsequential. In our society, the debate over the canon rests on an image of culture as "medicinal." Consuming the right kind of culture will produce healthy and desirable people. "The culture debaters turn out to share a secret suspicion of culture itself, as well as the anti-pornographer's belief that there is a simple, one-to-one correlation between books and behavior" (Pollitt 1991, 331).

Others who criticize the extremes on all sides likewise perceive culture as continually changing and being renegotiated. If American culture is always and necessarily a work in progress, says another critic, attempts by both the Right and the Left to fix it at any point do not make sense. There cannot be "only one path to virtuous American-ness" (Hughes 1992a, 45). In the current debates, there is no longer a Left and a Right, "just two puritan sects—one saying obscure Third World authors will replace Milton" and the other unable to "mount a satisfactory defense since it has burned most of its bridges to the culture at large." Those who rail against multiculturalism and those who "sanctify grievance" are equally to blame. Accusations of "a new McCarthyism of the left" are absurd, since "no conservative academics have been fired by the lefty thought police" (46). Yet the "extremists" of political correctness are equally absurd in their view that only blacks can write about slavery and only the oppressed deserve credibility (48).

Multiculturalism itself is to be approved of in its moderate versions but not as presented by its extremist advocates. Thus, "if multiculturalism is about learning to see through borders, one can be all in favor of it," but if it means "cultural separatism," one cannot (Hughes 1992a, 47). Multiculturalist prodding has made American history "more inclusive, representative, and accurate." But this change has failed to satisfy those multiculturalists who prefer "to describe the Western tradition as just one of many equally important contributors to the American identity" and thus "make hash of history" (P. Gray 1991, 16).

The very intensity of the debates about the canon or multicultural education also comes in for some criticism. One writer suggests that both sides should "lighten up." Conservatives must "realize that criticisms of the great books approach to learning do not amount to totalitarianism. And the advocates of multiculturalism need to regain the sense of humor that enabled their predecessors . . . to coin the term P.C. years ago—not in arrogance but in self-mockery" (Ehrenreich 1991, 84).

Another moderating view takes the culture warriors to task for confusion or simplification. Conservatives are accused of conflating "the whole intellectual heritage of the West with . . . capitalism and representative democracy," even though any great books curriculum would include the "hierarchical totalitarianism of Plato" and the "leveling totalitarianism of Marx" as well as novelists and poets who do not sing the praises of capitalism (Stanford 1989, 18). The allegation on the left that the traditional curriculum reinforces the status quo is equally wrongheaded, since Marx, Darwin, Nietzsche, and Freud hardly serve as "an inducement for voting Republican" (20).

Because moderation is so often equated with the good, claiming a position at the center is often seen as desirable. One conservative writer therefore rejects the right of liberals such as Robert Hughes or Arthur Schlesinger Jr. to appropriate the center for themselves. Terry Teachout argues that the center is getting crowded as liberals and "ageing leftists" now attack the "new left-wing cultural orthodoxy" that previously came in for criticism only from the right (1992, 53). This is progress of a sort, but the liberal centrists still cling to the idea that "there are two equally ominous threats to high culture, one from the Left and one from the Right." In truth, few conservative politicians take any interest in culture. "There certainly are right-wing zealots afoot, but they are mainly interested in such things as abortion, free condoms, and prayer in the schools, not deconstruction, phallocentrism, and clitoral hermeneutics" (54).

But while all are hostile or derisive toward those they consider extremists, the existence of a "center" is often questioned. Thus, Hughes, one of the liberals Teachout cites as attempting to monopolize the center, argues that there really is no such thing as a center. Conservatives such as Jesse Helms, Hughes maintains, believe that the National Endowment for the Arts must not stray "from what he fancies to be the center line of American ethical belief. The truth is, of course, that no such line exists—not in a society as vast, various and eclectic as the real America" (1989, 82). In similar fashion, a progressive contends that government funding for the arts cannot rely on "community standards" because this "rests on the idea of a homogenous community, with clearly demarcated standards, which does not in fact exist" (Mattick 1990, 357). And while Teachout mocks liberals for their eagerness to place themselves in the desirable center, he, too, suggests that the center does not exist. There is only good and bad, right and wrong. Liberals' center-seeking pattern persists because the "idea of choosing sides in the culture war makes them intensely uncomfortable" (1992, 54). Many other culture warriors undoubtedly would agree with Teachout that there is right and wrong and that they are in the right.

One of the major books in the canon wars dispute, Roger Kimball's *Tenured Radicals* (1990), closes by suggesting that the center has collapsed. "What we have witnessed is nothing less than the occupation of the center by a new academic establishment, the establishment of tenured radicals" (189). In response, Russell Jacoby suggests that conservatives have written the major books in the canon wars because the "leftist academics" are "secure employees of mainstream institutions." Because they are insiders, not outsiders, they "attack hegemony and conservatism from within hegemonic and conservative institutions" (1994, 162).

In fact, a 2006 national survey of political opinion among faculty members suggests that academics have become more centrist, at the expense largely of the conservatives, though there are also fewer liberals today than there were in 1969. Indeed, more faculty now describe themselves as "moderate" (47 percent) than as either liberal (44 percent) or conservative (9 percent), and the youngest cohort (those between the ages of twenty-six and thirty-five) contains the highest proportion of moderates and the lowest proportion of liberals (Gross and Simmons 2007; see also Zipp and Fenwick 2006).

Centrism or moderation is also an appealing position with respect to the issue of support for the arts. In the campaign against the National Endowment for the Arts, two forms of extremism are seen: the "self-appointed political guardians of American virtue" and those "who think any denial of a grant to 'experimental' art is cultural fascism." Most Americans lie between these extremes, supporting government funding for the arts with little government control (Hughes 1992b, 43). Put slightly differently, it is not a violation of the First Amendment to criticize the National Endowment for the Arts (as some on the left would have it), nor should art be tame, old, and heterosexual (as some on the right would have it) (Editorial 1990a, 7). As to the art itself, "for every neoconservative highbrow who denies that art can exist in the schlock-swollen flood of popular culture, there is a postmodernist leveler who insists that every morsel of schlock is art" (Bayles 1994, 65).

One spokesman for the arts sees them as being attacked from the left, the right, *and* the center. The politicization of the National Endowment for the Arts, Brustein argues, has brought the "assumption that any resources derived from the taxpayer's pocketbook should be distributed according to the taxpayer's preferences" rather than using expert judgment. So art is now attacked by "the politically correct left," "the right-wing minions of moral correctness," and "the middlebrow arbiters of culture . . . who bark at anything not immediately familiar to the middle-class public." Each side claims "endorsement from the majority." For the Right, this majority usually means "the clean-cut Americans who celebrate Thanksgiving in Norman Rockwell paintings." For the Left, it means "all those previously excluded from the cultural banquet"—in other words, multiculturalism and cultural diversity. For the center, it means effectively the marketplace's "bottom line" (1997d, 31–32).

The issues of family values and feminism also elicit writing of the "plague on all your houses" variety. A progressive feminist writer chooses to mock all sides. It is so easy, she says, to support "family values" and to find the culprits who are undermining it. "The right blames a left-wing cultural conspiracy: obscene rock lyrics, sex education, abortion, prayerless schools, working mothers, promiscuity, homosexuality, decline of respect for authority and hard work, welfare and, of course, feminism. . . . The left blames the ideology of postindustrial capitalism: consumerism, individualism, selfishness, alienation, lack of social supports for parents and children, atrophied communities, welfare and feminism. The center agonizes over teen sex, welfare moms, crime and divorce, unsure what the causes are beyond some sort of moral failure—probably related to feminism" (Pollitt 1992a, 88, 90). Though this is clearly a defense of the ever-beleaguered feminists, it is also a mockery of the rhetoric of family values.

Another commentator, not wedded to feminism, mocks both the feminists and the traditionalists who oppose them, assailing both "victim feminism" and "victim antifeminism." Conservatives who see women as miserable because of the changes wrought by feminism manifest a "pessimistic view" that "probably bears about the same relation to reality as the feminist view that discrimination and bias against women are running rampant in America." Both sides view the problems of contemporary women as social problems, so that feminists see stay-at-home mothers as victims of patriarchal oppression, while conservatives see working mothers as victims of feminist cultural coercion. The ideologies of both sides are "irrelevant to the lives of the majority of men and women who are interested neither in gender warfare nor in going back to a mythical idyllic past but are trying to find their own balance between the modern and the traditional" (Cathy Young 1999, 20–21). Once again, only the sensible moderates see things clearly.

Moderation may take the form of simply heaping epithets on both sides, as when Krauthammer proposes respect for civil religion while deriding "Bible thumpers" and "zealous relic-hunting secularists" (1984, 16). The idea of moderation may suggest that a particular population does not look like the descriptions given to it by the extremists. Thus, a gay writer suggests that neither the queers who spout liberation from convention nor the conservatives who advocate adherence to convention represent the gay population. Most gays combine "sex and taxes, passion and furniture," and "lesbian and gay differences are more various—and more public—than either Helms can hope to contain or than any few lesbian, gay or queer commentators can claim publicly to represent" (Abraham 1997, 6).

Another expression of moderation lies in finding the common ground between what appear to be extremes. Thus, one liberal writer suggests that the current culture war is not really about the "final battle between good and evil." Both sides share the goal of worldly success but reject the "purely individual strategy of salvation" of the how-to-get-rich gurus. Both seek "social rather than purely individual solutions to the achievement of the good life." But both operate within the confines of modern capitalism and can therefore steer things only a bit to the right or the left (Judis 1999, 56). In a rather different vein, a critic of both creationism and the "multicultural left" notes that both worldviews aim to indoctrinate children rather than encouraging them to make up their own minds. The creationists who say that evolution and creationism should receive equal time in schools are succumbing to the "relativistic trope" of multiculturalism despite their horror at the multiculturalists' insistence that "there is no single Truth." But a similar contradiction plagues the multiculturalists, who welcome the perspectives of gays, women, and racial minorities but not those of fundamentalist Christians (Zimmerman 1999, 13–14).

Even in such a seemingly irreconcilable argument as that between evolution and creationism, the sounds of moderation can be heard as both the creationists and those who use Darwinist explanations of all behavior are taken to task for similar failings. "In their insistence that the meaning of human life stands or falls on the truth or falsehood of evolution, the creationists resemble certain Darwinians who derive ethics from paleontology and biology, and have scientific explanations for the entirety of emotional and cultural life, and conflate the truths of evolution with a materialist view of human existence. . . . The explanations of the determinist Darwinians are not scientific, they are scientistic; and scientism, too, is only a faith" (Editorial 1999, 12). Similarly, a writer suggests that the current arguments are akin to a battle "between two 19th century fundamentalisms, one religious, the other scientific" (Glynn 1999, 44).

There is also a kind of centrism in such statements as, "In culture this year, as in politics, the extremes are touching. The tribunes of the people have joined forces with the conglomerated princes of capitalist darkness to defend the right of Ice-T and Body Count to arouse their listeners with fantasies of cop-killing" (Editorial 1992, 7). Being derisive about both sides—the "extremes"—is another typical manifestation of moderation. On the abortion issue, for example, numerous commentators see bad behavior or hypocrisy on both sides. "For a decade and a half, the abortion issue has made extremists and hypocrites of us all—pro-choicers enshrining trimesters in the Constitution, pro-lifers using an ostensible concern for the mothers' health to restrict the mother's freedom of choice" (Kinsley 1989, 96).

Finally, a kind of moderation is expressed in the repeated suggestion that culture warriors offer extremist proclamations for fund-raising purposes. A liberal notes that while the actual dollar amounts of government funding for the arts are trivial, conservatives use the issue in their direct-mail fund-raising as a "hot-button" issue (Kinsley 1992a, 6). And a conservative says that conservatives have failed to acknowledge all the ways in which they have been winning the culture wars—with divorce, illegitimacy, teen sexual activity, abortion, crime, and suicide rates all falling—because to do so would not be good for fund-raising; the apocalyptic style sells (Nadler 1998, 30).

If moderation has been something of a constant in American culture, is anything new about its current manifestations? To the degree that elites are now more polarized than was previously the case, moderation is unusual because it represents antipolarization among the polarized. The political pressures toward centrism present difficult choices for those whose views represent polar extremes in a culture war. In addition, the new awareness of subcultural variations in the population makes it more difficult to find the "center."

CHAPTER 8

Culture, Class, and American Exceptionalism

While this volume argues that there is no culture war, just newer iterations of long-standing American cultural dilemmas, the rhetoric and the social movements associated with the "culture wars" raise questions about the nature of the divisions within contemporary American society. Why is a culture war perceived to have broken out in the late 1980s and early 1990s? Are cultural issues generally displacing economic ones as the basis of political allegiances? Is the American pattern exceptional? What role does class division play within current American politics? Has polarization increased within the American polity? Do the presidential elections since 2000 exemplify the culture wars, with Sarah Palin the latest incarnation thereof? How do issues of economics versus culture play out in the internal discord of the partisans?

Cultural Politics

Inglehart's work on the movement from "materialism" to "postmaterialism" in European societies (1977) drew attention to the idea that cultural politics had become significant in advanced industrial societies. In the

American context, some scholars have argued that cultural or ethnoreligious conflicts have long been primary, though economic problems lead to their suppression at various times (Rae 1992). Other scholars contend that economic concerns dominated American politics from 1896 to 1964, when cultural politics came to the fore. In this new politics, Republicans increasingly supported the traditional values of an inherited culture, while Democrats embraced the rationalistic values of a progressive culture (Shafer 1985). Even economic and welfare issues came to be seen in cultural terms. Republicans objected to Democratic welfare state policies not only because of their high costs but because they "enshrined the values of dependency," and Democrats objected to the Republican reliance on the private sector not only because it lacked compassion but also because it ignored the demands of the new cultural claimants—especially feminists and homosexuals—who needed governmental action (227). Feminists, homosexuals, environmentalists, and peace movement activists helped fuel the Democrats' cultural politics, while religious evangelicals came to be central to the new Republican cultural politics.

The emergence of cultural politics exacerbated the internal divisions within both parties. Republicans suffered from the split between social and economic conservatives, who often represented different social class groups. On the Democratic side, division arose between progressive convention delegates and a heavily traditional rank and file (Shafer 1985, 230).

But the image of a culture war in which Democrats have become the party of religious modernists (from all faiths), while the Republicans are the party of religious conservatives (again, of all kinds) has not come to pass (Layman 2001, 301; Manza and Brooks 1997, 59). And the origins of any division between the parties along cultural/religious lines remain a matter of some dispute. Did the Republicans, as the minority party, see advantage in a campaign of "moral restoration"? (Fiorina, Abrams, and Pope 2005, 141; Leege et al. 2002). Or did the Democrats begin the cleavage when ultraliberal delegates took over the party's 1972 convention and focused on cultural issues (Layman 2001)?

In the first scenario, the Republican Party sought to chip away at the Democrats' "old New Deal coalition" by using cultural issues as a wedge, beginning with race in the 1960s, adding religion and gender in the 1970s, and thereafter "by cumulating the symbols of the 1960s counterculture (drugs, sexual permissiveness, lack of respect for traditional ways, etc.). [Later] as Republican campaigners gave increasing voice to their fears about moral degradation in America, evangelical Protestants mobilized heavily and entered the party's core by the 1990s" (Leege et al. 2002, 89).

Through the alternative lens, George McGovern, the 1972 Democratic presidential nominee, began the cultural divide by attempting to appeal to young people's "cultural liberalism" and antiwar sentiments. As these "secular activists" entered Democratic Party politics, they "shifted the party's mean position on cultural matters to the left." Not until 1980 did the minority Republican Party take "clear steps toward religious and cultural conservatism" (Layman 2001, 99, 306).

The rubric of a culture war, enunciated by Patrick Buchanan in 1992, has been seen as a social construction that helps conservatives by knitting together disparate issues into "a compelling narrative frame." It "invites religious conservatives to make their faith (rather than their gender, age, race, occupation, or neighborhood) their primary identity and to define this identity as germane to many political positions" (DiMaggio 2003, 92–93). To be sure, progressives made use of the same sort of logic, as seen, for example, in an editorial in *The Nation,* before the "culture war" idea had been widely propagated and discussed. The editorial responds to President Ronald Reagan's proposed constitutional amendment in favor of school prayer by suggesting that the matter does not simply involve constitutional arguments but rather is part of a campaign to impose right-wing cultural hegemony: "There's a cultural war on, and it will not be won by lawyers and logic alone" (Editorial 1984, 308).

An alignment between political parties and particular cultural positions is certainly not new in American life. Indeed, in the late nineteenth century, as today, the Republican Party supported "the pietist position that the state should regulate personal behavior to prevent sinners from engaging in public affronts to decency and virtue." As a result, the vast majority of northern Protestants—workers, farmers, and businessmen alike—supported the Republicans, while arrayed against them was "a Democratic coalition of the targets of pietistic wrath: slaveholders and later most white Southerners, Catholics, nonpietistic Protestant immigrants, . . . drinkers, and the wider urban subcultures of plebeian sensual pleasures." Immigrants and Catholic workers and businessmen supported the Democrats

(Oestreicher 1988, 1262). Such voting alignments suggest the significance of cultural rather than class politics. Issues such as "prohibition, enforced Sabbath observance, Bible reading in schools, immigration restriction, and bilingualism . . . mattered deeply to most Americans," and they voted accordingly (1275).

This phenomenon does not mean, however, that workers lacked class sentiments but merely suggests that the parties had not mobilized voters along class lines. The situation changed, of course, in the aftermath of the Great Depression, when class sentiments *were* translated into political consciousness (Oestreicher 1988, 1283). Yet even after class awareness trumped cultural and religious factors so that workers were much more likely to be Democrats than were professionals and business executives, Catholic workers remained more likely to be Democratic than were nonsouthern white Protestant workers (1264).

In this newer understanding of American history, cultural (or "ethnocultural" or "ethnoreligious") conflicts have long been most important. Such conflicts simply have recently reemerged after having been "temporarily suppressed by the class-based party politics of the New Deal era" (Rae 1992, 629). As the New Deal class alignments broke down during the 1960s, moral and cultural questions again came to the forefront. Even though the progressives had brought economic issues to the forefront between 1900 and 1916, their emphasis on "corruption" and "reform" made for "a powerful ethno-cultural resonance" (631). It is difficult to determine whether cultural conflicts have truly been primary in American politics or whether the newfound scholarly interest in cultural issues has made this seem to be the case. One must also be cautious to avoid assuming any kind of zero-sum relationship between class and cultural politics. Furthermore, recent American politics have strongly featured the cultural rather than economic aspects of social class.

Those who see American history as steeped in cultural conflict tend to inflate the realm of cultural issues. One could certainly quarrel with the idea that foreign policy or national security issues, for example, "are also rooted in cultural differences" (Rae 1992, 629) or with the idea that race is a cultural issue. In the context of late-twentieth-century political analysis, is race really a cultural issue rather than a question of the distribution of economic and political power? If multiculturalism and political correctness became political issues during the 1990s, how much of this language served as a cover for economic and political issues? Yet some analysts of American politics tend to treat race as a cultural factor—for example, when Leege and his colleagues suggest that no other cultural factor had the staying power of race between 1960 and 1996 (2002, 193).

Of interest, too, is the question raised by McCormick (1974, 371–72): if the majority of nineteenth-century voters cared mostly about cultural matters, why were only a small proportion of public policies culturally oriented? Why was so much government activity devoted to economic affairs? And even if a policy matter is a clearly cultural one—as was the case with temperance, for example—the meaning of voter reaction is not entirely clear. Was the fight over alcohol a matter of conflicting religious beliefs, differing lifestyles, or simple hatred for out-groups? Any or all might have been involved (367), as were class differences communicated in symbolic terms. Moreover, for all the talk of culture wars in American politics during the early 1990s, the Contract with America issued by the newly dominant congressional Republicans in 1994 "did not include a word about cultural or moral issues" (Layman 2001, 247). It did address some of these issues by indirection—for example, it argued against giving welfare payments to mothers who are minors and in favor of tax incentives for adoption and of stronger child pornography laws.

Few would deny, however, that precursors to modern-day culture wars are apparent in nineteenth-century American politics. Disputes about laws regarding the Sabbath or temperance or the abolition of slavery produced splits between those religious groups that favored government intervention to promote and protect morality and those that favored government neutrality. But then as now, issues of class and culture were not mutually exclusive; voters cared about both. When late-nineteenth- or early-twentieth-century workers participated simultaneously in work-based oppositional subcultures and neighborhood-based ethnic groups and churches that dictated different views, the prevailing attitude depended on the concrete choices and circumstances at hand. Modern-day Kansans who respond to Republican Party appeals seemingly against their class interests (Thomas Frank 2005) may also be acting on the basis of an antigovernment populism that links government actions to support for racial minorities and the "underclass."

Contemporary cultural politics may differ from earlier incarnations in being more self-conscious. Once the disputes became framed as a culture war, proponents on all sides sought to influence the culture by securing greater prominence for their perspectives. Organizations formed to track and publicize the coverage of various issues in the media, in school textbooks, and in college courses.

Beginning in the 1980s, for example, a voluminous literature appeared on the question of whether religion is absent or marginalized in American history textbooks. A study suggesting that such was the case received widespread publicity and generated further studies and lobbying. Curiously, however, a follow-on study that examined high school history textbooks since the late nineteenth century discovered that texts in the 1980s actually provided more coverage of fifteen major religious events than did those of the late nineteenth century. And an examination of more recent events in religious history in textbooks of the 1950s showed that they offered considerably less coverage than did textbooks published thirty years later. When still more recent events were examined and texts of the 1980s were compared with those of the 1990s, the latter showed significantly more coverage of both the recent events and the entire chronology. The author concluded that "the criticisms of the secondary school textbooks of the 1980s have apparently had an impact" (Carleton W. Young 1995, 270). Conversely, an American historian whose scholarly work focuses on religious history suggested that despite burgeoning scholarly interest, history textbooks tend to minimize discussions of religion largely to avoid controversy and potential parental reactions. "Ironically," he noted, "religion continues to receive insufficient attention" at least in part because of the politicization of the issue (Paul Boyer 1996, 205).

It is perhaps ironic, too, that for all the talk about how 1960s radicals have infiltrated academe, college-level American history textbooks published during the 1990s offer little in the way of sympathetic treatments of either the New Left or the counterculture. Discussions of the counterculture tend to be dismissive, and there is little examination of the connection between the counterculture and the New Left or of the enduring political consequences of these movements. However, the main culprit here may be not a heightened sensitivity to conservative criticism but rather "the triumph of multiculturalism on the political Left." The counterculture and the New Left are marginalized because "middle-class white radicals fit only uneasily into this story line" (Schulman 1999, 1533).

American Exceptionalism?

While cultural issues have become more significant politically in many of the affluent industrialized societies, value conflicts in the United States appear to differ from those in European nations. Affluent middle-class citizens elsewhere have moved to the left in support of such "postmaterialist" concerns as the environment and women's rights, while working-class citizens retain "materialist" values in support of economic growth and military security. In the United States, by contrast, progressive postmaterialist influences have brought forth a countermovement not from working-class materialists but from theologically conservative Christians (Layman and Carmines 1997, 753). As an example, only in the United States has a major political party included opposition to evolution as part of its political platform (Jon D. Miller, Scott, and Okamoto 2006, 766).

Unlike the situation in much of Europe, little connection exists in the United States between one's attitudes toward materialism or postmaterialism and one's opinions about abortion, women's rights, and alternative lifestyles. Opinions on these issues seem to be influenced more by "variables such as Jewish faith, church attendance, evangelicalism, and moral traditionalism that are linked directly to religious and moral values. Perhaps in the more secular environment of Western Europe these religious factors play less of a role in shaping cultural issue attitudes" (Carmines and Layman 1997, 304). Using American data, neither income nor age predicts materialism or postmaterialism, and positions on these indexes do not predict attitudes on social and political issues (Darren W. Davis and Davenport 1999, 662; Darren W. Davis 2000, 471).

The United States is indeed a "deviant case." Data from the World Values Survey illustrate that *preindustrial* societies tend to show "deference to parental authority, and the importance of family life, and are relatively authoritarian; most of them place strong emphasis on religion. Advanced industrial societies tend to have the opposite characteristics." The United States remains an exception to the cultural patterns of most other advanced industrial societies (Inglehart and Baker 2000, 23–24, 31). And while nations that resemble the United States—Canada, Britain, and Australia, for example—showed an increase in secular-rational values between the administration of the 1981 survey and those in the 1990s, the United States showed a very slight decrease in these values (40).

American society is exceptional, as Lipset and others have argued, because what makes one American is not birth or ancestry but subscribing to the American Creed. The United States started from a revolution and "has defined its raison d'etre ideologically" (Lipset 1996, 18). Americans "feel emotionally connected to one another" because of their shared "ideals, values, and aspirations. . . . This ideational foundation of America is a chief feature of American exceptionalism" (Baker 2005, 174). If American society rests on shared ideas, then the nature of these ideas would appear to be critical to understanding American exceptionalism. Yet Lipset and Baker emphasize very different core values. Lipset emphasizes individualism and voluntarism, whereas Baker believes that the key to the American culture lies in adherence to traditional moral authority. "America's traditional values—strong beliefs in religion and God, family values, absolute moral authority, national pride, and so on—are fundamental to what it means to be American" (Baker 2005, 54).

The relative lack of class consciousness and of political organizing along class lines and the absence of a socialist party of any strength have long been seen as part of "American exceptionalism." In this understanding, the sheer strength of U.S. economic individualism, coupled with animosity toward government power, rendered Americans unreceptive to any socialist movement. Lacking a history of feudalism, Americans were "born equal" and hence saw no need for European-style class politics. As a result, "even when Franklin Roosevelt adopted many of the quasi-collectivist measures of the European Liberal reformers, he did not use their language of class," and supporters of the New Deal did not drift into socialism any more than their progressive predecessors had. Early-twentieth-century progressive reformers championed individual social mobility through hard work and achievement (Hartz 1955, 205, 235).

In the late 1820s, workingmen's parties received substantial support in such major American cities as New York, Boston, and Philadelphia, garnering 10–15 percent of the vote in local elections. But their version of equality did not exclude private property or individual competition. Rather, they sought greater equality of opportunity. Thus, they proposed state financing of boarding schools so that all children could be raised in a common atmosphere and class-based advantages would be eliminated (Lipset 1996, 114). Wildavsky has suggested that this belief that "equality of opportunity, meticulously followed, would lead to an approximation of equality of result . . . made the United States truly exceptional" (1987, 19). Seen in a somewhat different light, instead of the usual class-related struggles, the late-nineteenth-century United States saw a kind of working-class republicanism that perceived a "contradiction between republican traditions of individual rights and personal independence and the realities of increasingly regimented lives and authoritarian work disciplines" (Oestreicher 1988, 1259). In this version, the class struggle was tinged with cultural considerations.

American workers may have lacked the class consciousness of many of their European counterparts but were by no means the bourgeois individualists that the American exceptionalism thesis suggests. Indeed, the frequency of strikes in the United States between 1902 and 1905 was higher than that in nine out of ten European countries for which data are available (Oestreicher 1988, 1257). Because U.S. workers did not have to struggle for the franchise, they were more easily drawn into cross-class coalition politics. But American labor unions—even the American Federation of Labor—were not apolitical (Kimeldorf and Stepan-Norris 1992, 496–97).

The thesis of American exceptionalism is something of an oversimplification insofar as it posits a single or unitary European pattern of working-class politics against which to measure American behavior. Neither in the period before World War I nor in the post–World War II era did Britain, France, and Germany have the same kind of labor movements and class politics (Kimeldorf and Stepan-Norris 1992; M. Nolan 1997; Tyrrell 1991). Weakness in socialist movements also characterized U.S. neighbors—neither Canada nor Mexico had strong socialist parties (Rodgers 2004, 40).

Some practitioners of the thesis of American exceptionalism overemphasize the significance of static values to the exclusion of both historical contingencies and the actions of particular political and institutional entities. Perhaps the most serious criticism of the thesis, however, is its tendency toward "chauvinistic nationalism" (Blau 2007, 1064). Expressions of such sentiments concerned critics in light of the return of the rhetoric of American exceptionalism in the aftermath of the 9/11 terrorist attacks (Blau 2007; Rodgers 2004).

Proponents of the idea of American exceptionalism are aware of this criticism and clearly assert that they do not intend exceptionalism to mean superiority. Lipset, for example, subtitled his book on the subject, "A Double-Edged Sword." He suggested that such "negative traits" as income inequality and high crime rates are "inherently linked" to American institutions. The American Creed, he argues, "fosters a high sense of personal responsibility, independent initiative, and voluntarism even as it also encourages self-serving behavior, atomism, and a disregard for communal good." It promotes excessive greed and self-promotion. Yet the emphasis on individualism also "represents a tremendous asset, encouraging the self-reflection necessary for responsible judgment, for fostering the strength of voluntary communal and civic bonds, for principled opposition to wars, and for patriotism" (1996, 268). On balance, Lipset's assessment of the costs and benefits of American individualism and voluntarism (major components of its exceptionalism) hardly seems impartial.

An uglier example of the negative side of American exceptionalism appears in the idea that racism in the United States has been particularly virulent precisely because of the individualistic and egalitarian nature of the American Creed. Thus, white prejudice against blacks "set them apart and denied their humanity more thoroughly than would the means of enforcing subordination in a less professedly democratic and more consistently hierarchical society" (Fredrickson 1995, 594).

For all the voluminous argumentation and scholarship about American exceptionalism, use of the term retains a Rorschach-like quality, in much the same way that *multiculturalism* evokes conflicting or contradictory images. Thus, Lipset uses survey data to support the idea that Americans to this day are more supportive of individualism than of egalitarian outcomes and are more opposed to social welfare policies than their European counterparts. Though there is support for social equality (at least for all white men), economic individualism remains dominant among the American populace. American exceptionalism reigns. But Wildavsky sees an end to American exceptionalism in contemporary Americans' willingness to believe that society is at least partly responsible for the ills that befall the poor, minorities, and women. Once Americans believe, as they now do, that "liberty and equality, competition and fair-shares are compatible with each other," American exceptionalism is dead (Wildavsky 1991, 137). For Daniel Bell, writing in 1975, the key to American exceptionalism lies in a "common political faith" that would allow American society to "escape the ideological vicissitudes and divisive passions of the European polity." This faith rests on "being entirely a middle-class society, without aristocracy or boheme. . . . As a liberal society providing individual opportunity, safeguarding liberties, and expanding the standard of living, it would escape the disaffection of the intelligentsia, the resentment of the poor, the frustrations of the young. . . . Today, the belief in American exceptionalism has vanished" (197).

Fourteen years later, however, Bell was once again willing to entertain the idea that an American exceptionalism existed. It resided in the fact that the United States "has been the complete civil society, perhaps the only one in political history" (1989, 48). The state always had a limited role. Even during periods of class warfare, which were at times of greater intensity than in Europe, workers' movements were not accompanied by attempts to seize state power. As the power of the central government grew beginning in the 1930s, the idea of civil society was threatened. But it is now revivified, emphasizing voluntary association, church, and community (56). Bell rejects the idea that the absence of socialist movements and the presence of evangelical and fundamentalist religious movements make for American exceptionalism. In both cases, he asserts, there are no general rules or laws of development against which to view the American case as exceptional. Rather, the strength of voluntary church and community organizations defines American exceptionalism.

Bell's definition of American exceptionalism does not accord with that of most commentators, who see it as including the absence of class consciousness and socialist movements, the presence of strong religious movements, and greater levels of individualism and voluntarism than are present elsewhere. Though historians are generally more dismissive of the idea of American exceptionalism than sociologists and political scientists have been, one American historian takes a somewhat different perspective, noting that "American exceptionalism is as old as the nation itself and, equally important, has played an integral part in the society's sense of its own identity" (Kammen 1993, 6). Another historian hostile to the idea of American exceptionalism also concedes that "in popular culture, exceptionalism remains strong" (Tyrrell 1991, 1032).

While the idea of American exceptionalism originated with eighteenth-century European observers who saw the United States as being free of "Old

World social evils," it was picked up by ordinary Americans in the nineteenth century and has remained a part of American consciousness. Notwithstanding the realities that Puritan religious leaders "openly embraced orthodoxy—banishing dissidents, whipping Baptists, even executing Quakers" and that "colonial legislators had been much more likely to jail their critics than to protect their speech," freedom of religion and freedom of speech became the "stuff of culture" in the United States. So, too, did the main tenets of American exceptionalism: autonomous individuals, a clean slate (denying history), and a belief in a uniform human nature that attributes universality to particular social traits. "Thinking that we create our own identities highlights volition and autonomy and minimizes the categorical force of race and gender in shaping our social existence. . . . Multicultural historians contest these comfortable illusions" (Appleby 1992, 420, 422, 425, 426 427).

Several points are of particular interest in this brief overview of debates about American exceptionalism. The first is that while historians and social scientists may engage in comparative studies to determine if and how the United States may be exceptional, American cultural lore has long accepted the idea. The second is the realization that even our understanding of American exceptionalism is fraught with uncertainty stemming from the individualism/republicanism dilemma and adherence to traditional versus self-expressive values. Are we exceptional because of our supreme individualism or because of our civic virtue? Is class conflict in the United States diminished by our unwillingness to enlarge the scope of government or by our refusal to accept the importance of groups and group cultures? Does our cultural unity rest on devotion to individualism or to traditional moral authority?

What may make the American culture wars exceptional, however, is the relative strength of the religious dimension. European politics is far less involved with such issues as abortion, gay rights, and prayer in the schools, though multiculturalism is becoming contentious in many countries and recent changes in the leadership of the Catholic Church have generated some renewed attention to abortion issues in Spain and Italy. Nevertheless, only in the United States has a major political party supported creationism; only the United States has instituted prohibition against alcohol and a ban on prostitution. Abortion as an issue has evoked stronger responses in the United States than in Europe's Catholic countries, where church opposition to abortion does not produce the "extreme actions" of their American coreligionists who "have assimilated to Protestant moralistic styles" (Lipset 1996, 67). And one might wonder how many European sociologists would agree that politics is fundamentally a struggle for power that "is in large part a struggle between competing truth claims which are, by their very nature 'religious' in character if not in content" (Hunter 1991, 58).

There is little doubt that those who attend church frequently have come to differ in both their voting patterns and their attitudes from those who seldom or never attend church. Even analysts who view the culture war idea as an exaggeration relevant only to partisan elites note the significance of church attendance in presidential voting in the elections of 1992–2000. Controlling for party, ideology, presidential performance, and candidate evaluation, church attendance was a highly significant predictor of presidential voting (Fiorina, Abrams, and Pope 2005, 101). In the 2004 election, a large difference existed in the voting behaviors and attitudes of white voters who regularly attended church and those who seldom or never did so (Abramowitz and Saunders 2005). And this pattern continued through the 2008 election, though Barack Obama won a slightly larger share of the votes of those who attend church more frequently than once a week than did John Kerry in 2004 and Al Gore in 2000 (Pew Forum 2008a).

The Continuing Significance of Class, Race, and Gender

While the United States may have had periods of greater class awareness than its mythology allows for, it is nevertheless a society that often has difficulty talking directly about social class, a society in which status injuries may remain "hidden" (Sennett and Cobb 1972). Not surprisingly, therefore, cultural issues serve as a convenient surrogate for social class. On the right, references to the "liberal elite," the "establishment," or the "new class" all invoke images not of money and achievement—which are beyond reproach in the American mainstream—but of intellectual snobbery and rarefied tastes. On the left, issues of race, ethnicity, and gender—replete with their "cultural" components—may serve as surrogates for social class. And the upsurge of religious sentiment associated with the culture wars has had strongly populist overtones, suggesting "protest and resistance against a secular elite" (P. L. Berger 1999, 11).

The increased significance of religious involvement does not mean that class is irrelevant in American political affiliations and voting. Indeed, from the 1970s to 2000, voting was more affected by differences in family income than by religious differences (Greeley and Hout 2006, 66). Who votes and who does not is certainly class related. While race and gender have increased in significance in presidential voting, class has remained stable (C. Brooks and Manza 1997). For all of religion's newfound significance in American politics, religious traditionalists with low incomes and no college education have not become much more Republican than religious modernists at the same status level (Layman 2001, 315).

The connection between class and voting becomes blurred, however, as both Left and Right are bifurcated. Just as social and economic conservatives often come from different social class groups, so too some analysts now see "two Lefts," one working class, the other middle class and "postmaterialist" (Hout, Brooks, and Manza 1995, 808). Who votes for which party may also depend on the ways in which political parties shape their appeals to voters (Manza, Hout, and Brooks 1995). The rightward turn of the Democratic Party on fiscal issues since the early 1990s, for example, made Democrats less distinguishable from Republicans, a development that may have complicated party identifications along class lines (Kaufmann 2002, 290).

Further complicating the situation is the fact that social class encompasses both economic and status dimensions. One study using British data finds that class factors clearly correlate with support for left or right parties, but status factors are responsible for attitudes on a libertarianism-authoritarianism scale. Higher-status groups are more likely to espouse libertarian rather than authoritarian views, disagreeing with such statements as "Censorship of films and magazines is necessary to uphold moral standards" and "Schools should teach children to obey authority" (Chan and Goldthorpe 2007).

The simple division into Left and Right does not adequately measure political attitudes precisely because it omits this dimension of libertarian versus authoritarian attitudes (Duch and Strom 2004), or what Wildavsky (1987) has called simply "hierarchy." This dimension at times is encompassed within scales that seek to measure other variables. Critics have pointed out that the materialism/postmaterialism scale is contaminated in this way, since items related to authority and the maintenance of social order are included within the "materialism" scales (Flanagan 1987). Perhaps as a result, the data do not confirm the existence of consistent political and social attitudes accompanying the values of materialism/postmaterialism (C. Brooks and Manza 1994; Brown and Carmines 1995; Darren W. Davis 2000; Darren W. Davis and Davenport 1999). The postmaterialist middle class may well have moved left while the working class has moved right (Flanagan 1987, 1305–7). In many countries, the more educated libertarians who had traditionally supported the Right for economic reasons have begun to move to the left for social reasons, while the less educated who had historically voted for the Left for economic reasons have moved to the right because of social issues (Flanagan and Lee 2003). Curiously, well-educated libertarians are more likely than authoritarians to support unions, perhaps because unions are seen as elite-challenging institutions. More likely, however, the union movement now has more white-collar than blue-collar members. The National Education Association in the United States, for example, has become the champion of many items on the New Left agenda (259).

As political parties in most economically developed nations appear to have moved away from an emphasis on class politics (labor and welfare issues) and toward "postindustrial" or "new" politics issues (ecology and the environment, women's rights, gay rights, animal rights, and so on) (Clark 2003), some analysts see a general decline in class politics (Pakulski and Waters 1996, 671). Other observers note that an inverse relationship exists between the strength of class politics and cultural politics. Thus, it has been argued that "culture wars" have come to the fore in American political discourse as a reflection of both the weakening of class politics and increasing contention over the scope of the centralized state. In this understanding, the very success of the limited U.S. class politics in the aftermath of the New Deal—reflected in an increase in welfare state provisions—has reduced its salience. Cutbacks in the welfare state might well revive class politics in the future. In the interim, however, groups have been mobilized when they see their values and norms challenged by a central authority that appears to intrude into the formerly more autonomous realms of family and schooling (Hechter 2004).

Other analysts argue, however, that it is a mistake to make zero-sum assumptions about "class" versus "new" or "postclass" politics, since they obviously coexist (Manza and Brooks 1996, 721). Defenders of the continuing significance of class maintain that one's class location shapes one's attitudes but does so in conjunction with a range of other factors. Moreover, attitudes are "often irreducibly idiographic." After all, it would be "hard to imagine a multivariate regression rooted in social structural variables that would 'predict' that Engels, a wealthy capitalist, would be a supporter of revolutionary socialism" (E. O. Wright 1996, 710). And if one's employment situation in the United States does not predict class loyalties as readily as it might in some European nations, class may still remain relevant in such labor-related issues as whether management should be able to hire replacement workers to break strikes (Gerteis and Savage 1998).

Class also remains relevant insofar as class cultures affect the ways in which people in different class positions organize and interact within social movements. The repeated accusations that movements of gays or feminists, for example, are too "middle class" is generally more a matter of style than of economic interests. Thus, working-class organizations and movements may be more likely to see the world as a matter of competing interests or powers, whereas middle-class organizations more often see the world in terms of opposing ideas (Rose 1997, 480). To be sure, movements that appear to be universal in nature—for example, draft resistance, affirmative action, and land use policies—often disproportionately benefit the middle classes. But even those concerns that do not offer any significant class benefits—for example, preserving obscure species such as the snail darter—may still entail class "interests." Because middle-class members of such organizations seek to define themselves through their work and knowledge, they may pursue their personal identities through engagement with activist social movements. In contrast to middle-class environmental organizations, the working-class antitoxics movement deals with issues of immediate need and challenges the existing system of benefits (483).

In contemporary American society, class is often mentioned alongside race and gender. But class, race, and gender—often jokingly referred to as the "holy trinity"—interact with culture in complex and varying ways. Not only are cultural differences presumed to exist among people of different class, race, and gender, but the imagery and rhetoric associated with each group may have political consequences. The significance of cultural images becomes clear if Thomas Frank (2005) is even partially correct that conservatives have succeeded in painting "liberals" as an "overclass" that dominates the media and the courts, telling "us" how to live. This imagery allows conservatives to distance themselves from elites such as "Hollywood liberals" and to speak instead on behalf of the "common man." Various less powerful groups have also used the rhetoric of culture to attain their goals, as people not previously seen in cultural terms have come to define themselves as worthy subcultures—the handicapped, the deaf, and the obese, for example.

Yet the use of culture as a framing device to attain equal rights does not work equally well for all groups. For example, racial and gender groups have employed culture in different ways. In American society, as Gunnar Myrdal asserted in 1944, the treatment of racial minorities has posed a serious "dilemma." Ideas of white supremacy clearly collided with ideas of egalitarianism. Indeed, as noted earlier, racism in the United States may have been especially virulent because the justification of racial inequality was often accomplished by positing the negative characteristics of nonwhites. A heightened sensitivity to issues of race in the post-civil-rights era, however, may have fastened on cultural dimensions to the detriment of economic and social progress for minority group members. Numerous commentators have noted that talking of "multiculturalism" may be harmful because it ignores the structural and class factors responsible for the failures of racial integration and the economic advancement of African Americans. The terms *multiculturalism* and *diversity* have become euphemisms that "ignore issues of justice, power, and equity" (Andersen 2001, 197). Respondents to in-depth interviews attempting to understand "the deep structure and cultural commonsense implicit in diversity discourse" reveal an "inability to talk about inequality in the context of a conversation about diversity" (J. M. Bell and Hartmann 2007, 898, 910). People appear to want to see "diversity without oppression"—they wish to acknowledge diversity while avoiding "any discussion of race and diversity that points to continuing inequity in group life chances" (Andersen 2001, 195).

An anthropologist with roots in South Africa has pointed out the benign intent underlying the American view that race and culture are independent of each other, that culture is responsible for who people are, and that cultural differences are to be respected. Nevertheless, from a South African perspective, these views would be seen as a justification for apartheid. Racial segregation was seen as proper because "only segregation would preserve cultural differences" (Kuper 1999, xiii). And for many progressive American social scientists, the "culture of poverty" thesis, which appeared to attribute poverty to "values" or "lifestyles," was enough to make all cultural explanations suspect (Patterson 2000, 204).

Cultural explanations seemed to operate differently with respect to inequalities of gender. Here, the distinction between culture and biology was used to support women's emancipation from subordinate roles. "For women, the idea of culture was inextricably part of their emancipation, . . . since changing the conditions of their subordination required the notion that sexual differences were culturally based ('gender')" (McCarthy 1996, 103). Though using culture in opposition to biology has been a successful tactic for women, all females clearly do not share the same values and attitudes. Quite the contrary: an enormous gap exists between the attitudes and concerns of young business and professional women and those of young homemakers. Indeed, one study of cultural politics between 1960 and 1996 finds that the gap between these two groups at the end of the period was "the largest gap of any kind found in our data on cultural politics," larger than racial differences or the "gender gap." The authors of this study suggest that the image of the two parties split along culture war lines is mostly the "end product of the collision among feminists' desire for a more egalitarian society, pietistic churches' sense of threat posed by changing norms, and political elites' needs to amalgamate winning coalitions" (Leege et al. 2002, 229, 217).

Despite the complex relationships among religious, racial, gender, and class identities, proponents of the culture war thesis tend to see the orthodox and progressive worldviews as existing independently of the social groups that espouse them. Empirical data certainly suggest links between a group's interests and its moral values, as in the well-known connection between women's educational and occupational attainment and their attitudes toward abortion (Luker 1984). Moreover, as John H. Evans has pointed out, without group interaction, any worldview would lose plausibility and cease to exist (1997, 397).

The idea that plausibility structures based on social interaction are critical to the maintenance of certain views is nicely illustrated in the case of attitudes toward premarital sexual behavior. Since the early 1970s, a substantial decline has occurred in the number of Americans who adhere to the orthodox Christian view that premarital sex is morally wrong. Only those conservative Protestants who are frequent churchgoers continue to see premarital sex as morally wrong. Conservative Protestants who attend church infrequently do not differ at all from mainline Protestants and Catholics in their attitudes toward premarital sex (L. R. Petersen and Donnenwerth 1997).

But cultural, religious, gender, and class positions are, of course, intertwined in complex ways. Evangelicals who are professional and managerial workers, for example, remain less liberal than other members of their class on attitudes toward sex while accommodating to the liberal ethos of their class on gender roles, abortion, and civil liberties (Schmalzbauer 1993). Once socioeconomic characteristics are controlled, the religiously orthodox are in fact more liberal than the religiously progressive regarding government help in providing jobs, support for organized labor, Social Security spending, and profit-sharing for workers (N. J. Davis and Robinson 1996a). Hostility to public schools that appears to be based on religious or moral orthodoxy is often more a matter of class-based cultural differences. The higher classes see secular school as legitimate, while the bureaucratic and rationalized sphere of public schools is alien to Pentecostals and Charismatics but not to Evangelicals or practicing Catholics (Sikkink 1999, 72, 76).

Intersections between gender and religious divisions are also complex. Women tend to be more supportive than men of government welfare and affirmative action programs and less supportive of war and defense spending. Women are thus more likely to vote Democratic. For religiously modernist (or "progressive") women, a convergence takes place between their cultural/religious and economic/political attitudes. The same is true for religiously traditional (or "orthodox") men. As a result, party identifications are reinforced: modernist women have become more Democratic, and traditional men have become more Republican. But for traditionalist women and modernist men, the conflict between their cultural and economic/political positions makes them likely to be independent of any party affiliation (Layman 2001, 319). Some analysts have suggested that issues of relative group position may be fueling what appear to be debates about cultural issues. White men have become increasingly resistant to the Democratic Party's liberal cultural agenda, possibly because abortion rights, female rights, and gay rights represent challenges from subordinate groups. The social welfare conservatism among lower-income men who might benefit from such programs might also represent a line of defense against such challenges. Women—who are generally more religious and morally traditional than men—have become more liberal in their orientations, while the defense of traditional lifestyles has come to play a more significant role in the political beliefs of men than of women (Kaufman 2002).

Social context matters, too. Thus, residents of states that have more Fundamentalists have more conservative gender attitudes, regardless of personal characteristics. It is not known whether this phenomenon occurs because conservative gender messages are conveyed in social interaction or through the media or the schools or whether some kind of self-selection operates so that people with more conservative gender attitudes are more likely to migrate to such areas (Moore and Vanneman 2003).

Even the role of education in influencing values and politics is less than clear. Over the course of the twentieth century, religious belief and practice increased among college graduates, while the religiosity of those with less than a high school education declined. This convergence appears to suggest that "the more-educated became increasingly integrated into central American institutions, and the less-educated less so" (Fischer and Hout 2006, 211). Yet strong religious beliefs may have more significance in affecting other beliefs than education does. Thus, among those conservative Protestants who reject a literal interpretation of the Bible, having a college or graduate school education substantially increases the probability of a belief in evolution. But among those who take the Bible literally, more education means more dissent from science (Greeley and Hout 2006, 36–37). One longitudinal study found that the negative influence of education on religious involvement came mainly through fostering participation in countercultural protests, an issue unique to the period being studied. Otherwise, education increases religious participation (Sherkat 1998, 1108).

A Polarized Population?

When advocates of the culture wars thesis see a tie between social groups and the two transcendent worldviews, the groups they refer to are political and cultural elites. Although the public as a whole does not show increased polarization of opinion, those who self-identify as Republicans or Democrats have become more polarized (DiMaggio, Evans, and Bryson 1996; J. H. Evans 2003; Layman and Carsey 2002). Whether this "raises troubling questions about the role of political parties in a pluralistic society" (DiMaggio, Evans, and Bryson 1996, 738) or "allows less sophisticated Americans to connect their values and interests with vote choice" (Hetherington 2001, 629), such partisan distinctiveness does not reflect a change in the attitudes of the citizenry as a whole, since partisans remain a small minority.

Some observers have argued that polarization is unlikely to remain confined to elites or to the significant minority of largely college-educated citizens who are partisan activists. "To imagine that extremist politics has been confined to the chattering classes is to believe that Congress, the media, and American interest groups operate in an ideological vacuum. I find that assumption implausible" (J. Q. Wilson 2006, 19). Others contend, however, that it is not clear that the "party sorting" now in evidence will eventually lead to attitudinal polarization on a more massive scale (J. H. Evans 2006, 4). The political parties are now more distinctive, but the distribution of attitudes and ideological positions among the citizenry has not changed much (Fiorina 2006, 3).

No simple one-to-one relationship appears to exist between elite and mass polarization. Rather, research findings vary depending on the issue being examined. Thus, one study found that increasing elite polarization between 1970 and 1999 (as measured by congressional roll-call votes) on the issues of gay rights and pornography was not matched by mass polarization (as measured by responses to the General Social Survey). Mass polarization did follow elite polarization on environmental issues. On the issue of gun control, the sequence was reversed: a kind of bottom-up polarization occurred, with leaders following the masses. The difference perhaps lies in the degree to which the issue was salient to the masses. A relative lack of interest in gay civil rights and pornography conceivably produced a lack of response to elite cues (Lindaman and Haider-Markel 2002).

The preferences and perspectives of party elites tend to be much more consistent and stable than those of the mass public, and communications between elites and masses are subject to misunderstanding and simplification (Jennings 1992). The mass public is not altogether ignorant regarding the meaning of conservative and liberal ideologies, but one study finds that "well over a third of the mass sample did not offer any definitions" of these labels. And while conservative elites do not see the conservative philosophy as a matter of preference for retaining the status quo, the mass sample does. Indeed, those in the mass electorate who identify themselves as conservatives have an understanding of conservative ideology that appears to be more akin to the views of liberal elites than of conservative ones (Herrera 1996–97, 624, 633–34). Similarly, a study of those who identify themselves as "conservative Democrats" finds that their views on issues are not really conservative, suggesting that perhaps their identification is sustained by the high regard in which contemporary elite discourse holds the conservative label (Schiffer 2000).

However differently masses and elites understand various issues, more American voters now see important differences between the parties and do care which party wins the presidential election. This number has grown steadily between 1976 and 2000 (Brewer 2005, 221). However, while partisan differences on economic issues have consistently remained large, the differences on cultural issues were very small from the 1960s through the 1980s. Only in the 1990s did partisan differences start to increase, first on abortion and then with respect to the role of women and school prayer. Yet the degree to which such cultural issues contribute to partisan identification is low—perhaps surprisingly so (224, 226).

Adding to the complexity of elite versus mass attitudes on culture war issues is the recognition that in some cases, little connection exists between who frames the issue and who wins in the public opinion contests. General Social Survey data from 1977–96 show that pro-life rather than pro-choice advocates have framed the way the majority of Americans think about abortion. Yet public opinion has become more "progressive" with respect to these attitudes. The pro-life side's connection between abortion and beliefs about the sanctity of human life has gained support, whereas pro-choice forces' attempts to link abortion to privacy rights, gender equality, and the idea that the state should not be co-opted by religious views has not. That success in framing the issue, however, has not led to increased opposition to abortion (Strickler and Danigelis 2002, 200).

Whatever the degree of popular polarization, disagreement has arisen about whether such a trend is beneficial or malevolent. Critics of the American party system have long attacked the absence of significant differences between Republicans and Democrats, chastising them for offering little more than Tweedledum and Tweedledee proposals. Yet the perception that the two parties may now reflect real cultural differences gives rise to fears about a polarized nation, incapable of uniting. But perhaps, as Layman suggests, the debates would be more bitter if the two major parties took similar positions on cultural issues, thus forcing "cultural extremists" into pursuing alternatives such as protests or third-party formations. Keeping such disputes within the dominant party structure may ensure a greater degree of compromise (2001, 330).

Concerns about polarization of attitudes or values are often based on fears of social conflict or disintegration. Yet the understanding of public opinion shared by most experts suggests that attitudes are rarely polarized, despite popular beliefs to the contrary. "Takeoff issues" that become the focus of attention (abortion or gays in the military, for example) often distract attention from the larger number of issues about which attitudes are not at all polarized. Similarly, while people experience homogeneity of attitudes within their own social networks, these same networks generally retain heterogeneity of attitudes overall. Attitude differences are underestimated because people discuss important issues selectively and may consequently experience more homogeneity than actually exists. What are the consequences of these paradoxical realities for collective action? On the one hand, polarized interaction structures and their accompanying heightened radicalism can indeed arise on single issues. On the other hand, polarization may remain confined to single issues, so that radicalization on such a limited scale will not have major disruptive consequences (Baldassarri and Bearman 2007). Yet whatever the actual probabilities of a "culture war," the concept appears to have taken hold of the collective imagination and become the lens through which many Americans view political contests. The case of Sarah Palin is illustrative.

Sarah Palin and a Renascent Culture War?

From virtually the moment in 2008 that Sarah Palin was named as the Republican vice presidential nominee, commentators began to talk of the culture war reentering the campaign. On September 5, David Kirkpatrick in the *New York Times* spoke of "Firing Up the Faithful with Echoes of Culture War Rhetoric." One week later, the *Christian Science Monitor* ran an editorial under the title "The Palin Factor in the 'Culture Wars.'" On September 23, Jay Tolson wrote in *U.S. News and World Report* that "Sarah Palin Sparks Revival of the Culture War." On October 4, *The Economist* discussed the "Endless Culture War." By her very presence on the ticket, this conservative

Christian whose infant son was born with Down syndrome appeared to have inserted the culture war into a campaign from which it had been noticeably absent.

Until Palin's entry, the culture war theme had not featured in the 2008 election for a number of different reasons. The Democratic campaign had sought compromises on abortion (keeping it legal but sponsoring programs that would cut down on the number of abortions), and the candidates agreed on same-sex unions. Barack Obama's very appearance on the national scene, in his speech to the Democratic National Convention in July 2004, was devoted to the idea of bridging the cultural divisions in the country. He spoke famously about religiosity in the Blue States and concern for civil liberties in the Red States. John McCain had equally famously railed against the intolerance of such culture warriors as Jerry Falwell and Pat Robertson in 2000, and McCain remained a figure not trusted by the Christian Right.

Internal wrangling among Evangelicals also complicated culture war politics. With an obvious intent to influence the course of the campaign, a group of more than eighty evangelical leaders issued an "Evangelical Manifesto" in May 2008. The manifesto explicitly called for "an expansion of our concern beyond single-issue politics, such as abortion and marriage" and repudiated "the two extremes that define the present culture wars in the United States" (Evangelical Manifesto Steering Committee 2008, 13, 16). The document asserted that Evangelicals should never be "completely equated with any party, partisan ideology, economic system, or nationality." They must participate in the public square but never in such a way that "Christian beliefs are used as weapons for political interests" (15). Many evangelical notables signed the manifesto, but missing from the signatories were such well-known culture warriors as Gary Bauer, Tony Perkins, and James Dobson (W. Smith 2008). Some conservative Catholics who had previously been allied to the politics of the Christian Right were beginning to break away as well (Peter J. Boyer 2008).

Given the Christian Right's lack of strong support for McCain, poll data that showed popular repudiation of George W. Bush's presidency, and the fact that Democratic social policies (for example, on health care) were more popular than Republican ones even among Evangelicals, it is not too surprising that the McCain campaign might have sought to reinvigorate the culture wars by selecting Palin. As *The Economist* noted, "If the election is fought about anything except culture, then the Republicans are on difficult ground" ("Endless Culture War" 2008, 23). But the cultural issues that Palin introduced into the campaign were not primarily those of the culture wars.

From the outset, her themes were of a different sort. Her acceptance speech to the Republican National Convention emphasized her ties to a small-town America of hardworking people. She described herself as "just your average hockey mom" and her husband as a "commercial fisherman," "a production operator in the oil fields," and "a proud member of the United Steel Workers' Union." She pledged advocacy for "children with special needs." And she assumed a populist stance against the "Washington elite." The rest of the speech was devoted to the need for energy independence (famously captured by McCain's exhortation to "Drill, baby, drill"), to praise for McCain's military service and patriotism, and to attacks on Obama's willingness to increase taxes and "forfeit" victory in Iraq (Palin 2008). Her stump speeches were essentially the same, except that she devoted more time to the classic vice presidential duty of attacking the opposition. She thus accused Obama of "palling around with terrorists" (Cooper 2008) and of supporting a "spread the wealth" policy that amounted to "socialism" (Bosman 2008). Criticisms of Obama aside, she repeatedly expressed her solidarity with "unpretentious folks," with "good, hardworking, patriotic Americans." She extolled the virtues of "Joe the Plumber" and other "average Joes." She said, "Man, I love small-town U.S.A." (Healy 2008).

These speeches completely lacked the culture war rhetoric that appeared so prominently in the campaigns of both major candidates in 2000. Bush, Gore, and Gore's running mate, Joe Lieberman, asserted the importance of faith in their lives and talked of the need to support faith-based programs. They advocated cleaning up popular culture to restore morality and reinforce family values. Palin did not talk about her faith, did not proclaim the virtues of prayer, did not assert the need to remoralize American society. She did not address same-sex marriage and seldom mentioned the "sanctity of life," though her decision not to abort a fetus with Down syndrome and her seventeen-year-old unwed daughter's unwillingness to end her pregnancy amply proclaimed the Palin family's pro-life values.

Unlike earlier rhetoric, the very meaning of "family values" in 2008 seems unclear. In the 1990s, the phrase clearly signaled a distaste for mothers in the workplace and a hostility to premarital sex. What might it mean in 2008, when the conservative candidate is a mother of five, one of whom is unmarried and pregnant? To die-hard believers in the culture war idea such as James Davison Hunter, the seeming confusion over "family values" simply indicates that "the lines of the culture war are changing," that "the gender views" once were "so much sharper, traditional versus modern. So much has changed in the last 28 years" (quoted in Tolson 2008). But in fact, the Christian Right has continued to proclaim hostility to premarital sex and to advocate abstinence-only sex education, even while the behavioral reality appears to contradict the belief system (Talbot 2008). How would Palin's supporters have reacted to the pregnancy of the unmarried daughter of either Hillary Clinton or Barack Obama?

Unlike the Democratic populism of Obama and Biden and John Edwards, who hailed the children of single mothers and steelworkers and coal miners who succeeded despite their disadvantages, Palin's populism proclaimed the steelworker's and the coal miner's superiority to Ivy League–educated elites. Herein lies her appeal.

Palin's enthusiastic audiences saw in her not an advocate of "orthodox" morality but someone "just like me." It is not a culture war; it is identity politics. Palin did not proclaim her faith; she proclaimed her solidarity with the white working class, as major figures on the right clearly saw. Patrick Buchanan (2008) said, "Barack and Michelle are affirmative action, Princeton, Columbia, Harvard Law. She is public schools and Idaho State." Ross Douthat observed that Palin "embodies a right-wing archetype of the Real America in much the way that Barack Obama embodies a left-wing archetype of Multicultural Man. . . . Identity politics can be constraining, but in the right circumstances it can be liberating as well—and the 'she's one of us' factor may end up giving Sarah Palin more room to maneuver than any conservative leader since Reagan" (2008, 40).

Though Palin may have been chosen in part because she was a female, as McCain hoped to win over some of Hillary Clinton's disaffected supporters, class and race rather than gender were dominant in her appeal. Numerous commentators noted that her most enthusiastic supporters were white men, and exit poll data suggest that she did not woo females away from the Democratic column. In fact, Obama's popularity among women was greater than that of either Kerry in 2004 or Gore in 2000 (*New York Times* 2008).

Her class and race appeals were evident in her repeated assertions that she represented "the real America." The white working-class audiences that Palin excited could not, of course, announce their support for "white power." Yet they represented a kind of identity politics that differs little from that initiated by the Black Power movements of the late 1960s. They manifested "a racial pride that dares not speak its name, and that defines itself through cultural cues instead—a suspicion of intellectual elites and city dwellers, a preference for folksiness and plainness of speech (whether real or feigned), and the association of a working-class white minority with 'the real America.'" (Hsu 2009, 54).

Is there any evidence to support the idea that Palin's presence on the ticket influenced voters who cared about the culture war divides? Among those who identified themselves as Evangelicals or born-again Christians, exit poll data indicate that Obama won more votes (26 percent) than Kerry did in 2004 (21 percent). The same holds true for white Catholics. Obama also made gains among those who attend church services more than weekly; 43 percent of such voters voted for Obama, compared to 35 percent for Kerry and 36 percent for Gore. At the other end of the religious spectrum, 67 percent of people who never attend church services voted for Obama, an increase from the 62 percent of such voters who supported Kerry and 61 percent who selected Gore (Pew Forum 2008a). Such results hardly indicate a resurgence of the culture war.

One way of checking more specifically for the possible influence of Palin's presence on the Republican ticket is by looking at two polls of white voters who attend church weekly. Gallup conducted the first poll in August 2008 (before her nomination) and the second the following October. The results were essentially unchanged: in August, McCain led Obama among these voters by 39 percent; in October, that margin was 37 percent. But if this minor decrease in support is set against the slippage in McCain's lead among white voters generally (from 7 percent to 2 percent), Palin's presence can be seen as helping Republicans retain support among highly religious voters (Newport 2008). The overwhelming majority of Republicans maintained a favorable view of Palin, while both Democratic and independent voters came to view her more negatively over time (Pew Research Center 2008).

Did Palin's candidacy make a difference in defining the issues that voters considered important? Here the evidence seems clear: it did not. The economy was far and away the dominant issue, with 91 percent of voters in mid-October saying it was most important. Another 80 percent said jobs were most important, followed by energy (78 percent), health care (77 percent), education (73 percent), taxes (71 percent), and Iraq (71 percent). At the bottom of the list were abortion (41 percent) and gay marriage (28 percent). Because the Pew survey asked the same questions in August and October, one can determine whether Palin's candidacy might have increased concerns about abortion and gay marriage. The percentage seeing gay marriage as a very important issue did not change; those seeing abortion as very important increased by 2 percent. However, those who saw abortion as very important still represented a smaller proportion of the electorate than in October 2004 (Pew Research Center 2008). Once again, then, there is no evidence of a resurgent culture war.

A contaminating factor in attempting to understand Palin's role in the election is the perception that she was inadequately prepared for the presidency. In a CNN exit poll, 60 percent of respondents believed that she was not qualified to be president should the need arise (CNN 2008). Because this view was widespread, some commentators speculated about a negative "Palin effect": voters who had intended to vote for McCain were persuaded not to do so because of her presence on the ticket. An attempt to study this Palin effect asked voters whether they were more or less likely to vote for McCain because Palin was his running mate. Asking the same question in both September and October, the survey found an increase in the number of independent voters who said that Palin had made them "less likely" to vote for McCain. But increases also occurred in the proportion of the population that said that Palin made no difference. By October, 50 percent of all the voters in the sample said that Palin made no difference (51 percent among Democrats, 48 percent among Republicans, and 49 percent among independents) (Cost 2008). Perhaps the growing significance of the economic crisis had rendered any kind of Palin effect less significant.

Whatever effect Palin had on the 2008 election, her presence did not introduce a culture war, despite the views of analysts wedded to the culture war hypothesis. Thus, James Davison Hunter says that although the culture war had never gone away, Palin's nomination moved it from the background to the foreground (quoted in Tolson 2008). Based on both the voting patterns and the issues most salient to voters as revealed in exit polls, the evidence does not appear to support that contention.

There is little evidence that the culture wars featured significantly in the two previous presidential elections either. John Kenneth White, a supporter of the culture war thesis, has interpreted Bush's 2000 victory as a repudiation of the Democratic Party because of its association with Bill Clinton's immorality. Bush appealed to voters "who were tired of Clinton and wanted a respite from the value challenges they had to face during his two terms" (2003, 168). Nearly two-thirds of the population—66 percent—believed that the Republican Party "stood for strong moral values," whereas only 44 percent viewed the Democrats that way. The election was therefore a matter of a "values divide." Yet White also presents data that undermine his arguments: a September 2000 poll found Bush and Gore tied at 44 percent when respondents were asked to select which of them would encourage high moral standards and values (162). More damning still is the revelation that an October 2000 poll showed that "if Americans could have chosen between Clinton and George W. Bush, they would have preferred Clinton 48 percent to 44 percent" (30).

The aftermath of the 2004 election saw a flurry of interest in the culture wars when exit poll data found that 22 percent of the voters chose "moral values" as the most important issue, compared to 20 percent who selected economy/jobs, 19 percent terrorism, and 15 percent Iraq. Since 80 percent of those who selected "moral values" voted for Bush, the immediate conclusion was that the culture wars were responsible for his reelection (Langer and Cohen 2005, 745–46). Furthermore, referenda about same-sex marriage in a number of states were seen as mobilizing the Christian Right to come out and vote, thereby helping Bush as well. More careful analysis shows that these premises were false.

The phrase *moral values* is, of course, something of a grab bag whose meaning is uncertain. Most polling experts considered the question "poorly devised." Though the term appealed to opponents of abortion and gay marriage, 12 percent of liberals and 15 percent of nonchurchgoers also selected it. When preelection polls asked open-ended questions, voters selected Iraq, the economy, and terrorism as their most important issues, and answers that could be characterized as moral values were in the low single digits (Langer 2004).

No surge occurred in the evangelical vote or in the number of voters who were pro-life (D. Brooks 2004), and white Protestants who attend church weekly made up a somewhat smaller share of the electorate than they had in 2000 (Langer and Cohen 2005, 750). Nor did Bush gain votes because same-sex marriage was on the ballot. In five of the eleven states in which such measures appeared, his share of the vote was lower than it had been four years earlier; in two others, his increased vote was lower than his increase nationally (Ashbee 2005, 213). Of those who defected from their party, many more did so because of their position on the Iraq war than because of their view of gay marriage (T. Jones 2005).

No one disputes the clear dominance of economic issues in the 2008 election. Whether this dominance had the effect of swamping the culture war or whether the culture war is otherwise moribund remains a matter of speculation. Some liberals in the first flush of victory proclaimed Palin the "last of the culture warriors" (Beinart 2008a). In effect, the war is over and we have won, they argued. Comparing the scene in Chicago's Grant Park on election night 2008 to the infamous 1968 riots there, Beinart argues that the cultural freedoms celebrated in that earlier era no longer seem alien to Americans. "Feminism is so mainstream that even Sarah Palin embraces the term; Chicago mayor Richard Daley, son of the man who told police to bash heads, marches in gay-rights parades. . . . Younger Americans—who voted overwhelmingly for Obama—largely embrace the legacy of the '60s" (Beinart 2008b, 31).

On the other side, an interesting exchange occurred in the pages of *National Review* in 2007, sparked by a libertarian who advised conservatives to bid "farewell to culture wars." Brink Lindsey argued that those who believed that "family life could not survive the exodus of women into the workforce" were wrong. Those who "believed that only a revival of faith in Christianity could stave off social breakdown" were also wrong, as cultural liberalism in New England now coexists with the "lowest levels of social dysfunction (crime, divorce, illegitimacy, etc.) in the country" (2007, 39–40). Ramesh Ponnuru countered that the culture wars remain relevant. After all, both parties follow what the survey data tell them. So it is interesting that Republicans emphasize "social conservatism rather than market economics" and Democrats stress "statist economics rather than social liberalism" (40).

Whatever the future may bring, it seems clear that the story of the Palin candidacy and the lessons of the two previous presidential campaigns lend support to the thesis of this book. The major themes of the 2000 election were not the conflict between "orthodox" and "progressive" morality. Bush, Gore, and Lieberman were all on the same side. In some senses, the winners in 2004 were Bush on the one hand and Obama on the other. Obama's 2004 "postpartisan" speech to the Democratic National Convention put him on the national radar screen and began his campaign for the presidency. He talked then of a common culture rather than a divided one.

During the 2008 campaign, Obama refused to answer the Reverend Rick Warren's question about when life begins, while McCain said simply "at conception." The Democrat nevertheless inserted provisions into his party's platform to help women prevent pregnancy or carry pregnancy to term, thereby reducing the number of abortions. He showed a similar sense of moderation and compromise concerning the role of religion. "Not every mention of God in public is a breach to the wall of separation—context matters," he said. "Having voluntary student prayer groups use school property to meet should not be a threat, any more than its use by the High School Republicans should threaten Democrats" (quoted in Peter J. Boyer 2008, 28).

The population, too, gives evidence of converging on issues of religion and morality. More Americans of all stripes have come to believe that churches should stay out of politics. Opposition to church involvement has increased among both Republicans and independents so that they now share the views of Democrats, and similar proportions of self-identified conservatives, moderates, and liberals oppose church involvement in politics (Pew Forum 2008b). A January 2009 survey about priorities for the new administration found that the proportions of Republicans and Democrats who thought that "dealing with moral breakdown" was a "top priority" were highly similar. Although this issue was well down on the list of priorities for members of both parties, the difference between them (4 percent) was among the smallest in the survey—second only to the gap in reducing the budget deficit (1 percent) (Pew Research Center 2009).

One final element of the Palin story is the high degree of internal dissension her candidacy generated among conservatives. Though she was allegedly promoted for the nomination by such stellar conservatives as William Kristol, Fred Barnes, Michael Gerson, Rich Lowry, and others (Mayer 2008), within short order she was rejected by such equally well-known conservatives as David Brooks, Christopher Buckley, George Will, and Peggy Noonan. In Noonan's view, Palin was "failin'" because "You must address America in its entirety, not as a sliver or a series of slivers but as a full and whole entity, a great nation trying to hold together" (2008).

A Multitude of Internal Divisions

If Palin's campaign was about the culture of class rather than the economics of class, issues of culture versus economics are implicated in many of the internal divisions that challenge both the Right and the Left. If the story of Palin's candidacy brings into focus discord within the conservative elite as well as within the evangelical elite, these difficulties do not differ from those faced on the left or in the feminist and gay social movements.

Because both the Left and the Right face conflicts between economic and cultural considerations as well as tensions between their libertarian and communitarian strands, each side easily derides the other for its internal contradictions. A progressive notes that the Right attacks the National Endowment for the Arts for eschewing market-based public tastes in favor of "cultural elitism" while blaming movie and media companies for giving the public what it wants (quoted in Sachs and Washburn 1995, 34). A conservative says, "American-style liberalism is schizophrenic. On the one side, it is profoundly communitarian; on the other, radically individualistic" (Neuhaus 1989b, 40).

Conservatives, a liberal argues, must reconcile the benefits of the market with its tendency to undermine "the moral character that the social conservative desires" (quoted in Sachs and Washburn 1995, 34–35). They cannot favor the use of public broadcasting to counter the market-based hedonistic media because this position reflects a liberal ideology. In fact, opposition to public broadcasting has allowed for some degree of agreement between economic and cultural conservatives. The latter decry pro-gay and antifamily programming, while the former attack it as an instance of "big government" interfering with the marketplace and traditional community life. Thus, in this instance, "cultural orthodoxy" and a "defense of free-market economics" can readily coexist (Hoynes 1996, 74). But conservatives cannot support the idea that public schools should instill moral character, since many of them favor giving parents vouchers to be redeemed at the private schools of their choice (R. Wright 1996, 44).

Social conservatives vie with economic conservatives on issues of popular culture, just as libertarian liberals vie with social welfare liberals. Although the Right favors regulation in the personal/moral sphere while preferring to leave the economic sphere unregulated, while the Left favors the reverse, libertarians dislike regulation in either sphere, and communitarians would like to see regulation in both spheres. Given this complexity, a "one-dimensional culture war" is implausible (Olson 1997, 256).

If conservatives must somehow juggle marketplace dominance against their more communitarian wing's desire to protect and defend society's values and morals, so too liberals disagree about whether to favor freedom of speech regardless of its content or to promote laws against hate speech. A conservative summarizes the liberal dilemma by referring to a campus speech code at the University of Wisconsin: "If a similar code were drawn up with right-wing imperatives in mind—one banning unpatriotic, irreligious or sexually explicit expression on campus—the people framing the Wisconsin-type rules would revert to their libertarian past" (Wills 1989, 71). And a writer in *The New Republic* expresses concern that "frank talk about race, sex, class, and sexuality" is impeded by our heightened awareness of what is and is not "politically correct." He fears that the "war against insensitive humor might end up generating the very social and racial tension it is trying to defuse" (David Segal 1992, 10).

In contests that pit economic and cultural priorities against each other, the case of immigration policy bedevils the Right, as some conservatives favor liberal immigration policies for economic reasons and others oppose such policies for cultural reasons. Those opposed to unlimited immigration argue that it is not even economically advantageous. The closing off of immigration during the 1920s reduced the amount of cheap labor available and thus stimulated capital-intensive investment that produced significant economic expansion (Auster 1992, 44). At the present time, another anti-immigration conservative argues, expansion of "the 'diversity' industry will mean less social stability and more ethnic and class tension—none of which bodes well for the market" (Custred 1997, 40). As detailed in chapter 5, conservatives argue among themselves about whether the United States is an immigrant nation or a nation like all others with a common culture and an emerging shared ethnicity.

Similar contention arises between the Cultural and Economic Lefts regarding the primacy of class versus race and gender. As one progressive writer sees it, the Cultural Left operates on high levels of abstraction that are "irrelevant and infuriating" to many Americans. Yet the class-based analysis of the Economic Left "appeals to neither the racism/sexism/homophobia crowd nor to the self-images of most Americans." The dilemma is made more complicated by the need to speak the language of the academic (cultural) leftists because faculty and graduate students from the postmodern literature and theory crowd volunteer in campaigns such as those to support a living wage (Alterman 1998, 10).

For other progressives, class remains dominant, and there is a simple need "to rediscover the language of class" (Tom Frank 1996, 19). Progressives should be wary of "postmodern multiculturalists" who emphasize racial identity. They often hinder the organizing efforts of progressives, as "the black postmodernists, no different from the whites they criticize, are often incapable of deracializing themselves and finding common cause with other progressives." Postmodern multiculturalists have a middle-class bias and so give only lip service to issues of class and thus hamper interracial organizing (Daryl Michael Scott 1998, 27).

But other progressives see class, race, and gender as intertwined; class is structured via race and gender. Unionization and increases in minimum wage alone will not fix the problems of inequality based on racism and sexism (Pollitt 1998b, 9). Class movements and movements for blacks, women, and gays should be seen as "natural allies." Critics who assume that the Left "can do class or culture, but not both are simply wrong. People's working lives, their sexual and domestic lives, their moral values, are intertwined" (Willis 1998, 19).

Another dimension of the economics versus culture debate on the left appears in an essay written for *Time* by a liberal commentator who suggests that America is now "tiptoeing" to the left on "lifestyle" issues. Michael Kinsley argues that while liberals are said to have made a mistake by abandoning economic issues for "lifestyle" or "identity" politics, "the country seems to be moving left" in precisely those lifestyle issues. His examples include support for medical marijuana, abortion, gay rights, and freedom on the Internet. While acknowledging that lifestyle libertarianism "is not a completely attractive phenomenon," since it favors self-indulgence over concern for the poor and the social welfare, he nevertheless sees it as a beneficial "counterweight" to both the social conservatives and the communitarians in both the liberal and conservative camps (1996, 38). In response, Thomas Frank, writing in *The Nation,* calls this essay a "banal contribution to the ongoing journalistic effort to solve the mystery of the vanishing left." If one forgets about the "efforts of the historical political left to control the vagaries of the market economy," then "this sort of lifestyle liberation sells." But in fact this approach is nothing more than the "liberation marketing" that portrays ads as telling lies, work as boring and exploitative, and bosses as bastards. Liberation comes from your Saab or your Doublemint gum. "Planet Reebok has offered the world a way to do without the troublesome historical left altogether" (1997, 10). Another commentary in *The New Republic* contends that "lifestyle as a value system grows steadily more powerful." Abortion, the author argues, has become part of the American lifestyle. "It's not a matter of monolithic, time-honored religion versus itty-bitty, flighty lifestyle. It's religion—marginal vestige, subculture, private matter—versus lifestyle—the engine, the symbol, the central organizing principle" of the nation (Caldwell 1999, 15).

Advocates commonly accuse their opponents of seeking to impose their views on the population. Conservative critics, for example, have seen the rigorous enforcement of feminism or "diversity" on campus as "liberal fascism" (Hart 1987, 46) or "soft fascism" (O'Sullivan 2000, 22) or "state-subsidized sensitivity fascism" (Teachout 1992, 54). What is perhaps surprising is that similar accusations are hurled at opponents within the same camp. In a relatively mild rebuke, for example, a conservative religious writer, hostile to the "religio-cultural mainline," contends that its view of "pluralism" is that "everybody should compromise its way" (Neuhaus 1986, 46). A much angrier denunciation of those on his own side comes from a progressive who is angered by the writings of some liberal intellectuals. Alexander Cockburn argues that the damages associated with the "rightward swerve of the Zeitgeist" have not been inflicted by Birchers or the Moral Majority but rather by respectable intellectuals such as Nathan Glazer, David Riesman, and Robert Coles. These liberals have supported "character education" and education to support "patriotism" and have argued that saluting the flag and reciting a school prayer should not become defined as problems. Thus, Cockburn concludes, "there's no Nazi like a liberal in search of the nation's soul" (1985, 70).

Such progressive anger at some liberals for favoring the communitarian over the libertarian side is matched by the anger of those who seek to overturn the libertarian bent within liberalism. Thus, an editorial in *The New Republic* emphatically rejects the overemphasis on individual rights. "Contemporary liberalism is so intellectually and psychologically invested in the doctrine of ever-expanding rights—the rights of privacy, the rights of children, the rights of criminals, the rights of pornographers, the rights of everyone to everything—that any suggestion of the baleful consequences of that doctrine appears to them as a threat to the liberal idea itself" (1988b, 7). As a result, "the issue of cultural degeneration has become taboo among liberals who mock Tipper Gore and her campaign to clean up rock lyrics. . . . But what is so wrong with . . . the protection of children from the numbing norms in our culture of random drugs, random sex, and random violence? . . . How strange it is that modern interventionist liberals would leave the determination of all this to a rapacious market" (8).

Questions of the role of economic versus cultural factors make for discord within the Left on the issue of feminism as well. Some feminists complain that the Left does not take their issues seriously enough because it relegates them to the culture wars, which are of less value than economic policy questions. One such writer argues that "no broad left will revive in this country until the men in it grasp the importance of culture wars. . . . The Christian conservatives' language of transformation and righteousness" cannot be countered simply with policy discourse. Women have been responsible for most of the activism over the past thirty years (Tax 1995, 378). Another feminist contends that "by marginalizing abortion as an issue of concern only to women and feminists, the left allows the right to control moral discourse, or what is now known as 'values,' and particularly 'family values'" (Gordon 1998, 5).

But there is also considerable disagreement on the left about how the feminist movement should proceed. A progressive commentator assails the "difference feminists," who emphasize aspects of "women's culture" that are different from and superior to "men's culture." She argues that difference feminism, "like other forms of multiculturalism . . . looks everywhere for its explanatory force—biology, psychology, sociology, cultural identity—except economics." Yet differences between men and women reside not in "universal features of male and female psychosexual development" but in "the economic and social positions men and women hold" (Pollitt 1992b, 801).

Other progressive feminists see both difference feminism and the emphasis on cultural rather than economic issues as something of a trap for the movement. They argue that cultural feminists only reinforce "oppressive cultural stereotypes" of women as peaceful nurturers. (Willis 1981, 495). Moreover, "the ultimate paradox of difference feminism is that it has come to the fore at a moment when the lives of the sexes are becoming less distinct than they ever have been in the West" (Pollitt 1992b, 806). Difference feminism is appealing because it makes women's "sacrifices . . . on behalf of domesticity and children" seem "legitimate, moral, even noble." Yet "the peaceful mother and the 'relational' woman are a kinder, gentler, leftish version of 'family values.'" It is as if "women don't really believe they are entitled to full citizenship unless they can make a special claim to virtue" (804). Another progressive asks why an alleged woman's culture has not altered business, medicine, and the law as more women have entered these occupations and posits women's desire to assimilate as an answer (Ehrenreich 1990, 15).

Disagreement also arises about which aspects of policy are of greatest concern. While some progressives argue that the harm connected with family breakdown is related to problems of money, not values (Pollitt 1992a; Stacey 1994), others contend that money is not the only problem. Male domination and institutionalized homophobia remain problems, too (Ehrenreich 1982). Yet the radical academic feminists who run many women's studies programs and emphasize the control that men exercise over women's "productive and reproductive labor" also come in for criticism: "Their moral authority comes from a widespread belief that they represent 'women.' In fact, their version of feminism falls short of being representative." Most American women subscribe to an older feminism whose goal is equity—that is, fair treatment (Sommers 1992, 32).

If divisions exist among feminists about whether they are basically similar to or different from men, an analogous disagreement occurs among gays and lesbians. Should they see themselves as essentially like heterosexuals and seek to be integrated among them, or should they celebrate their difference and seek to remain as outsiders—"queers"—who endeavor to change the society? Many observers agree that neither the model of gender nor the model of ethnicity fits the gay population, since every gay person already has both a gender and an ethnicity (Crain 1993, 16). Nor are gays an "oppressed minority" in the usual sense, since they are not denied the vote or education and are not necessarily poor (Rauch 1993, 18, 20). The issue in dispute is what gays should be fighting for.

A writer who identifies herself as a black lesbian complains about a "narrowness" of the gay movement in the 1990s that makes people of color feel excluded. "It's gay, white men's racial, gender and class privileges, as well as the vast numbers of them who identify with the system rather than distrust it, that have made the politics of the current gay movement so different from those of other identity-based movements for social and political change" (B. Smith 1993, 14). That the gay population has significant internal divisions—divisions of social class, race, gender, and lifestyle—is not a matter of dispute (see Abraham 1997; Bawer 1994; Ireland 1997; B. Smith 1993). At issue, however, is whether conflicts exist between the movement's leadership and its grassroots.

Gay conservatives express irritation that some gay leaders have aligned themselves with numerous progressive causes that do not really represent the allegiances of most American gays (Bawer 1994, 26). The idea of "sexuality as cultural subversion" is at odds with the view of most gays, "who not only accept the natural origin of their sexual orientation, but wish to be integrated into society as it is." Queer radicalism does not define gay identity but rather "may actually have to define itself in opposition to it" (Sullivan 1993, 32, 33). A progressive agrees that lesbian and gay students seem intent on "cultural assimilation. They want to be upright solid citizens. Openly gay solid citizens." But he cautions that such pragmatism is dangerous: "For once we accept that salvation comes in the form of a contract with straight society," we lose sight of the larger goals (Gevisser 1988, 414). The gay movement, though sanitized by those in power, has "radical roots" and "connections" to "the other great transformative struggles of these times, to the joyously skewed visions . . . that lie outside the conventions of the straight world, and occasionally stand it on its head" (Kopkind and d'Adesky 1993, 4). Another progressive expresses concern that "the publicly visible gay movement has become the gay right," despite the fact that queer theory has become important in academe. The gay conservatives find a ready audience because they say what many straight editors want to hear; queers must speak up and lobby both the gay and the straight press (M. Warner 1997, 18–19). But another progressive cautions that gays and lesbians are a highly diverse group of people whose differences are greater than those suggested by the commentators on either side (Abraham 1997, 6).

Within the pages of *The New Republic,* more and less conservative gays argue about whether the gay movement should maintain alliances with other social movements. Are coalitions with liberal black and women's groups ultimately harmful, since "many straight blacks and women have little enthusiasm for aligning their causes with that of gays"? The gay movement must face up to its "contradictions. Is it primarily now a public health organization, a civil rights movements, or another band to a defunct rainbow coalition?" (Blow 1987, 16). Do such coalitions hurt the gay movement by falsely implying that most gay people sympathize with progressive movements (Bawer 1994, 26)? Or do gays need to articulate what "a post-liberation society looks like"? Neither claiming to be just like everyone else (when others believe that gays are different) nor arguing for civil rights (when the Right has succeeded in shifting the meaning of this to "special rights") will succeed. Instead, gays need to seek equality not just for gay people but for all people (Vaid 1993, 28). Writers in *The Nation* applaud such coalitions, not only with blacks and women but also with labor, environmental, and pro-choice groups (see Ireland 1999; Kopkind 1993; B. Smith 1993).

According to gay conservatives, gay leaders who see themselves as waging a "cultural war" are framing the issue in the wrong way. What is truly at stake is the need to get America to accept homosexuality, and this is "a matter of education" (Bawer 1994, 26). But another gay conservative argues that any attempt to achieve gay freedom by changing heterosexuals' behavior is clearly flawed. The aim instead should be to ban all public discrimination against gays and to extend to homosexuals all the rights and responsibilities enjoyed by heterosexuals—including marriage and service in the military (Sullivan 1993, 36). Both of these writers agree that no inherent conflict exists between gays and the family—quite the contrary.

Yet ordinary gays and lesbians rather than the national leadership promoted the idea of gay marriage by applying for marriage licenses and filing lawsuits when those applications were denied. If the legalization of same-sex marriage occurs without the enthusiastic support of gay and progressive groups, it will be "one of the most breathtaking lapses of organizational vision in the history of the modern left," says one commentator (Rotello 1996, 18).

Advocates of "queer subculture," conversely, deride those gays who seek a happy lesbian or gay identity in a "normal, private home: secure, mature and demure." Such endorsement of assimilation and of state regulation of sex means the abandonment of queer ideals in favor of "moral respectability and self-esteem." These conservative gays "forget unconscious desire, or the tension between pleasure and normalization" (M. Warner 1997, 15). The idea of a "Queer Nation" may seem like an oxymoron, since how would unity be achieved among people "who define themselves by a perverse insistence on the individuality of their desires"? Yet the American experiment is all about just that: we are a nation composed of "millions of individuals busy protecting their private lives and liberties and pursuing their particular happinesses" (Crain 1993, 16). In this dispute, as in so many others in the culture wars, there is a spokesperson for the side of moderation, for rejecting the antithesis "between the newly ascendant gay conservatives and queers claiming the gay progressive political tradition for sexual liberation. Are these our options: to fight for a place at the table at which [Jesse] Helms exercises his authority; or to spend our lives acting out Helms's fantasy of our lives?" Both sides fail to reflect the reality of gay lives, in which there is diversity akin to that in the lives of straight people (Abraham 1997, 6).

Gays do not agree among themselves about whether same-sex marriage is ultimately a conservative or a radical idea. Some gays see it as a highly conservative proposition—an extension of "family values." Indeed, "it's one of the richest ironies of our society's blind spot toward gays that essentially conservative social goals should have the appearance of being so radical" (Sullivan 1989, 22). For others, same-sex marriage would have very radical implications for "the profoundly gendered structure at the heart of marriage." As lesbian and gay couples reconfigure marital roles, "who would be the 'husband' in a marriage of two men, or the 'wife' in a marriage of two women? . . . The absolute conflation of gender with role is shattered. What would be the impact on heterosexual marriage?" (Hunter 1991, 411). Same-sex marriage, says another, "is a breathtakingly subversive idea" because it will be "a direct hit against the religious right's goal of re-enshrining biology as destiny." Marriage law will have to become gender-blind and thus will act as a pressure toward more egalitarian marriages. Marriage is clearly a matter of cultural definition and choice; in each different era, "marriage institutionalizes the sexual bond in a way that makes sense for that society, that economy, that class" (Graff 1996, 12). But yet another progressive writer both supports same-sex marriage and sees it as fundamentally conservative, since gay and lesbian monogamous couples exhibit "the very family-values logic that otherwise bolsters conservatism" (Rotello 1996, 16). Similarly, some conservative gays see the entry of gays into the military as bolstering the conservative values of traditionalism and patriotism, while a progressive asserts that their entry would undercut "the patriarchal power of the military" (Kopkind 1993, 602).

Debate also arises about whether a gay culture exists. One conservative gay writer argues that gay culture is merely a response to persecution. "The gay subculture, like the speakeasy, 'flapper' era of Prohibition, or the so-called 'counterculture' of the Sixties and early Seventies, is a culture of rebellion against such persecution." Gays are, in fact, no more promiscuous or sex-obsessed than are heterosexuals. The real difference is that whereas heterosexuals can be anywhere, "a homosexual can be *safely* gay only in a gay environment" (Woolman 1986, 30). But a progressive writer argues that younger gay people "have created a queer culture that is rapidly reconfiguring American values, redesigning sensibilities and remodeling politics." Elements of gay culture "have infiltrated everyday life: the homoerotic advertising spreads, the ironic style in journalism and literature, the fashions on the street, the new political calculus" (Kopkind 1993, 595).

Whether among feminists, gays, or Evangelicals, issues of strategy and tactics often complicate the cultural struggles. It is sometimes difficult to ascertain whether particular actions and policies are the result of ideological commitment or of strategic or tactical pursuits in political conflicts. For example, was the attack against the National Endowment for the Arts and the National Endowment for Humanities in the late 1980s and early 1990s a matter of resuscitating the classical republican idea that government should promote virtue among the citizenry? Or was it rather about struggles within the conservative camp, as the Christian Right and other highly conservative groups attempted to subvert the more moderate Bush administration? Did they use the endowments and their various "cultural sins" as tools to energize their ranks (Jensen 1995)? Similarly, if prayer were again to be allowed in public schools, would this be a hindrance to those Evangelicals who favor school choice and do not want the public system to improve (Brookhiser 1994, 84)?

Conclusions

While the peace, environmental, and human rights movements have brought greater attention to cultural politics in many European societies, the cultural focus in American politics leans more to matters of a religious or moral nature. Among those who attend church regularly, religious views influence political attitudes and voting choices, though class, race, and gender also remain significant and interact with religion in complex ways.

Whether American-style cultural politics is a function of American exceptionalism remains an open question, however, since European societies also have growing concerns about religion and multiculturalism.

The culture war rubric that became widespread in the early 1990s probably intensified cultural politics and swept more subjects into its fold—arts funding and school and university curricula, for example. But the polarization implied in the military analogy has not developed. For all the public attention to "culture wars," mass and elite attitudes do not coincide in any simple way, and significant internal divisions remain within each camp.

CHAPTER 9

Concluding Comments

Defenders of the culture war idea contend that despite the moderation embraced by the American population, the "deep culture" that frames our understanding of social reality is divided into orthodox and progressive camps. This public culture, enunciated by elites, must be studied separately from public opinion. Examination of this culture will reveal that it does not allow for anything other than the binary choice: one either believes in absolute morality, or one does not.

After analyzing two decades of public discussion of culture war issues, I do not find such clarity. These complex debates reveal numerous convergences across the culture war divide and multiple internal divisions. They also manifest a distinctly American cast, since all participants subscribe to the enduring cultural ideas that frame the specific issues under dispute.

While the language of culture wars emerged only in the late twentieth century, cultural politics are decidedly not new in the United States. Battles about religion and morality and whether the individual or the community is primary have been present virtually from the outset. Nor are such cultural dilemmas likely to be resolved, since they are constantly revisited as new situations arise.

Economic, technological, and demographic changes constantly bring new challenges to cultural understandings. To take but one example, before the increase in both secular and non-Christian populations, the "one culture" of American pluralism was essentially Christian (or "Judeo-Christian") and European. Demographic and religious changes have thus brought renewed political struggles about both the role of religion and the nature of American pluralism.

But a lack of clarity prevails about the very nature of recent changes. Despite the enduring strength of religious belief in the United States, many believers now neither participate in religious practice nor have knowledge about the beliefs to which they subscribe. Does this indicate a weakening of religion or the continuation of remarkably strong adherence to nonsecular beliefs? Likewise, are ethnic and racial subcultures stronger or weaker than they have previously been? On the one hand, these subcultures so central to American cultural pluralism have weakened over time. On the other hand, they have gained new importance as many individuals now seek attachment to such groups. Has individualism become stronger as Americans withdraw their trust and participation from groups and institutions, as alleged by those who see a decrease in social capital? Or has individualism become more muted as Americans increasingly come to define their very selves in terms of the groups and subcultures to which they choose to belong? In light of our greater self-consciousness about matters cultural, have cultural elites gained or lost power?

There is no evidence of change in either the moralism or the moderation of the population. Yet moderation may have become at once more difficult and seemingly more necessary in the face of media that operate twenty-four hours per day and tend toward hyperbole and the magnification of small differences.

The culture wars are fueled by images—of "tenured radicals" in academe, of "secular humanists" and "Christian fundamentalists," of the sway of "modernity" or "postmodernity" and the vanquishing of the "traditional." Awareness of the role of such symbols leads interest groups and scholars alike to try to disentangle "reality" from imagery. Yet the reality of even such concepts as American exceptionalism remains a matter of dispute. Is the United States exceptional because of its treasured individualism and voluntarism or because of its enduring adherence to traditional morality? Does its exceptionalism reside in its minimal class-consciousness or its higher-than-usual devotion to religion?

If the culture wars are more muted now than when they were first named in the early 1990s, it may be because of some convergence in attitudes about sexual behavior and family life, feminism and gay rights, and even perhaps abortion. The polarization that culture war theorists imagine has not developed. Though unanimity on cultural issues is unlikely ever to occur, compromises appear to be possible and are now being discussed. Combining American morality and pragmatism is seen as a way of ending the culture wars (Saletan 2009). Federal protection of same-sex marriage could be combined with exemptions for religious groups, for example (Blankenhorn and Rauch 2009).

But whatever the progress of the culture wars, neither the culture that is its subject nor the very idea of culture is likely to remain constant. Conceptions of culture are likely to continue to change even as new battles for hegemony emerge.

Methodological Appendix

The Sample

The four magazines in the sample were chosen to represent the mainstream American political spectrum, from *National Review* on the right to *The Nation* on the left, with *Time* in the center and *The New Republic* in the more ambiguous position of a once clearly liberal magazine that veered rightward during the 1980s. *The Nation,* founded in 1865, is a venerable magazine of the Left. While newer liberal magazines such as the *American Prospect* and the somewhat more muckraking *Mother Jones* have captured progressive audiences as well, they lack the cultural heft of *The Nation. National Review,* founded in 1955 by William F. Buckley Jr. as the organ for conservative intellectuals, likewise has some younger competition—most notably, the *Weekly Standard,* founded in 1995 by neoconservatives William Kristol and Fred Barnes. Yet *National Review* retains its preeminence and devotes more attention to culture war issues than the newer publication does. And the *Weekly Standard* was, of course, unavailable during the first fifteen years of the study. *Time* magazine, established in 1923, has *Newsweek* (founded in 1933) as its principal competitor. *Time* was chosen because it generally has had higher circulation and greater visibility than *Newsweek.* Many *Time* covers, for example, have become cultural icons. *The New Republic* was founded in 1914 by well-known liberal thinkers Herbert Croly and Walter Lippmann. Its more diverse and less predictably liberal editorial stances during the 1980s and 1990s made it a source of some interest and perhaps greater prominence.

Although widespread circulation of the idea that a culture war was taking place did not occur until the early 1990s, discussion of such issues began in the previous decade. Soon after Ronald Reagan's 1980 election to the presidency, commentators began to talk about a "New Right." During the

1980s, Anita Bryant waged a nationwide campaign against laws promoting equal rights for homosexuals, and the foes of abortion clinics became more militant. Reagan blended traditional economic conservatism with a new social conservatism that advocated, for example, a constitutional amendment to allow for school prayer. This 1984 proposal provoked *The Nation* to declare the initiation of the cultural war (Editorial 1984, 308). For all these reasons, it made sense to begin the study of political magazines in 1980 rather than 1990. Though the coverage of culture war issues increased after 1990, a nonnegligible number of articles on the subject appeared during the 1980s.

DETAILED BREAKDOWN OF ARTICLES

The 436 articles published between 1980 and 2000 appeared in the magazines as follows:

National Review	148	(55 in 1980–90; 93 in 1991–2000)
Time	113	(33 in 1980–90; 80 in 1991–2000)
The New Republic	86	(22 in 1980–90; 64 in 1991–2000)
The Nation	89	(27 in 1980–90; 62 in 1991–2000)

The distribution of articles by topic is as follows:

Abortion	32
The Arts	40
Canon Wars	24
Culture Wars Generally	51
Family Values Issues	22
Feminism Issues	37
Homosexuality	62
Multiculturalism	38
Multicultural Education	27
Popular Culture	33
Religious Issues	55*
Sex Education	15

*24 pertain to church-state relations; 22 to internal disputes; 9 to creationism.

References

Abraham, Julie. 1997. "Sex and Taxes." *The Nation,* October 20, 6.

Abramowitz, Alan, and Kyle Saunders. 2005. "Why Can't We All Just Get Along? The Reality of a Polarized America." *The Forum* 3:1–22.

Abu-Lughod, Lila. 1999. "The Interpretation of Culture(s) after Television." In *The Fate of 'Culture': Geertz and Beyond,* ed. Sherry B. Ortner, 110–35. Berkeley: University of California Press.

Adams, James Truslow. 1926. "Our Dissolving Ethics." *Atlantic,* 138:577–83.

Alba, Richard. 1999. "Immigration and the American Realities of Assimilation and Multiculturalism." *Sociological Forum* 14:3–25.

Alexander, Charles P. 1990. "A Parent's View of Pop Sex and Violence." *Time,* May 7, 100.

Alexander, Jeffrey C. 2001. "Theorizing the 'Modes of Incorporation': Assimilation, Hyphenation, and Multiculturalism as Varieties of Civil Participation." *Sociological Theory* 19:237–49.

Alexander, Jeffrey C., and Philip Smith. 1993. "The Discourse of American Civil Society: A New Proposal for Cultural Studies." *Theory and Society* 22:151–207.

Alterman, Eric. 1998. "Making One and One Equal Two." *The Nation,* May 25, 10.

Alterman, Eric. 1999. "Fashion Statements." *The Nation,* November 8, 10.

"The America We Seek." 1996. *National Review,* March 25, 36, 38–41.

Andersen, Margaret L. 2001. "Restructuring for Whom? Race, Class, Gender, and the Ideology of Invisibility." *Sociological Forum* 16:181–201.

Angrosino, Michael. 2002. "Civil Religion Redux." *Anthropological Quarterly* 75: 239–67.

Appiah, Kwame Anthony. 1997. "The Multiculturalist Misunderstanding." *New York Review of Books,* October 9, 30–36.

Appleby, Joyce. 1985. "Republicanism and Ideology." *American Quarterly* 37:461–73.

Appleby, Joyce. 1992. "Recovering America's Historic Diversity: Beyond Exceptionalism." *Journal of American History* 79:419–31.

Arkes, Hadley. 1989. "Moral Obtuseness in America." *National Review,* June 16, 33–36.

Arkes, Hadley. 1993. "The Closet Straight." *National Review,* July 5, 43–45.

Asante, Molefi Kete. 1992. "Multiculturalism: An Exchange." In *Debating P.C.,* ed. Paul Berman, 299–311. New York: Dell.

Ashbee, Edward. 2005. "The 2004 Presidential Election, 'Moral Values,' and the Democrats' Dilemma." *Political Quarterly* 76:209–17.

Auster, Lawrence. 1992. "The Forbidden Topic." *National Review,* April 27, 42–44.

Auster, Lawrence. 1994. "Avoiding the Issue." *National Review,* February 21, 48–54.

Bacevich, A. J. 1993. "Gays and Military Culture." *National Review,* April 26, 26–31.

Bader, Veit. 1999. "Religious Pluralism, Secularism or Priority for Democracy?" *Political Theory* 27:597–633.

Baer, Douglas, James Curtis, Edward Grabb, and William Johnston. 1995. "Respect for Authority in Canada, the United States, Great Britain and Australia." *Sociological Focus* 28:177–95.

Baker, Wayne. 2005. *America's Crisis of Values.* Princeton: Princeton University Press.

Baldassarri, Delia, and Peter Bearman. 2007. "Dynamics of Political Polarization." *American Sociological Review* 72:784–811.

Barkalow, Jordon B. 2004. "Changing Patterns of Obligation and the Emergence of Individualism in American Political Thought." *Political Research Quarterly* 57: 491–500.

Barnett, Stephen R. 1991. "Get Back." *The New Republic,* February 18, 24, 26.

Barry, Brian. 2001. *Culture and Equality.* Cambridge: Harvard University Press.

Bates, Stephen. 1993. "The Textbook Wars." *National Review,* September 20, 65–66, 68–69.

Bawer, Bruce. 1994. "Notes on Stonewall." *The New Republic,* June 13, 24–27, 30.

Bayles, Martha. 1994. "How to Talk about Art." *National Review,* May 30, 64–65.

Beaman, Lori G. 2003. "The Myth of Pluralism, Diversity, and Vigor: The Constitutional Privilege of Protestantism in the United States and Canada." *Journal for the Scientific Study of Religion* 42:311–25.

Beinart, Peter. 2008a. "Last of the Culture Warriors." *Washington Post,* November 3, A21.

Beinart, Peter. 2008b. "The New Liberal Order." *Time,* November 24, 30–32.

Bell, Daniel. 1975. "The End of American Exceptionalism." *Public Interest* 41:193–224.

Bell, Daniel. 1989. "American Exceptionalism Revisited: The Role of Civil Society." *Public Interest* 95:38–56.

Bell, David A. 1986. "Ghosts of Leftists Past." *The New Republic,* August 11 and 18, 17.

Bell, Joyce M., and Douglas Hartmann. 2007. "Diversity in Everyday Discourse: The Cultural Ambiguities and Consequences of 'Happy Talk.'" *American Sociological Review* 72:895–914.

Bellafante, Ginia. 1998. "Feminism: It's All about Me!" *Time,* June 29, 54–60.

Bellah, Robert N. 1970. "Civil Religion in America." In *Beyond Belief,* by Robert N. Bellah, 168–86. New York: Harper and Row.

Bellah, Robert N. 1974. "American Civil Religion in the 1970s." In *American Civil Religion,* ed. Russell E. Richey and Donald G. Jones, 255–72. New York: Harper and Row.

Bellah, Robert N. 1975. *The Broken Covenant.* New York: Seabury.

Bellah, Robert N. 1976. "Response to the Panel on Civil Religion." *Sociological Analysis* 37:153–59.

Bellah, Robert N. 1978. "Religion and Legitimation in the American Republic." *Society* 15:193–201.

Bellah, Robert N. 2002. "The Protestant Structure of American Culture: Multiculture or Monoculture?" *Hedgehog Review* 4:7–28.

Bellah, Robert N., Richard Madsen, William M. Sullivan, Ann Swidler, and Steven M. Tipton. 1985/1996. *Habits of the Heart.* Berkeley: University of California Press.

Bellah, Robert N., Richard Madsen, William M. Sullivan, Ann Swidler, and Steven M. Tipton. 1991. *The Good Society.* New York: Random House.

Bennett, William J. 1992. *The De-Valuing of America.* New York: Summit.

Berger, Bennett M. 1995. *An Essay on Culture.* Berkeley: University of California Press.

Berger, Peter L. 1999. "The Desecularization of the World: A Global Overview." In *The Desecularization of the World,* ed. Peter L. Berger, 1–18. Grand Rapids, MI: Eerdmans.

Berger, Peter L., and Thomas Luckmann. 1966. *The Social Construction of Reality.* Garden City, NY: Doubleday.

Berns, Walter. 1990. "Saving the NEA." *National Review,* November 19, 34–36.

Bernstein, Richard. 1995. *Dictatorship of Virtue.* New York: Vintage.

Berreby, David. 2008. "The Case for Fitting In." *New York Times Magazine,* March 30, 25.

Bethell, Tom. 1997. "Smoking and Sex." *National Review,* May 19, 36.

Bickford, Susan. 1999. "Reconfiguring Pluralism: Identity and Institutions in the Inegalitarian Polity." *American Journal of Political Science* 43:86–108.

Billings, Dwight B., and Shaunna L. Scott. 1994. "Religion and Political Legitimation." *Annual Review of Sociology* 20:173–201.

Bishop, George. 1999. "Poll Trends: Americans' Belief in God." *Public Opinion Quarterly* 63:421–34.

Blankenhorn, David, and Jonathan Rauch. 2009. "A Reconciliation on Gay Marriage." *New York Times,* February 22, 11.

Blau, Judith. 2007. "What Would Sartre Say? And, Arendt's Reply?" *Social Forces* 85:1063–78.

Bloom, Allan. 1987. *The Closing of the American Mind.* New York: Simon and Schuster.

Blow, Richard. 1987. "Those Were the Gays." *The New Republic,* November 2, 14–16.

Bobo, Laurence. 1991. "Social Responsibility, Individualism, and Redistributive Policies." *Sociological Forum* 6:71–92.

Boggs, James P. 2002. "Anthropological Knowledge and Native American Cultural Practice in the Liberal Polity." *American Anthropologist* 104:599–610.

Bohman, James. 2003. "Deliberative Toleration." *Political Theory* 31:757–79.

Bolce, Louis, and Gerald De Maio. 1999a. "Religious Outlook, Culture War Politics, and Antipathy toward Christian Fundamentalists." *Public Opinion Quarterly* 63:29–61.

Bolce, Louis, and Gerald De Maio. 1999b. "The Anti-Christian Fundamentalist Factor in Contemporary Politics." *Public Opinion Quarterly* 63:508–42.

Bork, Robert H. 1989. "Why Do the Liberals Rage?" *National Review,* December 8, 26–27.

Bosman, Julie. 2008. "Election Eve: Palin's Final Pitch." *New York Times,* November 3, posted online at http://thecaucus.blogs.nytimes.com.

Bowen, Ezra. 1986. "A Courtroom Clash over Textbooks." *Time,* October 27, 94.
Bowen, Ezra. 1988. "The Canons under Fire." *Time,* April 11, 66–67.
Boyer, Paul. 1996. "In Search of the Fourth 'R': The Treatment of Religion in American History Textbooks and Survey Courses." *History Teacher* 29:195–216.
Boyer, Peter J. 2008. "Party Faithful." *New Yorker,* September 8, 24–31.
Breslauer, Jon. 1995. "Not-So-Clueless." *The New Republic,* September 4, 22–25.
Brewer, Mark D. 2005. "The Rise of Partisanship and the Expansion of Partisan Conflict within the American Electorate." *Political Research Quarterly* 58:219–29.
Broadway, Bill. 2001. "War Cry from the Pulpit; Some Fear Mix of Patriotism, Religion in Bush's Vow to Rid World of Evil." *Washington Post,* September 22, B09.
Bromwich, David. 1995. "Culturalism, the Euthanasia of Liberalism." *Dissent* 42:89–102.
Brookhiser, Richard. 1990. "Taming the Tribes of America." *National Review,* November 5, 63–65.
Brookhiser, Richard. 1991. "Of Church, Pews and Bedrooms." *Time,* August 26, 70.
Brookhiser, Richard. 1992. "We Can All Share American Culture." *Time,* August 31, 74.
Brookhiser, Richard. 1993a. "The Cultural Right Is Here to Stay." *Time,* May 31, 74.
Brookhiser, Richard. 1993b. "III Cheers for the WASPs." *Time,* December 2, 78–79.
Brookhiser, Richard. 1994. "Let Us Pray." *Time,* December 19, 84.
Brooks, Clem. 2002. "Religious Influence and the Politics of Family Decline Concern: Trends, Sources, and U.S. Political Behavior." *American Sociological Review* 67:191–211.
Brooks, Clem, and Jeff Manza. 1994. "Do Changing Values Explain the New Politics? A Critical Assessment of the 'Postmaterialist' Thesis." *Sociological Quarterly* 35:541–70.
Brooks, Clem, and Jeff Manza. 1997. "Social Cleavages and Political Alignments: U.S. Presidential Elections, 1960 to 1992." *American Sociological Review* 62:937–46.
Brooks, David. 2004. "The Values-Vote Myth." *New York Times,* November 6, A19.
Brown, Robert D., and Edward G. Carmines. 1995. "Materialists, Postmaterialists, and the Criteria for Political Choice in U.S. Presidential Elections." *Journal of Politics* 57:483–94.
Brumann, Christoph. 1999. "Writing for Culture: Why a Successful Concept Should Not Be Discarded." *Current Anthropology* 40:S1–S13.
Brustein, Robert. 1991. "The Use and Abuse of Multiculturalism." *The New Republic,* September 16–23, 31–34.
Brustein, Robert. 1992. "The War on the Arts." *The New Republic,* September 7–14, 35–38.
Brustein, Robert. 1995. "The Death of the Collective Ideal." *The New Republic,* September 11, 27–28, 30.
Brustein, Robert. 1997a. "On Cultural Power." *The New Republic,* March 3, 31–34.
Brustein, Robert. 1997b. "Funding Audiences." *The New Republic,* June 9, 32–33.
Brustein, Robert. 1997c. "Mend It, Don't End It." *The New Republic,* October 6, 29–31.
Brustein, Robert. 1997d. "The Decline of High Culture." *The New Republic,* November 3, 29–32.

Buchanan, Patrick. 2008. "The Palin Firestorm." September 9. http://www.realclearpolitics.com/articles/2008/09/one_of_them_and_one_of_us.html.
Buckley, William F., Jr. 1990a. "Are You 'Responsible'?" *National Review,* May 14, 62–63.
Buckley, William F., Jr. 1990b. "Cincinnati Censorship." *National Review,* May 14, 62.
Buckley, William F., Jr. 1992a. "Quayle versus Mapplethorpeism." *National Review,* July 20, 54–55.
Buckley, William F., Jr. 1992b. "A Fresh Deal for Gays." *National Review,* October 5, 71.
Buckley, William F., Jr. 1993a. "Senator Goldwater and the Gays." *National Review,* July 19, 70.
Buckley, William F., Jr. 1993b. "Is Multiculturalism the Answer?" *National Review,* August 9, 70–71.
Buckley, William F., Jr. 1994. "Let Us Pray?" *National Review,* October 10, 86–87.
Buckley, William F., Jr. 1995. "Excelsior the Counterculture." *National Review,* January 23, 78–79.
Buckley, William F., Jr. 1996. "Is There a God behind Religion?" *National Review,* February 12, 63.
Buckley, William F., Jr. 1997. "Re-Creating Creation." *National Review,* December 31, 62–63.
Caldwell, Christopher. 1999. "Pro-Lifestyle." *The New Republic,* April 5, 14–16.
Calhoon, Robert M. 1991. "Religion and Individualism in Early America." In *American Chameleon,* ed. Richard O. Curry and Lawrence B. Goodheart, 44–65. Kent, OH: Kent State University Press.
Campbell, David E. 2006. "Religious 'Threat' in Contemporary Presidential Elections." *Journal of Politics* 68:104–15.
Carey, James W. 1988. "Editor's Introduction: Taking Culture Seriously." In *Media, Myths, and Narratives: Television and the Press,* ed. James W. Carey, 8–18. Newbury Park, CA: Sage.
Carlson, Margaret. 1997. "Partial-Truth Abortion." *Time,* March 24, 40.
Carlson, Margaret. 1998. "The Passive Majority." *Time,* November 9, 60.
Carmines, Edward G., and Geoffrey C. Layman. 1997. "Value Priorities, Partisanship, and Electoral Choice." *Political Behavior* 19:283–316.
Carroll, Jackson W., and Penny Long Marler. 1995. "Culture Wars? Insights from Ethnographies of Two Protestant Seminaries." *Sociology of Religion* 56:1–20.
Casanova, José. 1992. "Private and Public Religions." *Social Research* 59:17–57.
Casanova, José. 1994. *Public Religions in the Modern World.* Chicago: University of Chicago Press.
Chait, Jonathan. 1997. "Illiberal Arts." *The New Republic,* September 29, 14, 16.
Chan, Tak Wing, and John H. Goldthorpe. 2007. "Class and Status: The Conceptual Distinction and Its Empirical Relevance." *American Sociological Review* 72:512–32.
Charen, Mona. 1984. "The Feminist Mistake." *National Review,* March 23, 24–27.
Chaves, Mark. 1994. "Secularization as Declining Religious Authority." *Social Forces* 72:749–74.
Chaves, Mark. 2002. "Abiding Faith." *Contexts* 1:19–26.

Chavez, Linda. 1994. "Demystifying Multiculturalism." *National Review,* February 21, 26, 28, 30, 32.

Chiusano, Michael. 1996. "Parents' Rights." *National Review,* September 30, 55–57.

Chock, Phyllis Pease. 1995. "Culturalism: Pluralism, Culture, and Race in the *Harvard Encyclopedia of American Ethnic Groups.*" *Identities* 1:301–23.

Christenson, James A., and Ronald C. Wimberley. 1978. "Who Is Civil Religious?" *Sociological Analysis* 39:17–83.

Christian Science Monitor. 2008. "The Palin Factor in the 'Culture Wars'." September 12, 8.

Church, George J. 1995. "Pro-Life and Pro-Choice? Yes!" *Time,* March 6, 108.

Citrin, Jack, David O. Sears, Christopher Muste, and Cara Wong. 2001. "Multiculturalism in American Public Opinion." *British Journal of Political Science* 31:247–75.

Clark, Terry Nicols. 2003. "The Breakdown of Class Politics." *American Sociologist* 34:17–32.

Clarke, Breena, and Susan Tifft Durham. 1991. "A 'Race Man' Argues for a Broader Curriculum." *Time,* April 22, 16, 18.

Cloud, John. 2000. "Can a Scout Be Gay?" *Time,* May 1, 34–36.

Clydesdale, Timothy T. 1997. "Family Behaviors among Early U.S. Baby Boomers: Exploring the Effects of Religion and Income Change, 1965–1982." *Social Forces* 76:605–35.

CNN. 2008. "Exit Polls: Obama Wins Big among Young, Minority Voters." November 4. http://www.cnn.com/2008/POLITICS/11/04/exit.polls/.

Cockburn, Alexander. 1985. "Jackboot Liberals." *The Nation,* January 26, 70.

Cockburn, Alexander. 1991. "Bush and P.C.—A Conspiracy So Immense." *The Nation,* May 27, 685, 690–91, 704.

Connell, Noreen. 1986. "Feminists and Families." *The Nation,* August 16–23, 106–8.

Cooper, Michael. 2008. "Palin on Offensive, Attacks Obama's Ties to 60's Radical." *New York Times,* October 5, A31.

Corliss, Richard. 1990. "X Rated." *Time,* May 7, 92, 94–95, 97–99.

Corse, Sarah M. 1995. "Nations and Novels: Cultural Politics and Literary Use." *Social Forces* 73:1279–1308.

Cost, Jay. 2008. "On the 'Palin Effect.'" October 15. http://www.realclearpolitics .com/horseraceblog/2008/10/on_the_palin_effect .html.

Cox, Harvey. 1996. "The Transcendent Dimension." *The Nation,* January 1, 20, 22–23.

Crain, Caleb. 1993. "Gay Glue." *The New Republic,* May 10, 16.

Cunningham, Mark. 1992. "The Abortion War." *National Review,* November 2, 42–48.

Curry, Richard O., and Karl E. Valois. 1991. "The Emergence of an Individualistic Ethos in American Society." In *American Chameleon,* ed. Richard O. Curry and Lawrence B. Goodheart, 20–43. Kent, OH: Kent State University Press.

Custred, Glynn. 1997. "Country Time." *National Review,* June 16, 39–40.

Danto, Arthur C. 1985. "Art." *The Nation,* June 22, 775–76.

Danto, Arthur C. 1997. "'Elitism' and the N.E.A." *The Nation,* November 17, 6–7.

Davis, Darren W. 2000. "Individual Level Examination of Postmaterialism in the U.S.: Political Tolerance, Racial Attitudes, Environmentalism, and Participatory Norms." *Political Research Quarterly* 53:455–75.

Davis, Darren W., and Christian Davenport. 1999. "Assessing the Validity of the Post-materialism Index." *American Political Science Review* 93:649–64.

Davis, Derek H. 1997. "Law, Morals, and Civil Religion in America." *Journal of Church and State* 39:411–25.

Davis, Nancy J., and Robert V. Robinson. 1996a. "Are the Rumors of War Exaggerated? Religious Orthodoxy and Moral Progressivism in America." *American Journal of Sociology* 102:756–87.

Davis, Nancy J., and Robert V. Robinson. 1996b. "Religious Orthodoxy in American Society: The Myth of a Monolithic Camp." *Journal for the Scientific Study of Religion* 35:229–45.

Davis, Nancy J., and Robert V. Robinson. 1997. "A War for America's Soul? The American Religious Landscape." In *Culture Wars in American Politics,* ed. Rhys H. Williams, 39–63. New York: Aldine De Gruyter.

Degler, Carl N. 1987. "In Pursuit of an American History." *American Historical Review* 92:1–12.

Demerath, N. J., III. 2002. "A Sinner among the Saints: Confessions of a Sociologist of Culture and Religion." *Sociological Forum* 17:1–19.

Demerath, N. J., III, and Karen S. Straight. 1997. "Lambs among the Lions: America's Culture Wars in Cross-Cultural Perspective." In *Culture Wars in American Politics,* ed. Rhys H. Williams, 199–219. New York: Aldine De Gruyter.

Demerath, N. J., III, and Rhys H. Williams. 1985. "Civil Religion in an Uncivil Society." *Annals of the American Academy of Political and Social Science* 480:154–66.

Demerath, N. J., III, and Yonghe Yang. 1997. "What American Culture War? A View from the Trenches as Opposed to the Command Posts and the Press Corps." In *Culture Wars in American Politics,* ed. Rhys H. Williams, 17–38. New York: Aldine de Gruyter.

Derbyshire, John. 2000. "First Amendment First." *National Review,* October 9, 32, 34.

di Leonardo, Micaela. 1996. "Patterns of Culture Wars." *The Nation,* April 8, 25–29.

Dillon, Michele. 1996. "The American Abortion Debate: Culture War or Normal Discourse?" In *The American Culture Wars,* ed. James L. Nolan Jr., 115–32. Charlottesville: University Press of Virginia.

DiMaggio, Paul. 1997. "Culture and Cognition." *Annual Review of Sociology* 23:263–87.

DiMaggio, Paul. 2003. "The Myth of Culture War." In *The Fractious Nation?* ed. Jonathan Rieder and Stephen Steinlight, 79–97. Berkeley: University of California Press.

DiMaggio, Paul, John Evans, and Bethany Bryson. 1996. "Have Americans' Social Attitudes Become More Polarized?" *American Journal of Sociology* 102:690–755.

Dionne, E. J., Jr. 2006. "Why the Culture War Is the Wrong War." *The Atlantic* 297:130–35.

Douthat, Ross. 2008. "Palin Fire." *National Review,* September 29, 39–41.

D'Souza, Dinesh. 1991. *Illiberal Education.* New York: Free Press.

Duberman, Martin. 1993. "A Matter of Difference." *The Nation,* July 5, 22–24.

Duch, Raymond M., and Kaare Strøm. 2004. "Liberty, Authority, and the New Politics." *Journal of Theoretical Politics* 16:233–62.

Eagleton, Terry. 2000. *The Idea of Culture.* Oxford: Blackwell.

Easterbrook, Gregg. 2000. "Abortion and Brain Waves." *The New Republic,* January 31, 21–25.

Edgell, Penny, Joseph Gerteis, and Douglas Hartmann. 2006. "Atheists as 'Other': Moral Boundaries and Cultural Membership in American Society." *American Sociological Review* 71:211–34.

Editorial. 1981a. "Creeping Sanity in Cambridge." *National Review,* February 20, 140–41.

Editorial. 1981b. "The Glorious Fourth." *National Review,* May 15, 532–33.

Editorial. 1984. "Prayer Power." *The Nation,* March 17, 307–8.

Editorial. 1988a. "A Cultural Conservative Manifesto." *National Review,* March 18, 21–22.

Editorial. 1988b. "The Culture of Apathy." *The New Republic,* February 8, 7–8.

Editorial. 1989. "Exhibitionism." *The New Republic,* July 17–24, 6.

Editorial. 1990a. "Art Appreciation." *The New Republic,* October 8, 7–8.

Editorial. 1990b. "The New Apartheid." *National Review,* July 23, 14.

Editorial. 1991a. "An American Culture." *National Review,* May 27, 18.

Editorial. 1991b. "Ex Uno, Plus" *National Review,* July 29, 16.

Editorial. 1991c. "Operation Rescue." *National Review,* October 7, 13.

Editorial. 1991d. "Mr. Sobol's Planet." *The New Republic,* July 15–22, 5–6.

Editorial. 1992. "Momma Dearest." *The New Republic,* August 10, 7.

Editorial. 1993a. "Don't Speak Its Name." *National Review,* August 9, 13–14.

Editorial. 1993b. "Queer Nation." *National Review,* August 9, 14, 16–17.

Editorial. 1993c. "Cross Purposes." *The Nation,* August 9, 157.

Editorial. 1994a. "Demagoguery in America." *The New Republic,* August 1, 7.

Editorial. 1994b. "Let Us Pray." *National Review,* December 19, 16–18.

Editorial. 1995a. "For Art's Sake." *The Nation,* February 6, 151–52.

Editorial. 1995b. "Polymorphous Perversity." *National Review,* November 27, 18.

Editorial. 1998a. "Dead Reckoning." *National Review,* January 26, 11–12, 14.

Editorial. 1998b. "Feminists Will Be Feminists." *National Review,* April 6, 17–18.

Editorial. 1998c. "Other Persuasions." *National Review,* August 3, 14, 16.

Editorial. 1999. "The Origin of Speciousness." *The New Republic,* September 6, 11–12.

Editorial. 2000a. "Separate but Equal?" *The New Republic,* January 10, 9.

Editorial. 2000b. "Crevices." *The New Republic,* July 24, 9.

Editorial. 2000c. "Holy Joe! A Culture War!" *The Nation,* October 9, 3.

Ehrenreich, Barbara. 1982. "Family Feud on the Left." *The Nation,* March 13, 234, 289, 303–6.

Ehrenreich, Barbara. 1990. "Sorry, Sisters, This Is Not the Revolution." *Time,* November 8, 15.

Ehrenreich, Barbara. 1991. "Teach Diversity—With a Smile." *Time,* April 8, 84.

Ehrenreich, Barbara. 1992a. ". . . Or Is It Creative Freedom?" *Time,* July 20, 89.

Ehrenreich, Barbara. 1992b. "Why the Religious Right Is Wrong." *Time,* September 17, 72.

Ehrenreich, Barbara. 1993a. "The Gap between Gay and Straight." *Time,* May 10, 76.

Ehrenreich, Barbara. 1993b. "Living Out the Wars of 1968." *Time,* June 7, 74.

Ehrenreich, Barbara. 1994. "Feminism Confronts Bobbittry." *Time,* January 24, 74.

Ehrenreich, Barbara. 1995. "In Defense of Talk Shows." *Time,* December 4, 92.
Ehrenreich, Barbara, and Janet McIntosh. 1997. "The New Creationism." *The Nation,* June 9, 11–13, 15–16.
Eichman, E. 1990. "Saving the Arts in Union Square." *National Review,* June 25, 23–24.
Eller, Jack David. 1997. "Anti-Anti-Multiculturalism." *American Anthropologist* 99: 249–56.
Elshtain, Jean Bethke. 1996. "Cardinal Virtue." *The New Republic,* December 9, 25.
Elshtain, Jean Bethke. 1998. "The Right Rights." *The New Republic,* June 15, 11–12.
Elson, John. 1994. "History, the Sequel." *Time,* November 7, 64.
"Endless Culture War." 2008. *The Economist,* October 4, 22–23.
Erikson, Kai T. 1976. *Everything in Its Path.* New York: Simon and Schuster.
Etzioni, Amitai. 1993. "How to Make Marriage Matter." *Time,* September 6, 76.
Evangelical Manifesto Steering Committee. 2008. *An Evangelical Manifesto.* May 7. http://www.anevangelicalmanifesto.com.
Evans, John H. 1997. "Worldviews or Social Groups as the Source of Moral Value Attitudes: Implications for the Culture Wars Thesis." *Sociological Forum* 12:371–404.
Evans, John H. 2002. "Polarization in Abortion Attitudes in U.S. Religious Traditions, 1972–1998." *Sociological Forum* 17:397–422.
Evans, John H. 2003. "Have Americans' Attitudes Become More Polarized?—An Update." *Social Science Quarterly* 84:71–90.
Evans, John H. 2006. "Polarized America? Letter to the Editor." *Commentary* 121:3–4.
Evans, M. Stanton. 1995. "What Wall?" *National Review,* January 23, 56–58, 60, 76.
Feldblum, Chai R. 2000. "Moral Law, Changing Morals." *The Nation,* October 9, 22, 24–25.
Feldman, Noah. 2007. "Universal Faith." *New York Times Magazine,* August 26, 13–15.
Ferber, Michael. 1985. "Religious Revival on the Left." *The Nation,* July 6–13, 9–13.
Ferguson, Andrew. 1989. "Mad about Mapplethorpe." *National Review,* August 4, 20–21.
Finifter, Ada W., ed. 1972. *Alienation and the Social System.* New York: Wiley.
Finn, Chester E., Jr. 1986. "Two Cheers for Education's G-Men." *National Review,* August 15, 35–37.
Fiorina, Morris P. 2006. "Polarized America? Letter to the Editor." *Commentary* 121:3.
Fiorina, Morris P., with Samuel J. Abrams and Jeremy C. Pope. 2005. *Culture War? The Myth of a Polarized America.* New York: Pearson Longman.
Fischer, Claude S. 2000. "Just How Is It That Americans Are Individualistic?" Paper presented at the American Sociological Association Meetings, Washington, D.C.
Fischer, Claude S. 2008. "Paradoxes of American Individualism." *Sociological Forum* 23:363–72.
Fischer, Claude S., and Michael Hout. 2006. *Century of Difference.* New York: Russell Sage Foundation.
FitzGerald, Frances. 1986. *Cities on a Hill.* New York: Simon and Schuster.
Flanagan, Scott. 1987. "Value Change in Industrial Societies." *American Political Science Review* 81:1303–19.
Flanagan, Scott C., and Aie-Rie Lee. 2003. "The New Politics, Culture Wars, and the

Authoritarian-Libertarian Value Change in Advanced Industrial Democracies." *Comparative Political Studies* 36:235–70.
Foner, Eric. 1995. "Bobbing History." *The Nation,* September 25, 302.
Fonte, John. 1996. "We the Peoples." *National Review,* March 25, 47–49.
Forsythe, Clarke D. 1999. "First Steps." *National Review,* December 20, 42, 44–45.
Frank, Thomas. 1997. "Liberation Marketing." *The Nation,* January 13–20, 10.
Frank, Thomas. 2001. *One Market under God.* New York: Anchor.
Frank, Thomas. 2005. *What's the Matter with Kansas?* New York: Holt.
Frank, Tom. 1996. "Hip Is Dead." *The Nation,* April 1, 16, 18–19.
Fredrickson, George M. 1995. "From Exceptionalism to Variability: Recent Developments in Cross-National Comparative History." *Journal of American History* 82:587–604.
Friend, Tad. 1992. "The Case for Middlebrow." *The New Republic,* March 2, 24–27.
Fukuyama, Francis. 1995. *Trust.* New York: Free Press.
Fukuyama, Francis. 1999. "How to Re-Moralize America." *Wilson Quarterly* 23:32–44.
Fumento, Michael J. 1988. "The Political Uses of an Epidemic." *The New Republic,* August 8–15, 19–23.
Gahr, Evan. 1997. "Tuning Out Religion." *National Review,* October 27, 44–46.
Gallagher, Maggie. 1987. "The New Pro-Life Rebels." *National Review,* February 27, 37–39.
Gallagher, Maggie. 1999. "Marriage-Saving." *National Review,* November 8, 38–40.
Gans, Herbert J. 1979. "Symbolic Ethnicity: The Future of Ethnic Groups and Cultures in America." In *On the Making of Americans: Essays in Honor of David Riesman,* ed. Herbert J. Gans, Nathan Glazer, Joseph R. Gusfield, and Christopher Jencks, 193–220. Philadelphia: University of Pennsylvania Press.
Gans, Herbert J. 1980. *Deciding What's News.* New York: Vintage.
Gans, Herbert J. 1988. *Middle American Individualism.* New York: Free Press.
Gates, Henry Louis, Jr. 1992. *Loose Canons.* New York: Oxford University Press.
Geertz, Clifford. 1973. *The Interpretation of Cultures.* New York: Basic Books.
Gergen, Kenneth J. 1991. *The Saturated Self.* New York: Basic Books.
Gerstle, Gary. 1994. "The Protean Character of American Liberalism." *American Historical Review* 99:1043–73.
Gerteis, Joseph, and Mike Savage. 1998. "The Salience of Class in Britain and America: A Comparative Analysis." *British Journal of Sociology* 49:252–74.
Gevisser, Mark. 1988. "Lesbian and Gay Students Choose." *The Nation,* March 26, 413–14.
Gibbs, Nancy. 1991. "America's Holy War." *Time,* December 9, 60–66, 68.
Gibbs, Nancy. 1992. "The War against Feminism." *Time,* March 9, 50–55.
Gibbs, Nancy. 1999. "America, Love It or Leave It." *Time,* April 5, 47.
Gibbs, Nancy. 2000. "Whose Bully Pulpit Now?" *Time,* September 11, 38.
Gibbs, Nancy, and Jeanne McDowell. 1992. "How to Revive a Revolution." *Time,* March 9, 56–57.
Gibson, James L. 1992. "The Political Consequences of Intolerance: Cultural Conformity and Political Freedom." *American Political Science Review* 86:338–56.
Giesea, Jeffrey R. 1997. "Western Sieve." *National Review,* September 15, 63–64, 84.

Gilder, George. 1986. "The Sexual Revolution at Home." *National Review,* October 10, 30–32, 34.

Gingrich, Newt. 1995. "Cutting Cultural Funding: A Reply." *Time,* August 21, 70–71.

Gitlin, Todd. 1995. *The Twilight of Common Dreams.* New York: Metropolitan.

Glazer, Nathan. 1988. "Canon Fodder." *The New Republic* August 22, 19–21.

Glazer, Nathan. 1991. "In Defense of Multiculturalism." *The New Republic,* September 2, 18–20, 22.

Glazer, Nathan. 1997. *We Are All Multiculturalists Now.* Cambridge: Harvard University Press.

Glynn, Patrick. 1999. "Monkey on Our Backs." *National Review,* September 13, 42, 44.

Goldberg, Jonah. 2000. "Violent Fantasy." *National Review,* October 23, 62–65.

Goldberg, Steven. 1991. "Feminism against Science." *National Review,* November 18, 30–33.

Goldberg, Steven. 1993. "Can Women Beat Men at Their Own Game?" *National Review,* December 27, 30, 32, 34–36.

Goode, Judith. 2001. "Teaching against Culturalist Essentialism." In *Cultural Diversity in the United States,* ed. Ida Susser and Thomas C. Patterson, 434–56. Malden, MA: Blackwell.

Goodheart, Lawrence B., and Richard O. Curry. 1991. "A Confusion of Voices: The Crisis of Individualism in Twentieth-Century America." In *American Chameleon,* ed. Richard O. Curry and Laurence B. Goodhart, 188–212. Kent, OH: Kent State University Press.

Gordon, Linda. 1998. "Back-Alley Abortion." *The Nation,* November 16, 5.

Gorski, Philip S. 2000. "Historicizing the Secularization Debate: Church, State, and Society in Late Medieval and Early Modern Europe, ca. 1300 to 1700." *American Sociological Review* 65:138–67.

Grabb, Edward, Douglas Baer, and James Curtis. 1999. "Origins of American Individualism: Reconsidering the Historical Evidence." *Canadian Journal of Sociology* 24:511–33.

Grabb, Edward, Douglas Baer, and James Curtis. 2000. "Pluralism and Toleration in Contemporary Political Philosophy." *Political Studies* 48:323–33.

Graff, E. J. 1996. "Retying the Knot." *The Nation,* June 24, 12.

Graff, Gerald, and William E. Cain. 1989. "Peace Plan for the Canon Wars." *The Nation,* March 6:310–13.

Grant, Daniel. 1999. "Bland Art in Every Pot." *The Nation,* November 29, 44–47.

Gray, John. 1992. "The Virtues of Toleration." *National Review,* October 5, 28, 30, 32, 34–36.

Gray, John. 2000. "Pluralism and Toleration in Contemporary Political Philosophy." *Political Studies* 48:323–33.

Gray, Paul. 1991. "Whose America?" *Time,* July 8, 12–17.

Greeley, Andrew. 1991. "American Exceptionalism: The Religious Phenomenon." In *Is America Different?* ed. Byron E. Shafer, 94–115. New York: Oxford University Press, 94–115.

Greeley, Andrew M., and Michael Hout. 1999. "Americans Increasing Belief in Life

after Death: Religious Competition and Acculturation." *American Sociological Review* 64:813–35.
Greeley, Andrew M., and Michael Hout. 2006. *The Truth about Conservative Christians.* Chicago: University of Chicago Press.
Green, Philip. 1989. "Abortion: The Abusable Past." *The Nation,* August 7–14, 177–79.
Gross, Neil, and Solon Simmons. 2007. "The Social and Political Views of American Professors." Working Paper, September 24.
Guinness, Os. 1993. *The American Hour.* New York: Free Press.
Hadaway, C. Kirk, Penny Long Marler, and Mark Chaves. 1993. "What the Polls Don't Show: A Closer Look at U.S. Church Attendance." *American Sociological Review* 58:741–52.
Hadden, Jeffrey K. 1987. "Toward Desacralizing Secularization Theory." *Social Forces* 65:587–611.
Hajda, Jan. 1961. "Alienation and Integration of Student Intellectuals." *American Sociological Review* 26:758–77.
Halman, Loek. 1996. "Individualism in Individualized Society? Results from the European Values Surveys." *International Journal of Comparative Sociology* 37:195–214.
Halman, Loek, and Veerle Draulans. 2006. "How Secular Is Europe?" *British Journal of Sociology* 57:263–88.
Hannerz, Ulf. 1992. *Cultural Complexity.* New York: Columbia University Press.
Harris, Michael P. 1988. "Second Thoughts about Abortion." *Time,* July 4, 44.
Harris, Sam. 2007. "God-Drunk Society." *The Atlantic* 300:44.
Hart, Jeffrey. 1987. "Ethnophobia, Heterophobia, and Liberal Fascism." *National Review,* February 13, 46.
Hart, Jeffrey. 1988. "Does the University Have a Future?" *National Review,* April 1, 32.
Hart, Jeffrey. 1989a. "Report from a Phallocrat." *National Review,* February 24, 45.
Hart, Jeffrey. 1989b. "Profscam." *National Review,* April 21, 39.
Hart, Jeffrey. 1996. "What Is an American?" *National Review,* April 22, 52, 54–56.
Hartmann, Douglas, and Joseph Gerteis. 2005. "Dealing with Diversity: Mapping Multiculturalism in Sociological Terms." *Sociological Theory* 23:208–40.
Hartz, Louis. 1955. *The Liberal Tradition in America.* New York: Harcourt, Brace and World.
Healy, Patrick. 2008. "A Riveting Speaker, Waving the Flag." *New York Times,* October 14, A19.
Hechter, Michael. 2004. "From Class to Culture." *American Journal of Sociology* 110:400–445.
Henry, William A., III. 1990. "Beyond the Melting Pot." *Time,* April 9, 28–31.
Henry, William A., III. 1991. "Upside Down in the Groves of Academe." *Time,* April 1, 66–69.
Henry, William A., III. 1993. "The Politics of Separation." *Time,* November 18, 73–75.
Hentoff, Nat. 1992. "Pro-Choice Bigots." *The New Republic,* November 30, 21, 24–25.
Herberg, Will. 1956. *Protestant-Catholic-Jew.* Garden City, NY: Doubleday.
Herberg, Will. 1974. "America's Civil Religion: What It Is and Whence It Comes." In *American Civil Religion,* ed. Russell E. Richey and Donald G. Jones, 76–88. New York: Harper and Row.

Herrera, Richard. 1996–97. "Understanding the Language of Politics: A Study of Elites and Masses." *Political Science Quarterly* 111:619–37.

Hetherington, Marc J. 2001. "Resurgent Mass Partisanship: The Role of Elite Polarization." *American Political Science Review* 95:619–31.

Hicks, Alexander. 2006. "Free-Market and Religious Fundamentalists versus Poor Relief." *American Sociological Review* 71:503–10.

Himmelfarb, Gertrude. 1999. *One Nation, Two Cultures*. New York: Knopf.

Hitchens, Christopher. 1984. "Minority Report." *The Nation,* September 22, 230.

Hitchens, Christopher. 1985. "Minority Report." *The Nation,* June 8, 694.

Hitchens, Christopher. 1991. "Minority Report." *The Nation,* October 21, 472.

Hollinger, David A. 1995. *Postethnic America.* New York: Basic Books.

Hollinger, David A. 2001. "The 'Secularization' Question and the United States in the Twentieth Century." *Church History* 70:132–43.

Hollinger, David A. 2002. "Why Is There So Much Christianity in the United States?" *Church History* 71:858–64.

Hook, Sidney. 1989. "Civilization and Its Malcontents." *National Review,* October 13, 30–33.

Hoover, Dennis R., Michael D. Martinez, Samuel H. Reimer, and Kenneth D. Wald. 2002. "Evangelicalism Meets the Continental Divide: Moral and Economic Conservatism in the United States and Canada." *Political Research Quarterly* 55:351–74.

Horton, Michael S. 1994. *Beyond Culture Wars*. Chicago: Moody.

Houppert, Karen. 2000. "The Meaning of Life." *The Nation,* March 13, 7.

Hout, Michael, Clem Brooks, and Jeff Manza. 1995. "The Democratic Class Struggle in the United States, 1948–1992." *American Sociological Review* 60:805–28.

Hout, Michael, and Claude S. Fischer. 2002. "Why More Americans Have No Religious Preference: Politics and Generations." *American Sociological Review* 67:165–90.

Hout, Michael, and Andrew Greeley. 1998. "What Church Officials' Reports Don't Show: Another Look at Church Attendance Data." *American Sociological Review* 63:113–19.

Howe, Irving. 1984. "Toward an Open Culture." *The New Republic,* March 5, 25–29.

Howe, Irving. 1991. "The Value of the Canon." *The New Republic,* February 18, 40–44, 46–47.

Hoynes, William. 1996. "Public Television and the Culture Wars." In *The American Culture Wars,* ed. James L. Nolan Jr., 61–87. Charlottesville: University Press of Virginia.

Hsu, Hua. 2009. "The End of White America?" *The Atlantic* 303:46–55.

Hudson, Deal W. 1996. "Thinking about God." *National Review,* September 30, 40, 42.

Hughes, Robert. 1989. "A Loony Parody of Cultural Democracy." *Time,* August 14, 82.

Hughes, Robert. 1990. "Whose Art Is It, Anyway?" *Time,* June 4, 46–48.

Hughes, Robert. 1992a. "The Fraying of America." *Time,* February 3, 44–49.

Hughes, Robert. 1992b. "The NEA: Trampled Again." *Time,* June 22, 43.

Hughes, Robert. 1995. "Pulling the Fuse on Culture." *Time,* August 7, 60–68.

Hunter, James Davison. 1991. *Culture Wars*. New York: Basic Books.

Hunter, James Davison. 1994. *Before the Shooting Begins*. New York: Free Press.

Hunter, James Davison. 1996. "Response to Davis and Robinson: Remembering Durkheim." *Journal for the Scientific Study of Religion* 35:246–48.

Hunter, James Davison. 1998. "The American Culture War." In *The Limits of Social Cohesion,* ed. Peter L. Berger, 1–37. Boulder, CO: Westview.

Hunter, James Davison. 2002. "Beyond Individualism? A Response to Robert Bellah." *Hedgehog Review* 4:42–48.

Hunter, James Davison. 2004. "Culture Wars Revisited." *Insight* 10:5–6.

Hunter, James Davison, and Alan Wolfe. 2006. *Is There a Culture War?* Washington, DC: Brookings Institution Press.

Hunter, Nan D. 1991. "Sexual Dissent and the Family." *The Nation,* October 7, 406, 408, 410–11.

Hyde, Henry J. 1990a. "The Culture War." *National Review,* April 30, 25–27.

Hyde, Henry J. 1990b. "Morals, Markets, and Freedom." *National Review,* November 5, 52–54.

Inglehart, Ronald. 1977. *The Silent Revolution* Princeton: Princeton University Press.

Inglehart, Ronald, and Wayne E. Baker. 2000. "Modernization, Cultural Change, and the Persistence of Traditional Values." *American Sociological Review* 65:19–51.

Inkeles, Alex. 1990–91. "National Character Revisited." *Tocqueville Review* 12:83–117.

Ireland, Doug. 1999. "Rebuilding the Gay Movement." *The Nation,* July 12, 11–12, 15–16, 18.

Jacoby, Russell. 1994. *Dogmatic Wisdom.* New York: Doubleday.

Jacoby, Tamar. 1991. "Psyched Out." *The New Republic,* February 18, 28–30.

Jelen, Ted G. 1990. "Religious Belief and Attitude Constraint." *Journal for the Scientific Study of Religion* 29:118–25.

Jelen, Ted. G., and Clyde Wilcox. 1997. "Conscientious Objectors in the Culture War? A Typology of Attitudes toward Church-State Relations." *Sociology of Religion* 58:277–87.

Jennings, M. Kent. 1992. "Ideological Thinking among Mass Publics and Political Elites." *Public Opinion Quarterly* 56:419–41.

Jensen, Richard. 1995. "The Culture Wars, 1965–1995: A Historian's Map." *Journal of Social History* 29:17–37.

Jones, Donald G., and Russell E. Richey. 1974. "The Civil Religion Debate." In *American Civil Religion,* ed. Donald G. Jones and Russell E. Richey, 3–18. New York: Harper and Row.

Jones, Terry. 2005. "Why They Voted." *St. Louis Journalism Review* June, 8, 24.

Joppke, Christian. 1996. "Multiculturalism and Immigration: A Comparison of the United States, Germany, and Great Britain." *Theory and Society* 25:449–500.

Judis, John B. 1999. "Value-Free." *The New Republic,* April 26–May 3, 53, 55–56.

Kallen, Horace M. 1956. *Cultural Pluralism and the American Idea.* Philadelphia: University of Pennsylvania Press.

Kallen, Horace M. 1957. "Alain Locke and Cultural Pluralism." *Journal of Philosophy* 54:119–27.

Kaminer, Wendy. 1996. "The Last Taboo." *The New Republic,* October 14, 24–28, 32.

Kammen, Michael. 1972. *People of Paradox*. New York: Knopf.

Kammen, Michael. 1993. "The Problem of American Exceptionalism: A Reconsideration." *American Quarterly* 45:1–43.

Kaufman, Jason. 2002. *For the Common Good? American Civic Life and the Golden Age of Fraternity*. New York: Oxford University Press.

Kaufmann, Karen M. 2002. "Culture Wars, Secular Realignment, and the Gender Gap in Party Identification." *Political Behavior* 24:283–307.

Kautz, Steven. 1993. "Liberalism and the Idea of Toleration." *American Journal of Political Science* 37:610–32.

Kazal, Russell A. 1995. "Revisiting Assimilation: The Rise, Fall, and Reappraisal of a Concept in American Ethnic History." *American Historical Review* 100:437–71.

Kazin, Michael. 1998. "The Politics of Devotion." *The Nation*, April 6, 16, 18–19.

Kidd, Dustin. 2006. "Rethinking the Culture Wars Concept." *Culture* 20:1, 4–6.

Kimball, Roger. 1990. *Tenured Radicals*. New York: Harper and Row.

Kimball, Roger. 2000. *The Long March: How the Cultural Revolution of the 1960's Changed America*. San Francisco: Encounter.

Kimeldorf, Howard, and Judith Stepan-Norris. 1992. "Historical Studies of Labor Movements in the United States." *Annual Review of Sociology* 18:495–517.

King, Florence. 1992. "She Dies in the End." *National Review*, July 6, 64.

Kinsley, Michael. 1989. "The New Politics of Abortion." *Time*, July 17, 96.

Kinsley, Michael. 1991. "P.C.B.S." *The New Republic*, May 20, 8, 50.

Kinsley, Michael. 1992a. "Arts and Crafts." *The New Republic*, March 16, 6, 41.

Kinsley, Michael. 1992b. "Happy Families." *The New Republic*, June 15, 6.

Kinsley, Michael. 1992c. "Ice-T: Is the Issue Social Responsibility . . ." *Time*, July 20, 88.

Kinsley, Michael. 1993. "Right-Wing P.C. Is Still P.C." *Time*, August 9, 66.

Kinsley, Michael. 1996. "America Tiptoes to the Left." *Time*, December 9, 38.

Kirk, Russell. 1983. "The Rediscovery of Creation." *National Review*, May 27, 626, 640–41.

Kirkpatrick, David D. 2007. "The Evangelical Crackup." *New York Times Magazine*, October 28, 38–45, 60, 64, 66.

Kirkpatrick, David D. 2008. "Firing Up the Faithful with Echoes of Culture War Rhetoric." *New York Times*, September 5, A23.

Klinghoffer, David. 1989. "Scenes from the Gay Life." *National Review*, August 4, 22–23.

Klinghoffer, David. 1996. "Kitsch Religion." *National Review*, June 3, 49–53.

Klinghoffer, David. 1998. "Gay Okay?" *National Review*, September 1, 24, 26.

Kohut, Andrew, John C. Green, Scott Keeter, and Robert C. Toth. 2000. *The Diminishing Divide*. Washington, DC: Brookings Institution Press.

Konig, Susan Brady. 1997. "They've Got to Be Carefully Taught." *National Review*, September 15, 46.

Koning, Hans. 1980. "Direct Line." *The Nation*, November 5, 501.

Kopkind, Andrew. 1993. "The Gay Moment." *The Nation*, May 3, 577, 590, 592, 594–96, 598, 600–602.

Kopkind, Andrew, and Anne-Christine d'Adesky. 1993. "A Queer Nation." *The Nation,* July 5, 3–4.

Kramer, Hilton. 1993. "Hold the Arts Page." *National Review,* June 21, 37–39.

Krauthammer, Charles. 1981. "The Humanist Phantom." *The New Republic,* July 25, 20–25.

Krauthammer, Charles. 1984. "America's Holy War." *The New Republic,* April 9, 15–19.

Krauthammer, Charles. 1990. "Education: Doing Bad and Feeling Good." *Time,* February 5, 78.

Krauthammer, Charles. 1991. "Hail Columbus, Dead White Male." *Time,* May 27, 74.

Krauthammer, Charles. 1995. "Quebec and the Death of Diversity." *Time,* November 13, 124.

Krauthammer, Charles. 1996. "When John and Jim Say 'I Do.'" *Time,* July 22, 102.

Krauthammer, Charles. 1998. "Will It Be Coffee, Tea or He?" *Time,* June 15, 92.

Krauthammer, Charles. 1999. "The Real Message of Creationism." *Time,* November 22, 120.

Kriegel, Leonard. 1984–85. "Who Cares about the Humanities?" *The Nation,* December 29–January 5, 712, 714–15.

Kroeber, A. L., and Clyde Kluckhohn. 1952. *Culture: A Critical Review of Concepts and Definitions.* Cambridge, MA: Peabody Museum.

Krugman, Paul. 2002. "For Richer: How the Permissive Capitalism of the Boom Destroyed American Equality." *New York Times Magazine,* October 20, 62–67, 76.

Kuper, Adam. 1999. *Culture: The Anthropologists' Account.* Cambridge: Harvard University Press.

Labi, Nadya. 1998. "Girl Power." *Time,* June 29, 60–62.

Lakoff, George. 2002. *Moral Politics.* Chicago: University of Chicago Press.

LaMarche, Gara, and William B. Rubenstein. 1990. "The Love That Dare Not Speak." *The Nation,* November 5, 524, 526.

Lamont, Michele, and Virag Molnar. 2002. "The Study of Boundaries in the Social Sciences." *Annual Review of Sociology* 28:167–95.

Langer, Gary. 2004. "A Question of Values." *New York Times,* November 6, A19.

Langer, Gary, and Jon Cohen. 2005. "Voters and Values in the 2004 Election." *Public Opinion Quarterly* 69:744–59.

Lasch, Christopher. 1979. *The Culture of Narcissism.* New York: Norton.

Layman, Geoffrey C. 1997. "Religion and Political Behavior in the United States." *Public Opinion Quarterly* 61:288–316.

Layman, Geoffrey C. 2001. *The Great Divide.* New York: Columbia University Press.

Layman, Geoffrey C., and Edward G. Carmines. 1997. "Cultural Conflict in American Politics: Religious Traditionalism, Postmaterialism, and U.S. Political Behavior." *Journal of Politics* 59:751–77.

Layman, Geoffrey C., and Thomas M. Carsey. 2002. "Party Polarization and 'Conflict Extension' in the American Electorate." *American Journal of Political Science* 46:786–802.

Layman, Geoffrey C., and John C. Green. 2006. "Wars and Rumours of Wars: The Contexts of Cultural Conflict in American Political Behaviour." *British Journal of Political Science* 36:61–89.

Leege, David C., Kenneth D. Wald, Brian S. Krueger, and Paul D. Mueller. 2002. *The Politics of Cultural Differences.* Princeton: Princeton University Press.

Leinberger, Paul, and Bruce Tucker. 1991. *The New Individualists.* New York: HarperCollins.

Leo, John. 1986. "Sex and Schools." *Time,* November 24, 54–63.

Levine, Lawrence W. 1996. *The Opening of the American Mind.* Boston: Beacon.

Lind, Michael. 1993. "Aliens among Us." *The New Republic,* August 23–30, 22–23.

Lindaman, Kara, and Donald P. Haider-Markel. 2002. "Issue Evolution, Political Parties, and the Culture Wars." *Political Research Quarterly* 55:91–110.

Lindsay, D. Michael. 2008. "Evangelicals in the Power Elite: Elite Cohesion Advancing a Movement." *American Sociological Review* 73:60–82.

Lindsey, Brink. 2007. "A Farewell to Culture Wars." *National Review,* June 25, 37–40.

Lipman, Samuel. 1991a. "The New American Arts Order." *National Review,* February 11, 39–40.

Lipman, Samuel. 1991b. "Can We Save Culture?" *National Review,* August 26, 36–38, 53.

Lipset, Seymour Martin. 1975. "The Paradox of American Politics." *Public Interest* 41:142–65.

Lipset, Seymour Martin. 1990. *Continental Divide.* New York: Routledge.

Lipset, Seymour Martin. 1996. *American Exceptionalism: A Double-Edged Sword.* New York: Norton.

Loftus, Jeni. 2001. "America's Liberalization in Attitudes toward Homosexuality, 1973 to 1998." *American Sociological Review* 66:762–82.

Loury, Glenn C. 1997. "Pride and Prejudice." *The New Republic,* May 19, 25.

Loury, Glenn C. 1998. "Legal Limits." *The New Republic,* February 23, 16–17.

Lowenthal, Leo. 1950. "Historical Perspectives of Popular Culture." *American Journal of Sociology* 55:323–32.

Luker, Kristin. 1984. *Abortion and the Politics of Motherhood.* Berkeley: University of California Press.

Machacek, David W. 2003. "The Problem of Pluralism." *Sociology of Religion* 64:145–61.

Mansfield, Harvey. 2000. "Where We Stand." *National Review,* July 3, 25–26.

Manza, Jeff, and Clem Brooks. 1996. "Does Class Analysis Still Have Anything to Contribute to the Study of Politics?" *Theory and Society* 25:717–24.

Manza, Jeff, and Clem Brooks. 1997. "The Religious Factor in U.S. Presidential Elections, 1960–1992." *American Journal of Sociology* 103:38–81.

Manza, Jeff, Michael Hout, and Clem Brooks. 1995. "Class Voting in Capitalist Democracies since World War II: Dealignment, Realignment, or Trendless Fluctuation?" *Annual Review of Sociology* 21:137–62.

Marshner, Connaught C. 1988. "What Social Conservatives Really Want." *National Review,* September 2, 38–40.

Martin, David. 1991. "What Makes People Good?" *National Review,* September 9, 25–29.

Marty, Martin E. 1985. "Transpositions: American Religion in the 1980s." *Annals of the American Academy of Political and Social Science* 480:11–23.

Mathewes-Green, Frederica. 1997. "Beyond 'It's a Baby.'" *National Review,* December 31, 40–42.
Mattick, Paul, Jr. 1990. "Arts and the State." *The Nation,* October 1, 348–58.
Mayer, Jane. 2008. "The Insiders." *New Yorker,* October 27, 38–42.
McCarter, Jeremy. 1999. "Arts and Craft." *The New Republic,* February 8, 15–17.
McCarthy, E. Doyle. 1996. *Knowledge as Culture.* London: Routledge.
McClay, Wilfred M. 2004. "The Soul of a Nation." *Public Interest* 155:4–19.
McConkey, Dale. 2001. "Whither Hunter's Culture War? Shifts in Evangelical Morality, 1988–1998." *Sociology of Religion* 62:149–74.
McConnell, Scott, and Eric Breindel. 1990. "Head to Come." *The New Republic,* January 8–15, 18–21.
McCormick, Richard L. 1974. "Ethno-Cultural Interpretations of Nineteenth-Century American Voting Behavior." *Political Science Quarterly* 89:351–77.
Melzer, Arthur M. 1991. "Tolerance 101." *The New Republic,* July 1, 10–12.
Merelman, Richard M. 1994. "Racial Conflict and Cultural Politics in the United States." *Journal of Politics* 56:1–20.
Meyrowitz, Joshua, and John Maguire. 1993. "Media, Place, and Multiculturalism." *Society* 30:41–48.
Miceli, Melinda S. 2005. "Morality Politics vs. Identity Politics: Framing Processes and Competition among Christian Right and Gay Social Movement Organizations." *Sociological Forum* 20:589–612.
Miller, Alan S., and John P. Hoffmann. 1999. "The Growing Divisiveness: Culture Wars or a War of Words?" *Social Forces* 78:721–45.
Miller, John J. 1993. "Afrocentrism in the Suburbs." *National Review,* September 20, 58, 60.
Miller, Jon D., Eugenie C. Scott, and Shinji Okamoto. 2006. "Public Acceptance of Evolution." *Science* 313:765–66.
Mindus, Daniel. 2000. "What to Tell the Children." *National Review,* September 11, 44, 46.
Minogue, Kenneth. 1991. "The Goddess That Failed." *National Review,* November 18, 46–48.
Mondak, Jeffery J., and Mitchell S. Sanders. 2003. "Tolerance and Intolerance, 1976–1998." *American Journal of Political Science* 47:492–502.
Moore, Laura M., and Reeve Vanneman. 2003. "Context Matters: Effects of the Proportion of Fundamentalists on Gender Attitudes." *Social Forces* 82:115–39.
Morley, Jefferson. 1986. "Shoving Time." *The New Republic,* July 28, 11–13.
Morrow, Lance. 1981. "To Revive Responsibility." *Time,* February 23, 72–74.
Morrow, Lance. 1992a. "But Seriously, Folks . . ." *Time,* June 1, 28–31.
Morrow, Lance. 1992b. "Family Values." *Time,* August 31, 22–27.
Morrow, Lance. 1994a. "Men: Are They Really That Bad?" *Time,* February 14, 52–59.
Morrow, Lance. 1994b. "Yin and Yang, Sleaze and Moralizing." *Time,* December 26, 158.
Morrow, Lance. 1995. "Fifteen Cheers for Abstinence." *Time,* October 2, 90.
Mouw, Ted, and Michael E. Sobel. 2001. "Culture Wars and Opinion Polarization: The Case of Abortion." *American Journal of Sociology* 106:913–43.

Muller, Jerry Z. 1995. "The Conservative Case for Abortion." *The New Republic,* August 21, 27–29.
Myrdal, Gunnar. 1944. *An American Dilemma.* New York: Harper.
Nadler, Richard. 1997. "Abstaining from Sex Education." *National Review,* September 15, 50–51.
Nadler, Richard. 1998. "Glum and Glummer." *National Review,* September 28, 26, 28, 30.
Neier, Aryeh. 1980. "Statues Have Free Speech Too." *The Nation,* October 18, 375–76.
Nelson, Jill. 1995. "Talk Is Cheap." *The Nation,* June 5, 800–802.
Neuhaus, Richard John. 1986. "The Catholic Moment." *National Review,* November 7, 46.
Neuhaus, Richard John. 1988a. "The Church of Your Political Choice." *National Review,* September 30, 46.
Neuhaus, Richard John. 1988b. "To See as God Sees." *National Review,* October 28, 24.
Neuhaus, Richard John. 1989a. "So Little Change, So Much Difference." *National Review,* March 24, 20.
Neuhaus, Richard John. 1989b. "After Roe." *National Review,* April 7, 38–42.
Neuhaus, Richard John. 1995. "Alien Notion." *National Review,* February 6, 62, 64–66.
Neusner, Jacob. 1984. "Ethnic Studies, Campus Ghettos." *National Review,* June 15, 42, 44, 61.
Newport, Frank. 2008. "McCain Retains Support of Highly Religious White Voters." October 27. http://www.gallup.com/poll/111463/McCain-Retains-Support-Highly-Religious-White-Voters.aspx.
New York Times. 2008. "National Exit Polls Table." November 5. http://elections.nytimes.com/2008/results/president/national-exit-polls.html.
Nolan, James L., Jr. 1996. "Contrasting Styles of Political Discourse in America's Past and Present Culture Wars." In *The American Culture Wars,* ed. James L. Nolan Jr., 155–88. Charlottesville: University Press of Virginia.
Nolan, Mary. 1997. "Against Exceptionalism." *American Historical Review* 102:769–74.
Noonan, Peggy. 2008. "Palin's Failin'." *Wall Street Journal,* October 17. http://online.wsj.com/article/SB122419210832542317.html.
"Notes and Asides." 1990. *National Review,* July 9, 16–18.
Novak, Michael. 1972. *The Rise of the Unmeltable Ethnics.* New York: Macmillan.
Novak, Michael. 1984. "The Revolt against Our Public Culture." *National Review,* May 4, 48.
Novak, Michael. 1997. "Personally Opposed." *National Review,* May 5, 47–48.
Nussbaum, Martha. 1992. "The Softness of Reason." *The New Republic,* July 13–20, 26–27, 30, 32, 34–35.
Oestreicher, Richard. 1988. "Urban Working-Class Political Behavior and Theories of American Electoral Politics, 1870–1940." *Journal of American History* 74:1257–86.
Olson, Daniel V. A. 1997. "Dimensions of Cultural Tension among the American Public." In *Culture Wars in American Politics,* ed. Rhys H. Williams, 237–58. New York: Aldine De Gruyter.
Olson, Daniel V. A., and Jackson W. Carroll. 1992. "Religiously Based Politics: Religious Elites and the Public." *Social Forces* 70:765–86.

Ortner, Sherry B. 1999. Introduction to *The Fate of "Culture": Geertz and Beyond,* ed. Sherry B. Ortner, 1–13. Berkeley: University of California Press.

Ostling, Richard N. 1989. "The Mainline Blues." *Time,* May 22, 94–96.

Ostling, Richard N. 1991. "What Does God Really Think about Sex?" *Time,* June 24, 48–50.

O'Sullivan, John. 1994a. "Nationhood: An American Activity." *National Review,* February 21, 36–45.

O'Sullivan, John. 1994b. "America's Identity Crisis." *National Review,* November 21, 36–41, 44–45, 76.

O'Sullivan, John. 2000. "Our Inglorious Revolution." *National Review,* April 3, 22.

Pakulski, Jan, and Malcolm Waters. 1996. "The Reshaping and Dissolution of Social Class in Advanced Society." *Theory and Society* 25:667–91.

Palin, Sarah. 2008. "Character, Hope and Change." Address to the Republican National Convention, September 2. *Vital Speeches of the Day* 74:486–89.

Parrillo, Vincent N. 1994. "Diversity in America: A Sociohistorical Analysis." *Sociological Forum* 9:523–45.

Pasley, Jeffrey L. 1987. "Not-So-Good Books." *The New Republic,* April 27, 20–22.

Patterson, Orlando. 2000. "Taking Culture Seriously: A Framework and an Afro-American Illustration." In *Culture Matters,* ed. Laurence E. Harrison and Samuel P. Huntington, 202–18. New York: Basic Books.

Payne, James L. 1995. "Education versus the American Way." *National Review,* September 25, 58, 60, 62.

Petchesky, Rosalind. 1990. "Giving Women a Real Choice." *The Nation,* May 28, 732–35.

Petersen, Larry R., and Gregory V. Donnenwerth. 1997. "Secularization and the Influence of Religion on Beliefs about Premarital Sex." *Social Forces* 75:1071–89.

Peterson, Richard A. 2002. "Roll over Beethoven, There's a New Way to Be Cool." *Contexts* 1:34–39.

Pew Forum on Religion and Public Life. 2008a. "How the Faithful Voted." November 10. http://pewforum.org/docs/?DocID=367.

Pew Forum on Religion and Public Life. 2008b. "More Americans Question Religion's Role in Politics." August 21. http://pewforum.org/docs/?DocID=334.

Pew Research Center for the People and the Press. 2002. "Americans Struggle with Religion's Role at Home and Abroad." March 20. http://people-press.org/report/150/americans-struggle-with-religions-role-at-home-and-abroad.

Pew Research Center for the People and the Press. 2003. "The 2004 Political Landscape." November 5. http://people-press.org/report/196/.

Pew Research Center for the People and the Press. 2005. "Religion a Strength and Weakness for Both Parties: Public Divided on Origins of Life." August 30. http://people-press.org/report/254/religion-a-strength-and-weakness-for-both-parties.

Pew Research Center for the People and the Press. 2006a. "Many Americans Uneasy with Mix of Religion and Politics." August 24. http://people-press.org/report/287/many-americans-uneasy-with-mix-of-religion-and-politics.

Pew Research Center for the People and the Press. 2006b. "Pragmatic Americans Lib-

eral and Conservative on Social Issues." August 3. http://people-press.org/report/283/pragmatic-americans-liberal-and-conservative-on-social-issues.
Pew Research Center for the People and the Press. 2008. "Growing Doubts about McCain's Judgment, Age and Campaign Conduct." October 21. http://people-press.org/report/462/obamas-lead-widens.
Pew Research Center for the People and the Press. 2009. "On Obama's Desk: Economy, Jobs Trump All Other Policy Priorities in 2009." January 22. http://pewresearch.org/pubs/1087/economy-jobs-top-public-priorities-2009.
Pochoda, Elizabeth. 1991. "Multicultural Watch." *The Nation,* November 18, 615.
Pochoda, Elizabeth. 1992. "Browbeating." *The Nation,* March 16, 344.
Pollitt, Katha. 1983. "Bookends." *The Nation,* July 2, 23–24.
Pollitt, Katha. 1990. "Georgie Porgie Is a Bully." *Time,* November 1, 24.
Pollitt, Katha. 1991. "Canon to the Right of Me . . ." *The Nation,* September 23, 328–31.
Pollitt, Katha. 1992a. "Why I Hate 'Family Values' (Let Me Count the Ways)." *The Nation,* July 20, 88, 90–92, 94.
Pollitt, Katha. 1992b. "Are Women Morally Superior to Men?" *The Nation,* December 28, 799–807.
Pollitt, Katha. 1994a. "Subject to Debate." *The Nation,* February 21, 224.
Pollitt, Katha. 1994b. "Subject to Debate." *The Nation,* December 26, 788.
Pollitt, Katha. 1996. "No God, No Master." *The Nation,* January 22, 9.
Pollitt, Katha. 1997. "Honk If You Like Art." *The Nation,* August 11–18, 10.
Pollitt, Katha. 1998a. "I'm O.K., You're P.C." *The Nation,* January 26, 10.
Pollitt, Katha. 1998b. "Race and Gender and Class, Oh My!" *The Nation,* June 8, 9.
Pollitt, Katha. 1998c. "Dead Again." *The Nation,* July 31, 10.
Pollitt, Katha. 2000. "Freedom from Religion, Si!" *The Nation,* September 18–25, 10.
Ponnuru, Ramesh. 1999. "Not Dead Yet." *National Review,* May 17, 41–44.
Ponnuru, Ramesh. 2007. "A Reply [to Brink Lindsey]." *National Review,* June 25, 40.
Postman, Neil, and Marc Postman. 1986. "Teach Creationism." *The Nation,* January 11, 5.
Presser, Stanley, and Linda Stinson. 1998. "Data Collection Mode and Social Desirability Bias in Self-Reported Religious Attendance." *American Sociological Review* 63:137–45.
Putnam, Robert D. 2000. *Bowling Alone.* New York: Simon and Schuster.
Rae, Nicol C. 1992. "Class and Culture: American Political Cleavages in the Twentieth Century." *Western Political Quarterly* 45:629–50.
Rauch, Jonathan. 1993. "Beyond Oppression." *The New Republic,* May 10, 18, 20, 23.
Ravitch, Diane. 1990. "Multiculturalism: E Pluribus Plures." In *Debating P.C.,* ed. Paul Berman, 271–98. New York: Dell.
Raz, Joseph. 1994. "Multiculturalism: A Liberal Perspective." *Dissent* 41:67–79.
Regnerus, Mark D., David Sikkink, and Christian Smith. 1999. "Voting with the Christian Right: Contextual and Individual Patterns of Electoral Influence." *Social Forces* 77:1375–1401.
Regnerus, Mark D., and Christian Smith. 1998. "Selective Deprivatization among

American Religious Traditions: The Reversal of the Great Reversal." *Social Forces* 76:1347–72.

Reilly, Robert R. 1996. "Culture of Vice." *National Review,* November 25, 60–61.

Reimer, Samuel H. 1995. "A Look at Cultural Effects on Religiosity: A Comparison between the United States and Canada." *Journal for the Scientific Study of Religion* 34:445–57.

Robertson, Roland. 1992. *Globalization: Social Theory and Global Culture.* London: Sage.

Robinson, Lillian S. 1989. "What Culture Should Mean." *The Nation,* September 25, 319–21.

Roche, John P. 1989. "The New Left Vigilantes." *National Review,* December 8, 34–35.

Rodgers, Daniel T. 1992. "Republicanism: The Career of a Concept." *Journal of American History* 79:11–38.

Rodgers, Daniel T. 2004. "American Exceptionalism Revisited." *Raritan* 24:21–47.

Rodriguez, Richard. 1988. "The Fear of Losing a Culture." *Time,* July 11, 84.

Rose, Fred. 1997. "Toward a Class-Cultural Theory of Social Movements: Reinterpreting New Social Movements." *Sociological Forum* 12:461–94.

Rosin, Hanna. 2005. "Beyond Belief." *The Atlantic* 295:117–20.

Rotello, Gabriel. 1996. "To Have and to Hold." *The Nation,* June 24, 11, 13, 15–16, 18.

Rothman, Stanley. 1992. "Is Dan Quayle Right?" *National Review,* October 5, 34–35.

Russell, George. 1991. "Reading, Writing—And Iroquois Politics." *Time,* November 11, 20, 24–25.

Sachs, Andrea, and Susanne Washburn. 1995. "Tough Talk on Entertainment." *Time,* June 12, 32–35.

Sahlins, Marshall. 1999. "Two or Three Things That I Know about Culture." *Journal of the Royal Anthropological Institute* 5:399–421.

Saletan, William. 2009. "This Is the Way the Culture Wars End." *New York Times,* February 22, 11.

Schiffer, Adam J. 2000. "I'm Not That Liberal: Explaining Conservative Democratic Identification." *Political Behavior* 22:293–310.

Schlesinger, Arthur, Jr. 1991. "The Cult of Ethnicity, Good and Bad." *Time,* July 8, 21.

Schlosberg, David. 1998. "Resurrecting the Pluralist Universe." *Political Research Quarterly* 51:583–615.

Schmalzbauer, John. 1993. "Evangelicals in the New Class: Class versus Subcultural Predictors of Ideology." *Journal for the Scientific Study of Religion* 32:330–42.

Schudson, Michael. 1989. "How Culture Works: Perspectives from Media Studies on the Efficacy of Symbols." *Theory and Society* 18:153–80.

Schulman, Bruce J. 1999. "Out of the Streets and into the Classroom? The New Left and the Counterculture in United States History Textbooks." *Journal of American History* 85:1527–34.

Scott, Daryl Michael. 1998. "Postmodern Daze." *The Nation,* December 14, 26–29.

Scott, David. 1992. "Criticism and Culture." *Critique of Anthropology* 12:371–94.

Scott, David. 2003. "Culture in Political Theory." *Political Theory* 31:92–115.

Scully, Matthew. 1993. "Joining the Cultural War." *National Review,* June 7, 26–27.

Segal, Daniel A., and Richard Handler. 1995. "U.S. Multiculturalism and the Concept of Culture." *Identities* 1:391–407.

Segal, David. 1992. "Excuuuse Me." *The New Republic,* May 11, 9–10.

Seligman, Daniel. 1993. "PC Comes to the Newsroom." *National Review,* June 21, 28, 30–32, 34.

Sennett, Richard, and Jonathan Cobb. 1972. *The Hidden Injuries of Class.* New York: Random House.

Sewell, William H., Jr. 1999. "The Concept(s) of Culture." In *Beyond the Cultural Turn,* ed. Victoria E. Bonnell and Lynn Hunt, 35–61. Berkeley: University of California Press.

Shafer, Byron E. 1985. "The New Cultural Politics." *PS* 18:221–31.

Shalit, Ruth. 1993. "Family-Mongers." *The New Republic,* August 16, 12–14.

Shalit, Wendy. 1998. "Whose Choice?" *National Review,* May 18, 28–30.

Sherkat, Darren E. 1998. "Counterculture or Continuity? Competing Influences on Baby Boomers' Religious Orientations and Participation." *Social Forces* 76:1087–1114.

Short, Thomas. 1990. "Gay Rights or Closet Virtues." *National Review,* September 17, 43–44.

Sidanius, Jim, Seymour Feshbach, Shana Levin, and Felicia Pratto. 1997. "The Interface between Ethnic and National Attachment." *Public Opinion Quarterly* 61: 102–33.

Siegel, Fred. 1991. "The Cult of Multiculturalism." *The New Republic,* February 18, 34–36, 38, 40.

Siegel, Judith S., and Edwin J. Delattre. 1981. "Blackboard Jumble." *The New Republic,* April 18, 17–18.

Sikkink, David. 1999. "The Social Sources of Alienation from Public Schools." *Social Forces* 78:51–86.

Simmel, Georg. 1908/1971. *On Individuality and Social Forms.* Repr. Ed. Donald N. Levine. Chicago: University of Chicago Press.

Simon, William E. 1993. "The Missing Issue." *National Review,* March 15, 20–21.

Sirius, R. U. 1998. "The New Counterculture." *Time,* November 9, 88–89.

Slater, Philip. 1976. *The Pursuit of Loneliness.* Boston: Beacon.

Smith, Barbara. 1993. "Where's the Revolution?" *The Nation,* July 5, 12–14, 16.

Smith, Christian. 2000. *Christian America? What Evangelicals Really Want.* Berkeley: University of California Press.

Smith, Christian, with Michael Emerson, Sally Gallagher, Paul Kennedy, and David Sikkink. 1997. "The Myth of Culture Wars: The Case of American Protestantism." In *Culture Wars in American Politics,* ed. Rhys H. Williams, 175–95. New York: Aldine De Gruyter.

Smith, Philip. 1998. "The New American Cultural Sociology: An Introduction." In *The New American Cultural Sociology,* ed. Philip Smith, 1–14. Cambridge: Cambridge University Press.

Smith, Warren. 2008. "Whose 'Evangelical Manifesto'?" OneNewsNow.com, April 17. http://www.onenewsnow.com/Printer.aspx?id=76376.

Sobran, Joseph. 1986. "The Politics of AIDS." *National Review,* May 23, 22, 24, 26, 51, 52.

Sommers, Christina Hoff. 1992. "Sister Soldiers." *The New Republic,* October 5, 29–30, 32–33.

Spencer, Martin E. 1994. "Multiculturalism, 'Political Correctness,' and the Politics of Identity." *Sociological Forum* 9:547–67.

Spillane, Margaret. 1990. "The Culture of Narcissism." *The Nation,* December 10, 737–40.

Stacey, Judith. 1994. "The New Family Values Crusaders." *The Nation,* July 25–August 1, 119–22.

Stanford, Michael. 1989. "The Stanford Library." *The New Republic,* October 2, 18–20.

Stark, Rodney. 1999. "Secularization, R.I.P." *Sociology of Religion* 60:249–73.

Steel, Ronald. 1998. "Who Is Us?" *The New Republic,* September 14–21, 13–14.

Stein, Joel. 1997. "The God Squad." *Time,* September 22, 97–100.

Stein, Maurice R. 1960. *The Eclipse of Community.* Princeton: Princeton University Press.

Stengel, Richard. 1986. "Sex Busters." *Time,* July 21, 12–18, 21.

Strickler, Jennifer, and Nicholas L. Danigelis. 2002. "Changing Frameworks in Attitudes toward Abortion." *Sociological Forum* 17:187–201.

Sullivan, Andrew. 1989. "Here Comes the Groom (A Conservative Case for Gay Marriage)." *The New Republic,* August 28, 20, 22.

Sullivan, Andrew. 1990. "Racism 101." *The New Republic,* November 26, 18, 20–21.

Sullivan, Andrew. 1993. "The Politics of Homosexuality." *The New Republic,* May 10, 24–26, 32–37.

Sullivan, Andrew. 1996. "Three's a Crowd." *The New Republic,* June 17, 10, 12.

Sullivan, Andrew. 2000. "Dumb and Dumber." *The New Republic,* June 26, 6.

Suny, Ronald Grigor. 2002. "Back and Beyond: Reversing the Cultural Turn?" *American Historical Review* 107:1476–99.

Swatos, William H., Jr., and Kevin J. Christiano. 1999. "Secularization Theory: The Course of a Concept." *Sociology of Religion* 60:209–28.

Swidler, Ann. 1986. "Culture in Action: Symbols and Strategies." *American Sociological Review* 51:273–86.

Swidler, Ann. 2001. *Talk of Love: How Culture Matters.* Chicago: University of Chicago Press.

Swidler, Ann. 2002. "Cultural Power and Social Movements." In *Cultural Sociology,* ed. Lyn Spillman, 311–23. Malden, MA: Blackwell.

Sykes, Charles J., and Brad Miner. 1991. "Sense and Sensitivity." *National Review,* March 18, 30–31.

Talbot, Margaret. 2008. "Red Sex, Blue Sex." *The New Yorker,* November 3, 64–69.

Tax, Meredith. 1989. "March to a Crossroads on Abortion." *The Nation,* May 8, 613, 631–33.

Tax, Meredith. 1995. "My Censorship—And Ours." *The Nation,* March 20, 374, 376–78.

Taylor, Charles. 1992. *Multiculturalism and "The Politics of Recognition."* Princeton: Princeton University Press.

Taylor, Charles. 1995. "Response to David Bromwich." *Dissent* 42:103–4.
Teachout, Terry. 1983. "Gay Rights and Straight Realities." *National Review,* November 11, 1408–12, 1433.
Teachout, Terry. 1992. "Dead Center: The Myth of the Middle." *National Review,* November 2, 53–55.
Thernstrom, Abigail M. 1981. "Bilingual Mis-Education." *The New Republic,* April 18, 15–17.
Thomas, Michael C., and Charles C. Flippen. 1972. "American Civil Religion: An Empirical Study." *Social Forces* 51:218–25.
Thomson, Irene Taviss. 2000. *In Conflict No Longer: Self and Society in Contemporary America.* Lanham, MD: Rowman and Littlefield.
Thomson, Irene Taviss. 2005. "The Theory That Won't Die: From Mass Society to the Decline of Social Capital." *Sociological Forum.* 20:421–48.
Tifft, Susan. 1990. "Of, by and for—Whom?" *Time,* September 24, 95–96.
Tocqueville, Alexis de. 1848/1961. *Democracy in America.* Repr. New York: Vintage.
Todorov, Tzvetan. 1989. "Crimes against Humanities." *The New Republic,* July 3, 26–30.
Tolson, Jay. 2008. "Sarah Palin Sparks Revival of the Culture War." *U.S. News and World Report,* September 23. http://www.usnews.com/articles/news/campaign-2008/2008/09/23/sarah-palin-sparks-revival-of-the-culture-war.html.
Traube, Elizabeth G. 1996. " 'The Popular' in American Culture." *Annual Review of Anthropology* 25:127–51.
Tucker, William. 1993. "Monogamy and Its Discontents." *National Review,* October 4, 28, 30, 32, 34–38.
Tyrrell, Ian. 1991. "American Exceptionalism in an Age of International History." *American Historical Review* 96:1031–55.
Vaid, Urvashi. 1993. "After Identity." *The New Republic,* May 10, 28.
Vaisey, Stephen. 2007. "On Justification (and Motivation): A Dual-Process Model of Culture in Action." *Culture* 21:1, 3–5.
van den Haag, Ernest. 1991. "Sodom and Begorrah." *National Review,* April 29, 35–38.
van Elteren, Mel. 1998. "The Riddles of Individualism and Community in American and Dutch Society." *Journal of American Culture* 21:43–80.
Vidal, Gore. 1997. "The New Theocrats." *The Nation,* July 21, 19–21.
Wacker, R. Fred. 1979. "Assimilation and Cultural Pluralism in American Social Thought." *Phylon* 40:325–33.
Wagner, David. 1986. "The New Right and the New Pluralism." *National Review,* May 23, 28–29, 32, 52.
Walzer, Michael. 1994. "Multiculturalism and Individualism" *Dissent* 41:185–91.
Walzer, Michael. 1995. "Response to David Bromwich." *Dissent* 42:105–6.
Walzer, Michael. 1996. "For Identity." *The New Republic,* December 2, 39.
Walzer, Michael. 1999. "What Does It Mean to Be an 'American'?" *Social Research* 57:591–614.
Warner, Michael. 1997. "Media Gays: A New Stone Wall." *The Nation,* July 14, 15–16, 18–19.
Warner, R. Stephen. 1993. "Work in Progress toward a New Paradigm for the Socio-

logical Study of Religion in the United States." *American Journal of Sociology* 98:1044–93.

Waters, Mary C. 1990. *Ethnic Options.* Berkeley: University of California Press.

Wedeen, Lisa. 2002. "Conceptualizing Culture: Possibilities for Political Science." *American Political Science Review* 96:713–28.

"What Do We Have in Common?" 1991. *Time,* July 8, 19–20.

White, John Kenneth. 2003. *The Values Divide.* Washington, DC: CQ Press.

Whitman, David. 1999. "More Moral." *The New Republic,* February 22, 18–19.

Whyte, William H., Jr. 1956. *The Organization Man.* Garden City, NY: Doubleday.

Wieseltier, Leon. 1994. "Against Identity." *The New Republic,* November 28, 24, 26, 28, 30, 32.

Wildavsky, Aaron. 1987. "Choosing Preferences by Constructing Institutions: Cultural Theory of Preference Formation." *American Political Science Review* 81:3–21.

Wildavsky, Aaron. 1991. "Resolved, That Individualism and Egalitarianism Be Made Compatible in America: Political-Cultural Roots of Exceptionalism." In *Is America Different?* ed. Byron E. Shafer, 116–37. New York: Oxford University Press.

Williams, Rhys H. 1997. "Culture Wars, Social Movements, and Institutional Politics." In *Culture Wars in American Politics,* ed. Rhys H. Williams, 283–95. New York: Aldine De Gruyter.

Williams, Rhys H., and Susan M. Alexander. 1994. "Religious Rhetoric in American Populism: Civil Religion as Movement Ideology." *Journal for the Scientific Study of Religion* 33:1–15.

Williams, Robin M., Jr. 1957. *American Society.* New York: Knopf.

Willis, Ellen. 1981. "Betty Friedan's 'Second Stage': A Step Backward." *The Nation,* November 14, 494–96.

Willis, Ellen. 1996. "Bring in the Noise." *The Nation,* April 1, 19, 22–23.

Willis, Ellen. 1998. "We Need a Radical Left." *The Nation,* June 29, 18–21.

Wills, Garry. 1989. "In Praise of Censure." *Time,* July 31, 71–72.

Wilson, James Q. 2006. "How Divided Are We?" *Commentary* 121:15–21.

Wilson, Thomas C. 1994. "Trends in Tolerance toward Rightist and Leftist Groups, 1976–1988: Effects of Attitude Change and Cohort Succession." *Public Opinion Quarterly* 58:539–56.

Wimberley, Ronald C., Donald A. Clelland, Thomas C. Hood, and C. M. Lipsey. 1976. "The Civil Religious Dimension: Is It There?" *Social Forces* 54:890–900.

Wolf, Naomi. 1992. "Father Figures." *The New Republic,* October 5, 22, 24–25.

Wolf, Naomi. 1995. "Our Bodies, Our Souls." *The New Republic,* October 16, 26, 28–29, 32–34.

Wolfe, Alan. 1998. *One Nation, after All.* New York: Viking Penguin.

Wolfe, Alan. 2001. *Moral Freedom.* New York: Norton.

Wood, Gordon S. 1987. "Ideology and the Origins of Liberal America." *William and Mary Quarterly* 44:628–40.

Woodberry, Robert D. 1998. "When Surveys Lie and People Tell the Truth: How Surveys Oversample Church Attenders." *American Sociological Review* 63:119–22.

Woodberry, Robert D., and Christian S. Smith. 1998. "Fundamentalism et al.: Conservative Protestants in America." *Annual Review of Sociology* 24:25–56.

Woolman, John. 1986. "Letter from a Friend: A Conservative Speaks Out for Gay Rights." *National Review,* September 12, 28–31, 58–59.

Wright, Erik Olin. 1996. "The Continuing Relevance of Class Analysis—Comments." *Theory and Society* 25:693–716.

Wright, Robert. 1996. "The False Politics of Values." *Time,* September 9, 42–45.

Wright, Susan. 1998. "The Politicization of 'Culture.'" *Anthropology Today* 14:7–15.

Wrong, Dennis H. 1961. "The Oversocialized Conception of Man in Modern Sociology." *American Sociological Review* 26:183–93.

Wrong, Dennis H. 1990. "The Influence of Sociological Ideas on American Culture." In *Sociology in America,* ed. Herbert J. Gans, 19–30. Newbury Park, CA: Sage.

Wrong, Dennis H. 1997. "Cultural Relativism as Ideology." *Critical Review* 11:291–300.

Wuthnow, Robert. 1988. *The Restructuring of American Religion: Society and Faith Since World War II.* Princeton: Princeton University Press.

Wuthnow, Robert. 1996. "Restructuring of American Religion: Further Evidence." *Sociological Inquiry* 66:303–29.

Wuthnow, Robert. 2005. "Democratic Renewal and Cultural Inertia: Why Our Best Efforts Fall Short." *Sociological Forum* 20:343–67.

Wuthnow, Robert. 2006. *American Mythos: Why Our Best Efforts to Be a Better Nation Fall Short.* Princeton: Princeton University Press.

Yeoman, Barry. 1998. "Art and States' Rights." *The Nation,* June 29, 31–33.

Young, Carleton W. 1995. "Religion in United States History Textbooks." *History Teacher* 28:265–71.

Young, Cathy. 1999. "Victimizers." *The New Republic,* April 12, 18, 20–21.

Zimmerman, Jonathan. 1999. "Relatively Speaking." *The New Republic,* September 6, 13–14.

Zipp, John F., and Rudy Fenwick. 2006. "Is the Academy a Liberal Hegemony? The Political Orientations and Educational Values of Professors." *Public Opinion Quarterly* 70:304–26.

Zukin, Cliff, Scott Keeter, Molly Andolina, Krista Jenkins, and Michael X. Delli Carpini. 2006. *A New Engagement?* New York: Oxford University Press.

Index